Tanks for the Memories

An oral history of the 712th Tank Battalion from World War II

as told to Aaron C. Elson

Published by
Chi Chi Press
Hackensack, N.J.
(201) 489-3982

Printed at
Ted Weiss Printing
Bensalem, PA

For my dad.

Maurice Elson
1914 - 1980

712th TANK BATTALION COMBAT ROUTE

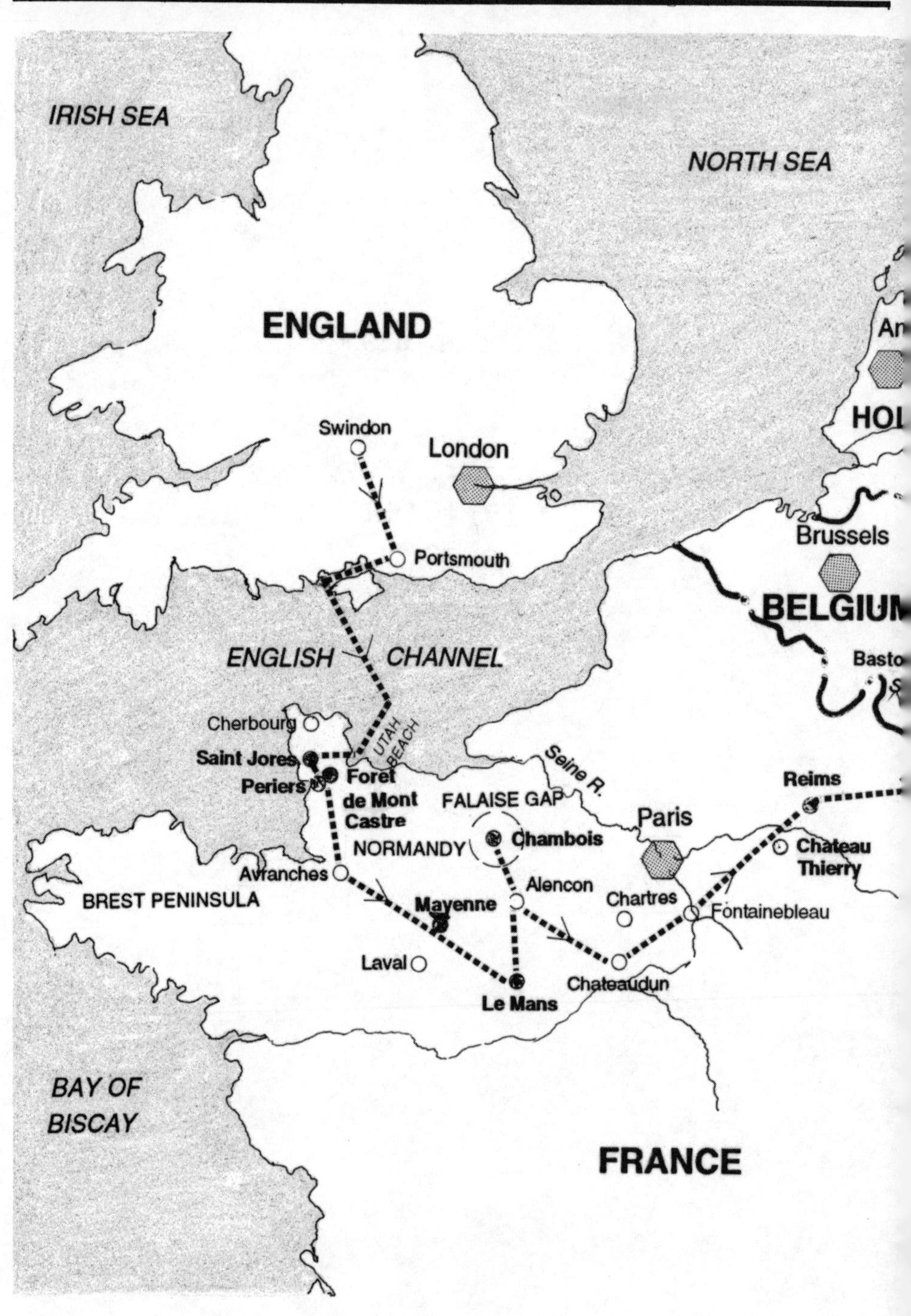

POLAND
GERMANY
Leipzig
Vacha
Hof
Prague
Bonn
Fulda
Coblenz
Frankfurt
Weiden
Suscice
Nuremburg
Amberg
Ziewsel
CZECHO-
SLOVAKIA
Moselle R.
Mainz
Main R.
OCCUPATION AREA
Dillingen
Siegfried Line
Rhine R.
Vienna
Stuttgart
AUSTRIA
Bern
SWITZERLAND
ITALY
N
Battle Sites
Not To Scale

PHOTO BY STEVE KRYSKO

Six A Company officers in Amberg, Germany, after the war in Europe ended. Back row, from left: Morse Johnson (inset, in 1993) and the late Sam MacFarland. Front row: Bob Hagerty (below left, in 1993), Ellsworth Howard, Howard "Olie" Olsen (below right, in 1993) and Jule Braatz. Of the six, all except Howard, who already was an officer, received battlefield commissions.

"There's a lot of things a man can laugh about now, that wouldn't have been a bit funny back when it happened. A lot of people say veterans never talk to them. Most of them don't. The reason they don't talk is they couldn't get the picture over to somebody that wasn't there. They talk to each other. They know what I'm talking about, and I know what they're saying. Somebody that wasn't there, he would think that you're making that story up."

--Otha Martin, tank commander, C Company, 712th Tank Battalion

Table of Contents

Preface

When I was a child, I loved hearing my father's stories about World War II. He managed to make the act of being wounded sound funny. "I had never been in a battle," he used to say, "so I stuck my head up to see what was going on." Among other things, he said, a bullet went through his helmet, but some tissue paper wadded inside kept his skull from being penetrated.

My father, Maurice Elson, trained with the infantry, went to Officers Candidate School at Fort Benning, Ga., and was assigned to the 712th Tank Battalion in Normandy as a replacement.

I only heard him talk once about the second time he was wounded. It was in December and there was snow on the ground, it was at night and in a place called Dillingen. He said he was hit by a German machine gun bullet that entered his chest an inch from his heart, and that the bullet was extracted from his arm. The doctors even gave him the bullet.

Several years after he died of a heart attack in 1980, I came across a newsletter addressed to my father. It was put out by the 712th Tank Battalion, and it chronicled the ordinary, but rarely mundane, lives of the battalion's members. It mentioned the grandchildren, the retirements, the visits, the surgeries, and it reminded its readers that nobody was growing any younger.

I wrote to the newsletter's editor, Ray Griffin, in Aurora, Neb., and asked if he would put in a notice asking anyone who remembered my father to contact me. Griffin passed my letter on to Sam MacFarland, who was in A Company, to which my father had been assigned. MacFarland wrote and said he didn't remember my father, but that I would be welcome to attend the next reunion, where I might find some people who did.

That reunion was in Niagara Falls, in 1987. I met three people -- Jule Braatz, Charlie Vinson and Ellsworth Howard -- who remembered my dad, and the stories I only vaguely remembered suddenly came to life. It was an exhilarating feeling.

The battalion members welcomed me as if I were part of a large, extended family, and I have been to several reunions since.

The 712th Tank Battalion landed in Normandy on June 28, 1944, and was on the front lines for 11 months. It was in the forefront of the Breakout from Normandy, helped encircle and trap the German 7th Army at the Falaise Gap, probed deep into enemy territory during General Patton's vaunted dash across France, and rushed up from the south to join in the Battle of the Bulge. It helped break the Siegfried Line, and at times was so far forward that identifying panels were placed on the tanks so Allied planes wouldn't bomb them. The battalion guarded the treasures of the Merkers Salt Mine, and helped liberate the Flossenburg concentration camp.

Jim Gifford joined the battalion as a replacement in Normandy, and was wounded during the Battle of the Bulge. Today Gifford is a lawyer in Yonkers, N.Y., where he also runs a used-car lot. He works seven days a week, and still has a country-lawyer charm that came from growing up in Gloversville, N.Y.

In a philosophical moment, Gifford says that during the war he experienced a kind of calm he did not feel before and has not felt since, because he didn't expect to survive. Therefore, all the pressure of worrying about school, about a career, about making a living, was lifted from his shoulders.

Forrest Dixon also says he didn't expect Jim Gifford to survive. "If the tank pulled up in front of a building," Dixon says, chuckling, "Lieutenant Gifford would get out and go around in back of the building to see if any Germans were hiding there with a bazooka."

Tony D'Arpino lives in the Boston suburb of Milton, and Ruby Goldstein in the Boston suburb of Hull. After the war, Goldstein opened a dry cleaning establishment and D'Arpino was one of his customers. It wasn't until they met at a reunion that D'Arpino, who was in C Company, and Goldstein, of A Company, realized they had belonged to the same outfit. Goldstein, a tank commander, was wounded at the Falaise Gap. D'Arpino, a driver, was one of only six of C Company's 75 original members to make it from Normandy to Czechoslovakia without being wounded, unless you count the fact that his eardrums were perforated when his tank went over a mine, and he has suffered from ringing in his ears ever since.

As I was interviewing Bob Hagerty in a hallway outside a meeting room at the Harrisburg, Pa., Sheraton during the 1992 reunion, one of the tankers' wives passed by. She leaned toward the microphone of the walkman-size tape recorder and said, a little giddily: "Every year they fight the war all over again, and every year it comes out the same!"

In a way, she was right. Every year, though, it has fewer participants. Most of the battalion members are in their seventies. Some wear hearing aids, and a portion of each reunion is spent catching up on medical histories. Several are in remission from cancer.

For a few days each year, though, they are young again, clattering in M4A3 tanks across rivers on pontoon bridges, barreling full tilt along ice-slicked roads, and bringing back to life, for a few flickering moments, the memories of those who are buried in the cemeteries of France and Belgium and Luxembourg and Germany, or whose ashes remain in the fields and orchards where they burned inside their tanks.

During the course of my research for this book, I visited the battalion's monument outside the Patton Museum in Fort Knox, Ky. It was a sobering moment. I had interviewed so many tankers, and heard so many anecdotes, that I thought I knew a great deal about the history of the 712th. But when I started going through the names of 97 battalion members killed in action, I recognized barely half of them.

This is by no means a comprehensive history of the battalion. It virtually ignores the stories of B Company and D Company, largely because most of the people I spoke to were in A Company or C Company. Rather, it is a collection of anecdotes, of images and memories and vignettes as related by a few dozen of the 1,235 men, including replacements, who passed through the ranks of the 712th.

CHAPTER 1

Muzzle and Steel

"I wouldn't take a million dollars for what I went through," George Bussell says, "but I wouldn't go through it again for a million dollars, either."

Bussell, a slight man of about 5-foot-6, approaching 80, was born and raised in Indianapolis, where he still lives. From the stories I had heard about him, I expected to meet somebody much heavier, but he has lost a great deal of weight in the last few years.

When I asked how he got into the Army, Bussell reflected for a moment, chuckled, and said: "Well, my father never knew it, but I volunteered."

"What do you mean?"

"My mom knew it," he said. "In front of my name there was a 'V,' but it looked like a check, and that's what I told Dad.

"He went to his grave never knowing I volunteered. Because he told me, 'Don't you volunteer. They'll get you soon enough.'

"My buddy and I, we got three sheets to the wind, and I said to him, 'Hell, let's volunteer.' So we went downtown. And they took me first, but my buddy Carl, he was married. When he got ready to sign up, they said, 'Are you married?' And he said 'Yeah.' They said 'Well, you can't sign.'

"We were figuring on going into the same outfit together. Instead, he waved goodbye to me when I went in."

Bob Hagerty was drafted in 1942. He was tall, gangly, and just out of high school, with dark brown hair and intense blue eyes.

He initially went to Fort Thomas, across the Mississippi River from his home in Norwood, Ohio. Then he was sent to Fort Riley, Kan., which was a horse cavalry replacement training center.

"I didn't even know how to mount a horse," Hagerty recalls. "I was afraid of horses. When they'd snort and throw that hoof, you could think of that hoof just breaking your leg. I had a fear of being kicked. I had a fear of being thrown when we were out riding. We had guys in basic training in Fort Riley, they just dissolved in tears. All their manliness was stripped away, and these guys would say, 'Sergeant, I can't do it,' and the sergeant would say, 'Get in there and fight!' They'd kind of shame you."

From Fort Riley, Hagerty was sent to Camp Lockett in California.

"In Lockett they had an amused look, 'Ahh, Fort Riley, eh?'" Hagerty says. "Many of the men had been there 18 months already, and they could quickly tell that you didn't know a hell of a lot.

"Even though I was at Lockett, I was there a brief time, so I wasn't a real cavalry man. The guys who were real cavalry men had been there so long they had a streak on their face from the strap of their campaign hat. They would wear the campaign hat kind of forward and the strap would cut under their nose. They wouldn't wear it under their chin, that was a rookie who fit it under his chin. Some of these guys had a sunburn all except for the strap, and they were proud of that look."

Shortly after Hagerty joined the 11th Cavalry Regiment at Camp Lockett, and not long after Bussell went into the 4th Armored Division at Pine Camp, both units were transferred to Fort Benning, Ga., where they became the cadre, or training corps, for the 10th Armored Division.

In the summer of 1943, the 10th Armored participated in the Tennessee maneuvers, bouncing through farmland and forest, knocking down fences and destroying crops that the government had to pay for, fording the muddy Cumberland River and getting bogged down on its banks, learning to corduroy roads by placing logs in the mud and to change track blocks on tanks and do a hundred other things that in a little over a year would save their lives a dozen times over.

On Sept. 20, 1943, shortly after returning from the Tennessee maneuvers, the 712th Tank Battalion was separated from the 10th Armored Division. It was one of a number of experimental "bastard battalions," self-sufficient units that were more streamlined than the cumbersome armored divisions and that could quickly be assigned where needed in combat. For the 712th, that versatility would enable it in Normandy to help out the 90th, 82nd Airborne, and 8th infantry divisions, although after the breakout it would work exclusively with the 90th.

Tony D'Arpino

Tony D'Arpino, from Whitman, Mass., was a tank driver in C Company.

I was working in a foundry when I got drafted. The day that I was supposed to go for my physical, I told my father -- he also worked at the foundry -- I said, "Don't tell them where I am." They were deferring guys because they were doing government work, and I didn't want to get deferred.

I can remember my father being shocked, because the morning I didn't go to work, the foreman comes to him and says, "Where's Tony?"

And my father says, "I don't know, he didn't come home last night."

And the foreman says to my father, "Is he shacking up?"

And of course my father, his Tony would never do anything like that. Anyway, I passed the physical, and they gave us two weeks to report. So the next morning I didn't go to work. I wasn't going to go to work no more, the hell with it. I was making 35 cents an hour. That's what they were paying. Thirty-five cents an hour. I take it back, it was 45 cents an hour.

Smoky Stuever

Ed "Smoky" Stuever was a sergeant in Service Company.

I was the first draftee out of Winnetka, Illinois. There were 29 volunteers ahead of me, so I was No. 30. Roosevelt picked me out of a cherry bowl.

The first number picked was 158, and mine was 185. The headline in the paper said 158 was the No. 1 draftee. I thought that was me, my equilibrium was off, and I gave the damn paper a kick, and the boss came running out of the house in his bathrobe. "What in the hell is the matter with you lad, you going be-zerk?" He was a corporate lawyer, with a red nose and cheeks from drinking scotch. I was his driver.

I picked up the paper and told him, "I'm sorry, sir...Oh, lookit here, 158, that ain't me. My number is 185."

"Oh, that's a good reason to celebrate. Come on in, me lad." And he pours me a shot of scotch. I'd never drank scotch in my life. I had four of 'em.

So I drove him to work, downtown Chicago, in an open touring car. I pull up, drop him off. He says, "Ed, take the car and enjoy yourself. Have a good day. Take your lady out to dinner." So I drove up to where my wife was working and said, "Come on, take the day off."

Jim Gifford

Lieutenant James L. Gifford, from Gloversville, N.Y., joined the battalion as a replacement in Normandy.

I was in Louisville, Kentucky -- a bunch of us had taken a hotel room for the night; that was the cheapest way out for soldiers -- when I heard a noise down the street. I looked out the window, and people were running around. So I went down to the lobby, and someone says, "We just got attacked in Pearl Harbor."

I said, "Where's Pearl Harbor?"

Someone said, "All I know is that they're telling soldiers to get back to camp."

So I went upstairs, I told the guys, and we all grabbed our stuff and went into the street. The civilians were pulling up in their cars and saying, "Soldier, we'll take you back to camp." Soon every car was full of soldiers, and we're all heading back from Louisville to Fort Knox, which was about thirty miles.

The next morning they lined us up, and they started reading off names: You're going to Fort Lewis, Washington. They thought the Japs were gonna hit the West Coast. Fort Lewis, Washington, they're reading all these names out. When they came to Jim Gifford, they said, "Armored Force School."

I said, "What? I don't believe this. There's a goddamn war on and I'm going to school?"

Russell Loop

Corporal Russell Loop, from Indianola, Ill., was a gunner in C Company.

I was drafted for a year, and I almost had the year in before Pearl Harbor. At the time, another boy named Jim Mills and I were carrying a major's horses in one end of a boxcar and his furniture in the other, and he was going to Fort Riley. He had a radio in his car, and he came out and said, "Boys, you'd just as well quit. I'm not going anywhere."

We had no idea what he was talking about.

So he said, "They've started a war. Pearl Harbor."

Then he went across the street, got a case of beer and a fifth of whiskey, and we sat in his car and drank beer and listened to the news the rest of the day.

Forrest Dixon

Major Forrest Dixon, from Munith, Mich., was the battalion maintenance officer.

I was commissioned a cavalry officer in the ROTC at Michigan State University, but when I got hauled in the Army, I went directly to Fort Knox, to go to school. From Fort Knox I was sent to the 4th Armored Division at Pine Camp, N.Y. Then the 4th Armored became the cadre of the 10th Armored Division at Fort Benning.

Meanwhile, the 11th Cavalry Regiment was supposed to ship out for Australia, but a lot of its members came down with jaundice from their yellow fever vaccinations. So they sat out there in California, and all of a sudden somebody decided to send them to Fort Benning to be part of the 10th Armored. So the 10th Armored had a cadre from the 4th Armored plus the 11th Cavalry.

For a while, the armored people and the horse cavalry didn't get along. Each outfit was allowed so many 24-hour passes, so many weekend passes, and so many furloughs. But the armored force people couldn't get them. It seemed like they all went to the cavalry. That's when I got in trouble. I gave three 24-hour passes to a kid who supposedly had a sick mother. See, a company commander could give a 24-hour pass, but he was limited in number. So I gave him three 24-hour passes, because the regiment wouldn't give him a three-day pass.

Then he went AWOL. He was supposed to be back for reveille on Monday morning, and he finally made it Wednesday afternoon. He came into the orderly room and said, "Sergeant Hensley reporting for duty, Sir."

I said, "Well, Private Hensley, explain."

He looked at me. "Private Hensley?"

"I reduced you to the grade of private this morning," I said. "I don't know what they're gonna do to me."

I got called over to regimental headquarters, and I got chewed out good. Then each of the majors there put a letter in my personnel file. So I was the oldest first lieutenant in the 10th Armored Division. I didn't get promoted for a long, long time.

Les Suter

Sergeant Lester J. Suter, from St. Louis, Mo., belonged to Service Company of the 712th.

I didn't want to be in the tanks. Fort Benning had a parachute school, and I said, "I'm going over and join the paratroopers." I liked the way they wore their hat, and the clothes they wore, they wore better boots than we did. They had a rugged attitude, too, like a commando attitude.

I wanted to be a tough guy, so I was going to go over there and join the paratroopers. And when I got over there, they said, okay, so they took me up this big goddamn tower, 750 feet. I looked down at the ground, and they said, "Now you put on this parachute and you jump." I said, "No way, I'm not jumping off this son of a bitch, take me down!" So they took me down and let me out. I went back to the tank battalion and was happy.

Bob Rossi

Pfc. Robert E. Rossi, from Jersey City, N.J., joined C Company as a replacement.

My brother Johnny was in the 4th Armored Division. Another of my brothers, Charlie, he's 72 years old now, he went to the draft board three or four times, and they kept turning him down.

The kids used to write in chalk out in the street, on the asphalt: "Charlie Rossi, 100 pounds soaking wet." I think they were exaggerating.

The fourth time he went, two doctors were arguing, one said we'll take him, the other said we're not gonna take him, and my mother went to the draft board and told them:

"You've got two of my sons already, how many more do you want?" So they deferred him.

Louis Gerrard

Corporal Louis Gerrard, from Philadelphia, was a gunner in C Company.

I got hurt coming back from the maneuvers in Tennessee. We were going down this road to the railroad yards to put the tanks on flatcars and take them back to Camp Gordon -- at that time it was Camp Gordon, it's Fort Gordon now -- and we were all very tired. We had been up getting the tanks prepared and everything, and the driver fell asleep. He hit this big tree, and I was thrown backward. The tank seats, they have prongs sticking up, they hit me in the back.

I was in a hospital in Camp Forrest, Tennessee, for quite a while, and then they transferred me back to Camp Gordon.

In the meantime, our battalion was taken out of the 10th Armored Division, and they made us a separate tank battalion. When I came back, all the guys said to me, "What the hell are you doing back here? You can get out of the Army. You've got the best deal going with your back injury."

I didn't want to get out of the Army. I told the guys, "I've got two brothers in the service, and they're both in North Africa, and I'd feel like hell if I got out of the Army. It wouldn't look good if I come home and they're still over there." So I stayed in."

Smoky Stuever

At Camp Lockett, there was a lieutenant who seemed to have a kid every year. This one particular time when he became a father he gave each one of us a cigar. That morning I lit my cigar, and there was a horse brought in that had a stub in its rear foot.

I knew that horse, he was a mean one to work on, and nobody dared to tackle him. I had worked on him before, and I said, "Ohhh, watch my smoke!"

I had this cigar in my mouth, and I picked up that horse's foot, and I said, "All right, give me those tongs," and I was about ready to pull the stub out when that horse started laying down on me, so I turned my head, that cigar hit the horse's hind end, and I went flying through the air.

"There goes Smoky!" someone said, and the nickname stuck with me.

Tony D'Arpino

When we were getting ready to go overseas, we all had our dental work done. Guys like me, if you had a cavity, you lost the whole tooth. They lined you up and they'd put you in the chair, "Yeah, that's got to come out." They'd give you novocaine, you'd get out and go back to the end of the line. And then when you came around again they pulled it.

Stanley Klapkowski, who was a gunner in most of the tanks I was in, had such perfect teeth, and white, they were beautiful. He had one little cavity, so they didn't want to yank it. They were gonna fill it. Now this is a true story. The dentist was Mexican, a little short guy, and he starts drilling. And Klapkowski knocks the drill out of his hand, he must have hit the nerve.

One more time, the dentist starts drilling, Klapkowski knocks the drill out of his hand. And the dentist says to Klapkowski, "What's the matter, can't you take it?"

And Klapkowski says, "You come outside, you son of a bitch, I'll show you if I can take it." He got restricted to the company grounds for a week for that.

In Fort Benning, I used to go to Mass with Klapkowski every Sunday. I never went in town with him, because I knew he was crazy. I hung around with the guys from Massachusetts, and that was it.

One Sunday morning, I wake up Klap -- we used to call him Klap -- and the blanket's over his head. I'm shaking him, and he isn't waking up. So I pulled the covers down. I didn't recognize him. His eyes were closed. His face was twice as big as it usually was. It scared me. I went and got the motor sergeant, he used to have his room right in the barracks, and we took Klapkowski to the medics.

He had gone in town the night before, and he saw this paratrooper, and he picked a fight with him. He said there were three or four of them who jumped him. He was in the hospital for a week.

Ruby Goldstein

Reuben Goldstein, from Dorchester, Mass., was a tank commander in A Company.

I had a similar incident. My driver, George Bussell, he was so stocky that when we went through basic training, they had like a ditch, in order to help somebody who got hurt, you had to carry them. You'd have to get on your back and crawl with him. I'm a hundred and fifty pounds or so, Bussell is two-fifty. It's like putting an automobile on you. That's how heavy he was. But I carried him.

We go into town, to Phenix City, Alabama, right over the little bridge from Columbus, Georgia, and they've got a barroom here, a barroom there, no matter which one you go to there's girls with the dice to sucker in the soldiers. So we go into one of the bars, and we stand at the bar, George and I, we have a drink. And we hear this music coming from a room.

We go into the room, and there's a couple of civilians sitting there, and a couple of girls. I go back to the bar, and George asks a girl to dance. She accepts. He's on the dance floor with her, then all of a sudden I hear something. I don't know what the hell it is; I hear a lot of noise.

So I run in there. George is on the floor, the girl is on the side, and this guy's got a chair and he's whacking at him. He objected, the Southerners objected to him dancing with one of their girls. This guy was gonna lift the chair up to hit George with it. I grabbed him, and I suckered him one. A guy got up from the table, grabbed me and suckered me one. Now we're all on the floor.

I got up. I went crazy. And George was banged up real bad. Now I've got to get him out of there, because I know the two of us are not gonna last too long.

I got ahold of him, we got him out, and I know damn well the MPs, if they grabbed us, we're locked up, forget it. I got him out of there, I got him back to camp, and his face was all puffed up.

Forrest Dixon

One of my boys came up to the officer's club at Fort Benning and said, "Captain, there's something you should know."

I said, "What?"

"Well," he said, "you know we're going to do some maneuvers over in Alabama tomorrow." And he said, "You know, Bussell was over in Alabama and he got rolled, and he was over there last night checking things out, and Mom's Place" -- that's where he got rolled -- "there's no basement under it.

"Now tomorrow, when you go over the bridge, you're gonna have a brake lock and your tank is going through Mom's Place -- in the front door and out the back. I thought you ought to know."

I said, "Thank you."

I didn't say a thing to Bussell. So the next day, why, here we go over the bridge, and I look, and I see Mom's Place. I open up the mike and I say, "Bussell, there's Mom's Place. Now you make god damn sure that we don't go in the front door."

He looked up at me and burst out laughing. "Who told you!" And that was the end of that. He was going right through it. He would have, too.

George Bussell

Sergeant George Bussell was a tank driver in A Company.

Sonofagun I wanted to do that! I said to Dixon, "Let's take it through the house." I was afraid of a basement. Boy, I'd have loved that.

Hell, that was some fight we got in in Phenix City. I ended up with a busted nose and a black eye, and I had six stitches in the top of my head. That guy really whupped me over with a walking cane.

I was in this place, and in the back you could dance. So I was back there playing the jukebox for this girl.

Before the fight started there were beer bottles and everything else laying around on the tables. Whiskey bottles. I asked her if she wanted to dance, and this guy was standing there, and he said, "What did you say to her?"

I said, "Hell, I asked her to dance. You don't mind, do you?"

That's all it took. He peeled off, and three or four of them started coming at me. I started backing up, and when I was backing up I fell over a chair and fell right down on a table. And this one guy jumped up there with a walking cane and hit me about four times across the head, broke my nose and busted my head open.

Of course, with all that rumpus back there, a bunch of other GIs came in there and stopped it.

CHAPTER 2

Baptism of Fire

July 3, 1944

Trigger 1 -- that was the radio call name of Jim Rothschadl's tank -- was the last to clamber into the hold of the LST in Weymouth, England, on the morning of June 27, 1944, because as platoon leader Jim Flowers' tank it would be the first one off. Rothschadl, the tank's gunner, had neglected to lower the .50-caliber machine gun mounted on the turret, and the top of the LST's huge door almost snapped it off, but after a few epithets from an officer at the loading dock the 33-ton medium tank was inside and the door clattered shut.

It took almost 30 hours to cross the English Channel. The tanks, packed as close as five inches apart, would rub together with a screech when the hull pitched in the water.

The hold reeked from a combination of the rotten egglike odor of the Bostic used to waterproof the tanks and the vomit from some of the seasick tankers. The crews were told to stay near the tanks and didn't go topside.

When the order finally came to enter the tanks and the big door opened, Utah Beach looked very far away as Rothschadl peered through the gunner's periscope. He could see a big ship laying on its side like a monster on the beach. Then the driver fired up the Wright-Whirlwind engine and the tank proceeded down the ramp and into the water.

Rothschadl couldn't see a thing as the periscope stuck out only five or six inches above the water line, and he said to himself, "My God, we're going to drown!" Then he felt the tracks catch hold on the sandy bottom, and heard the engine churning the water underneath, and he breathed a sigh of relief.

The 712th was one of 87 independent tank battalions used in World War II: 762 enlisted men and officers, 57 medium tanks, 17 light tanks, three 105-millimeter assault guns, its own maintenance and headquarters companies, and assorted jeeps and trucks. Although it was the seventh tank battalion to land in Normandy, it was one of the first to get ashore with virtually all of its equipment intact.

The battalion's B, C and D Companies were assigned to the 90th Infantry Division in Normandy, and A Company was sent to the 82nd Airborne Division.

By the end of their first day in combat -- July 3rd -- several of the tankers had been killed, many more wounded, and approximately half of the battalion's tanks were knocked out, bogged down, tipped over, or otherwise disabled.

"At this rate," Captain Forrest Dixon remarked to Lieutenant Colonel George B. Randolph early the following morning, "we'll be good for one more day."

"No," said Colonel Randolph, the battalion commander, who was a schoolteacher in civilian life. "If we lost half our tanks yesterday, and we lose half of the ones remaining today, and half of those that are left tomorrow, we'll be good for several days."[1]

Bob Hagerty

It's funny, you remember not the tragic things, like when you see somebody who just died, because no matter how much you mourn him you're not going to bring him back. What you tend to think of is the goofy things. Like the time, I think Big Andy [Bob Anderson] was my tank driver, and we were supporting the infantry. We came across a little clearing, and I remember we came to some small trees, and I had to urinate. We didn't see anything out in front of us. I said, "Andy, hold it right here, I'm gonna get out a minute," and I jumped out and started to urinate right by the tracks.

A couple of the other guys decided to get out of the tank as well. And we all were about half-finished when we heard some small arms fire. There were Germans, we hadn't seen them. Whatever we were doing, the process stopped right there. We jumped onto the back of the turret, and we had the turret between us and them, we were able to duck inside the tank. You know, that's so many years ago, but I still remember that. Or a time right after we'd been committed in France, I think it was even before the first person in the battalion was killed, and our tanks were being brought up to a certain place in support of the 82nd Airborne. They were dug in, and they fancied themselves as super soldiers. They had these distinctive outfits and they carried grenades hooked onto their uniform legs, and they had big knives, they said they killed quietly rather than shooting, so it all sounded very grizzly. We were supposed to take our platoon of tanks -- Ed Forrest was our platoon leader -- into position just slightly behind where the infantry would be. That meant we had to go up a little dirt road and make a turn onto a smaller dirt road and that would bring us into position.

Forrest went first, then the Number 2 tank, the Number 3 tank, and I was Number 4, I was the platoon sergeant. Somebody had told Forrest, "Look, when you go up this road and you take the right turn, hit the gas, don't worry about sliding around the turn or maybe running into some small saplings, hit the gas, because there's a German gun that's trained on the road."

[1]The 712th Tank Battalion would spend 311 days in combat, most of them actively engaged with the enemy.

So he goes up, and gets around there, and he goes over where this infantry position is, and Number 2 goes up, and Number 3 goes up, and then I went up, and as I made the turn, I heard this loud metallic sound, but the tank kept moving, so I thought, "We haven't been hit?" Then Number 5 tank came along behind me.

When we got up behind the infantry, and we got out to see if anything had happened, there was a big hole in an apparatus on the back end of the tank that was useful for a tank that was discharged into the water, it redirected your exhaust portals. What the German had done, he'd fired as I rounded that corner, and his shell went through this shield. We were a millisecond away from him penetrating our tank.

People who knew said, "Oh, that was an 88," you could tell by the size of the hole. Well, an 88 was big enough to knock out our tanks any day in the week.

After that, the guys in the company who hadn't yet been exposed to battle, you know, they didn't have any war stories -- they were gonna have damn shortly, but they didn't have them then -- they could say, "Look at Hagerty's tank, look at that hole."

George Bussell

We still had those big shrouds on the tanks from landing in the water. Hagerty was the tank commander and I was his driver[1]. We were coming down this road, we stopped at this crossroad, and boy, one came in close. Because they had everything zeroed in.

I said to Bob, "We'd better move." So we moved on up to a hedgerow, and backed around so we could get a shot at anything coming.

I got out of the tank, and went back and was eating a sandwich. I leaned over on the tank with my hand, and in that shroud that comes up, just below the end of the tank, there was a big hole. That 88 went clear through it. I said to Bob, "That's pretty damn close, ain't it?"

And we were carrying Bangalore torpedoes on the back of the tank. They came in two pieces, and you could hook them together. Then instead of blowing up, they blew down. You could use them to blow a hole through a hedgerow. I saw that hole, it was inches from those Bangalore torpedoes. I said to Hagerty, "Look at that. I don't know about you, but I'm getting rid of these torpedoes." I threw 'em over the hedgerow. That was too close for comfort.

[1]Bussell drove Hagerty's tank in Normandy. There was considerable shifting of personnel among crews. As the platoon sergeant, Hagerty rode in the fourth tank. Later, when he received a battlefield commission, he moved to the first tank. It is possible that that is when Bob Anderson became his driver.

Jim Gifford

After we landed at the beach, we got up into Ste. Mere Eglise,[1] that was the first town that was in the process of being taken, and there were gliders all over the place. Loaded with gliders. Every field had gliders tipped up, turned over, there were ten, fifteen guys in the nose of them, still laying there, and all their equipment, dead. There were so many gliders that struck things and killed all the men in them. It was pathetic.

I walked up to a glider and I saw these guys all in there and there was nobody you could help, they were all dead, no question about it, some guys spilled out on the ground.

I saw a Reader's Digest laying on the ground by a glider, and on the side of it, it had an American flag, about an inch wide. I cut that off the Reader's Digest, and I picked up a piece of plastic from the windshield of the glider.

Later, I took the handle off my .45 and I carved a new handle with the plastic, and I put the American flag from the Reader's Digest underneath it. I've still got the gun. It was on my hip all through the war. It was my buddy wherever I was, and I was damn well sure I was gonna bring it home. We were supposed to turn that stuff in when we got back. I said to hell with it, let them find me, I'm keeping this, and I've still got it. I even have a permit for it.

Smoky Stuever

My first mission was to retrieve an A Company tank that lost a track on Hill 122, a shell blew off some blocks of track.

On my way up there, the mortar fire started coming in pretty heavy, so I had my driver, Shorty [Marion Kubeczko], shut off the tank. I ran around behind the tank and dove underneath the engine. There was a limb about two inches in diameter, and I was hanging onto that, with my head turned sideways, and all of a sudden I look and there's a piece of shrapnel dug into that limb. When I saw that piece of hot metal smoking in that wood, I thought, "I've got to get out of here!" So I stood behind the tank and crouched over, I thought, well, the most I could do is lose a leg.

Then the mortar fire ceased and I saw where I had to go. I ran back to the tank retriever, and I said, "Let's go." We got up there and I made a very quick surmise of it because the tank was right out in the open, and I told the men to bring in a section of five track blocks. It took us only ten minutes to change them and put the tank back on the road, and we got out of there.

[1]Although he was not assigned to the 712th until mid-July, Gifford landed at Utah Beach within a few days of D-Day.

The next day we had to go to the middle of Hill 122, and over to the right, where there was a D Company tank turned over in a ditch. We turned it over, and in order to get it out of there we had to tow it about a quarter of a mile farther up the road into an opening that looked like a picnic area.

There was a cottage there, and some of the guys went over and examined that cottage. My tank was towing the D Company tank, and as we backed it around, I stood behind a great big tree that was at least two feet in diameter, and directed the movements. Then the sniper fire got heavy, and the bark of the tree was peeling off right next to me, so I told Shorty to get out of there on the double, and as he went out I ran around the tank on the opposite side and I crawled on it.

As we got down a little ways, the Army had laid a big, heavy smokescreen so the Germans couldn't see where I was. And right at that time one of the pins wobbled out of the towbar because one of the men didn't lock it in with a cotter pin, and it vibrated out of there. The tank went back in the ditch and bent my towbar and it bent my patience.

We hooked it up again and pulled it into a group of apple trees and we shut it off, because the mortar fire was starting to come in quite heavy.

A little bit farther up ahead on the right side of the road was a big gravel pit, a stone quarry that they used for building roads. There was a bunch of foxholes in there that the Germans must have dug, and as I jumped into one of the foxholes, I saw this shiny piece of piano wire, and underneath some leaves was a German potato masher[1] on the other end of that wire. I almost fainted, or was on the verge of it, and I just rolled up out of that hole, and I couldn't yell or talk, I just pointed, and old Chap -- that's Sergeant Kochan -- saw me and he said "What the hell's the matter with you, Smoky?" And I kept pointing at that hole, I couldn't talk, and then I finally was able to say, "Don't go in there."

Then he saw it and said "Everybody lay low." He threw a piece of a log in the foxhole, and it wasn't long before that piece flew out of there and it was shredded.

I finally regained my strength. I couldn't do anything. I had to go over by the tank, sit down, and drink some good old cider, because the water wasn't fit for humans, and I regained my ego, and we continued to fix that D Company tank.

Mike Anderson

Mike Anderson, from Needham, Mass., drove one of the three 105-millimeter assault guns in Headquarters Company. The assault guns were mounted on medium tanks.

We were on a hardtop road, and we came by a farmhouse. I was in the first tank, and they let us go through. The second tank got hit and burned. That's the one in which Richard Howell was killed.

[1]Concussion grenade

After we passed the farmhouse, we got into the orchard, and we were weaving back and forth around the trees. There was a German tank in the corner. He shot at us a couple of times. The first one hit the ground, and the second one knocked our track off. We fired back, and our first round went over it. The gunner dropped the barrel as far as he could, and let the next round go, and it caught that German tank right under the big gun, right above where the driver was sitting.

After we got squared away, we walked over and looked at this tank. The driver was still in there, he was dead. The rest of the crew had jumped out and gone back. But they had another round in the gun, and that breach was almost closed completely. If they'd have closed it, I think that's the one that would have got us before we got them.

CHAPTER 3

Hill 122

July 3-13, 1944

Hill 122, so named because of its height in meters above sea level, had a commanding view of the invasion beaches.

To the French, it was part of the Foret de Mont Castre. To the Germans, it was a strong point in the Mahlmann Line, which was to be held at any cost.

To the 712th Tank Battalion, which had never been in combat; and the 90th Infantry Division, which had struggled since D-Day, it was a crucible, in the fires and the mud and the blood of which would be forged one of the most effective tank-and-infantry teams in the European Theater of Operation.

Virtually the entire tank battalion was on or around Hill 122 in the first few days of fighting, in villages with names such as Pretot and Beau Coudray and Les Sablons and La Haye du Puits and Ste. Suzanne and St. Jores. The terrain was rugged: small fields divided by hedgerows, which the tankers describe as if they were designed by the devil: chest-high networks of bushes and shrubs that had a thousand years to intertwine their roots until they were solid as rock, with Germans on one side and Americans on the other, or Americans behind one hedgerow and Germans behind the next, or suicidal snipers invisible inside them. Fields interspersed with hedgerows, thick forest, dense underbrush, one blacktop road running from La Haye du Puits on the north toward Periers on the south, a few sunken dirt roads, a sclitary railroad track. Clay soil that made it difficult for the tread of a 33-ton tank to take hold and swamp that made it impossible.

Reuben Goldstein and Charles Bahrke of A Company would earn the battalion's first Silver Stars near Hill 122, crawling back under their tank after it was hit, climbing up through the escape hatch in its belly, and knocking out the German 88-millimeter gun that had been firing at them. Smoky Stuever would lose his closest buddy, Marion "Shorty" Kubeczko, on Hill 122 when a mortar shell came down through the open hatch of the tank recovery unit Kubeczko was driving. Pfc. Richard Howell, who had mailed three postdated letters to his wife, Lillian, in Arcadia, La., would be killed at the base of Hill 122 when a shell from a German Mark IV tank penetrated the gun shield of Howell's 105-millimeter assault gun.

Today a monument stands on Hill 122. The names of nine members of First Platoon, C Company who were killed on July 10, 1944, are inscribed on it.

"On the morning of July 3rd, 1944," Jim Flowers, who was a 30-year-old lieutenant at the time, says, "the 712th Tank Battalion, being attached to the 90th Infantry Division, was making an assault toward Hill 122."

Jim Flowers stands about 6-foot-2, and speaks with a rich Texas drawl. He walks with some delicacy, is quick to smile, and exudes a contagious sort of warmth. He has very little patience for people who ask him to cut to the chase.

"First Platoon, Company C, had been assigned to work with the First Battalion of the 359th Infantry, part of the 90th Infantry Division. Company A was assigned to work with the 82nd Airborne.

"I'd moved my tanks up with the First Battalion of the 359 the evening before. Sometime early in the morning the artillery shelled the area in front of us, a little preparation fire, where there was a little town, Pretot.

"An infantry colonel named Paul Hamilton was the commander of the First Battalion of the 359. When Hamilton and I were planning how to make this attack, we had gone out and climbed a tree so we had better observation. Now, I've got better sense than that, but Hamilton, he wanted to, so hell, I'm not gonna let an infantry soldier outdo me at anything.

"We were looking down a slight hill toward a creek. After the artillery lifted, Colonel Hamilton took two companies of infantry and jumped off toward Pretot going down the hill and across the creek, and up the other side to the village, which was about a mile in front of us.

"My tanks were off on the left-hand side of the road. I couldn't go down to the creek and cross it because the banks were too steep, and I couldn't take my tanks down the road because the road was mined, so I had to wait for the engineers.

"It wasn't long after Hamilton left with his two companies until somebody said that Hamilton had been wounded down near the creek. There's a boy named Leroy Pond from Fayetteville, Arkansas, he was a captain at the time, he took command of the battalion and they continued the attack.

"About this time, I heard some tanks, and no tanks are supposed to be coming down this road. I was about 50 yards off the road, and I ran out to the road and looked, and hell, here comes a column of five tanks, and George Tarr[1] is leading them. Then he stopped, and I said, 'What the hell are you doing here?' And he's looking for where he's supposed to be.

"'You're in the wrong place,' I told him. 'You're supposed to go on the other side of the road. The 82nd Airborne is over there, and you're supposed to go through them.'

[1]George Tarr was a lieutenant in A Company.

"Tarr said, 'Well, I want to go down here.'

"They got maybe three hundred yards down the road, when the lieutenant who was in charge of the mine removal squad came back and told me that the lieutenant who was leading the tanks down there had been killed.

"He said Tarr stopped and got down off his tank, and came over and was talking to him, and almost immediately, his tanks are drawing artillery fire. And this infantry lieutenant says, "Get the hell out of here, fella, you're bringing fire in on us." So Tarr turned around, went back to his tank and started climbing up the side of it. You put your foot up on a bogey wheel, and then up on the track. Then he thought of something else and he turned around, and he went back to the infantry lieutenant, and after the infantry lieutenant answered his question, he turned around and started to climb back up on the tank, and a shell landed on the road beside the tank and right behind George.

"They dragged George over in the ditch beside the road. I can still see him, he's over there in the ditch, leaning back, like he was taking a nap."

Jim Rothschadl

Corporal Jim Rothschadl, from Waubun, Minn., was Jim Flowers' gunner on Hill 122.

I took my basic training at Fort Benning. Tough training, too. You had to go through a two- or three-week period called Tiger Camp that would kill an ordinary guy. They kept you on the go 24 hours a day practically. They'd just about drive you out of your mind. I wouldn't last half a day at it now.

At first there was no 712th Tank Battalion. We were Company I of the 10th Armored Division. I was in Company I, 11th Armored Regiment, 10th Armored Division. Later on the whole battalion was split off.

They had an armored school at Fort Benning. Each company was supposed to send one or two guys, and I was asked to go. It lasted about six weeks. After it was over with, one morning in formation the captain read off a commendation for me. Out of 500, I was the second highest. It surprised me. Later on, he sent me to gunnery school at Fort Knox for two months.

When I got back, there was a position that I thought might be opening. The armory had a person who assigned weapons and kept them repaired and made sure they were all brought in after they were taken out. I was in the armory when Jim Flowers came by and started talking to me. I had never met him before. He had only recently transferred to our unit.

We had quite a chat there. He came back another time and we talked some more. The third time he came back was several days later. "I'd like to have you in my tank," he said, "as a gunner."

"I'd rather not, really," I said. I didn't want to be inside of a tank. I'd been in a tank quite a bit. I drove a tank, and fired out of a tank for weeks and months. There isn't a lot of room in that turret. It's claustrophobic when you're locked in there.

Flowers didn't say much. He left, and then he came back a few days later and said, "Well, that's the way it's gonna be. You're gonna be my gunner."

Jim Flowers

I took my tanks on into Pretot, and I found Leroy Pond and his battalion staff out in the edge of an apple orchard. There are a lot of apple orchards in Normandy. I went over and told him I'm there, I'm ready to go to work, words to that effect. We were planning how we were gonna get everything organized and get up on the line where we were supposed to be, and maintain contact with the units on our left and right.

The thing I'll never forget was that some replacements came up for the First Battalion, and some of these boys, you could look at them and tell that they were scared half to death before they ever actually came under enemy fire. One boy that I remember in particular was a young captain, he reported in to Pond, and as they'd come in, Pond would assign them to whatever job he wanted them to do, and have a sergeant take them out to where they're supposed to be.

Pond sent this young captain up to take command of one of the companies where the company commander had become a casualty, and that kid, he didn't make it all the way up there, he fell apart before he got there. The sergeant brought him back, and he says, "He can't make it." He was sitting over on the ground, shaking like he had a bad chill.

If it were one of my boys, I would have gone over and grabbed that young fellow in the front of his shirt and shook the hell out of him and told him, "Now look, you've been trained to do a job. You're a captain in the infantry, and it's your job to do this, and all of us are frightened. Now you get your butt up from here and you go up there and take command of that company."

But Pond didn't do that. He sent the captain back. I think the common terminology to describe that boy's condition was battle fatigue, and he'd never been in a battle.

On July 6, Pond and I got the word to make the assault for Hill 122. People had been there before, some tried to get up and couldn't do it.

The north side of Hill 122 is pretty steep, and there's no way we're going to get the infantry or anything else up there. But you don't need to, because on each end it's not all that steep. That's the reason we approached it from the ends instead of making a frontal assault.

Pond and I were going to go up the west side of Hill 122 and the Second Battalion, under the command of Colonel Don Gorton, was going to come up the east side.

There's sparse vegetation on this slope where we were. No place to hide anything. Maybe a bird could hide in there, and maybe a cottontail rabbit could, but certainly nothing so large as a tank. So after I crossed the railroad tracks I'm drawing fire.

I've got to get out of there and I've got to do it in a hurry. The only thing I can do is run down the road toward the east end of the hill, and I'm under observation all the way. So I took my tanks and went barreling down there, and got down to a wooded area between the road and the railroad, and ran into Lieutenant Lombardi [Lt. Charles Lombardi led the third platoon of C Company]. And Don Gorton with his Second Battalion is there, they're waiting to get the word to move out and go up on the hill. So Gorton and I plan that when we get the word we'll move up the east end. I went over and told Lombardi what I was gonna do.

Hill 122 had been occupied by the Roman legions back in the third, fourth century a.d. Matter of fact, there's a stone quarry I called it, an excavation, up there to this day, and I think there's a building or the foundations for some buildings that the Romans had built there fifteen, sixteen hundred years ago.

I took my tanks and ran up this gully on the east side of the hill, expecting that the next moment would be the last of me, but I didn't draw any fire. Lombardi's tanks were right behind me, and the infantry was right with us.

We got up on the top of the hill from the east side, but I can't stay there. I'm supposed to be down on the west end, where Pond is bringing his infantry people up.

I dashed on down to the other end of the hill, and some of Pond's people were already there. Pond stayed there long enough to catch his breath. He hadn't had all that much opposition anyhow. Then he moved part of his battalion in a southwesterly direction, and got out onto a gently sloping hill on the other side of Hill 122.

The Germans probably let him get out there, and then moved in behind him and cut him off. So he's sitting out there with a couple of companies from his battalion, and the Germans had cut their wire line, their telephone line, so the only communication he has is with his radio.

George Porter, who at that time was headquarters company commander of that battalion, asked me if I could take some stuff out there. I said why hell, yes. They needed rations. They needed water. They needed medical supplies. They needed ammunition. Plus they needed batteries for the radio.

I said, "You get the stuff up here, and I'll load it on the decks of my tanks and make a dash out there to him."

While they're bringing the stuff up, we get word that the Second Battalion of the 358th Infantry, which was also up on the hill by then, had encountered some pretty terrific fighting in the woods. So I took my tanks in there to drive the Germans back.

There was a heavy mist. I couldn't see very far anyhow, so I got inside the tank, closed the turret hatches, and tried to see out of the damn periscope. Only there's no good way to get the water off of the front glass of the periscope. The only way you can clean it is

HILL 122 - July 3, 1944

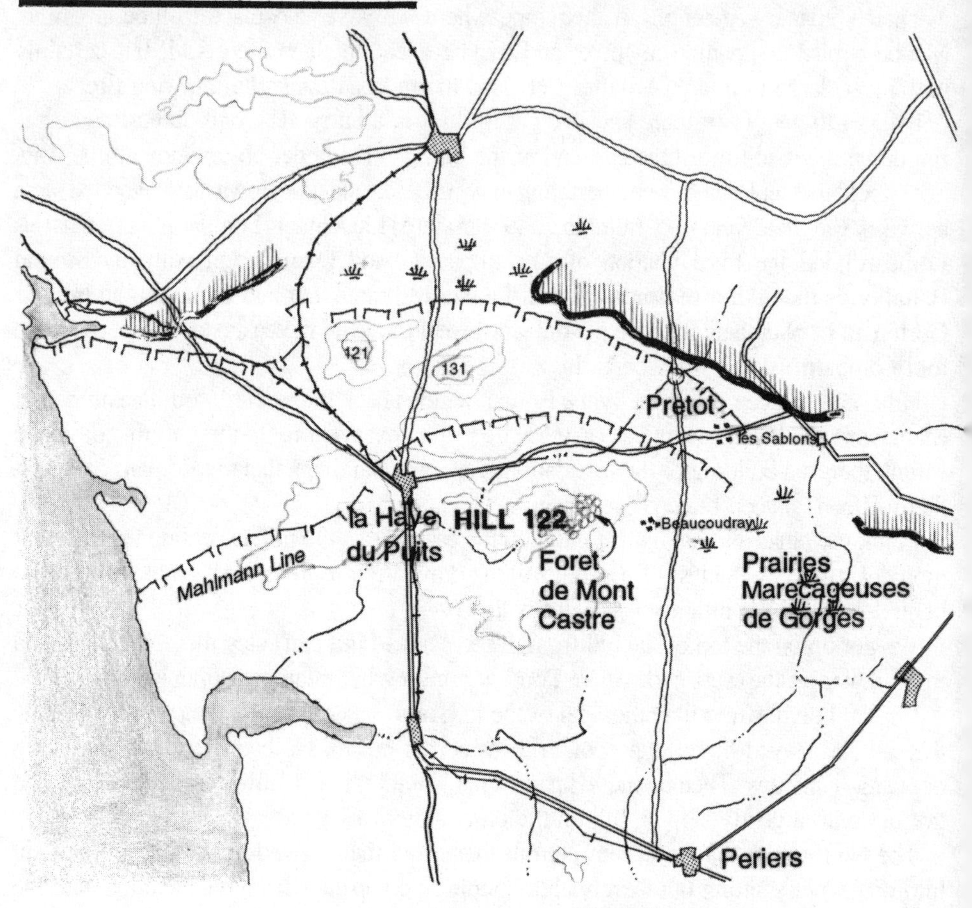

HILL 122 - July 15, 1944

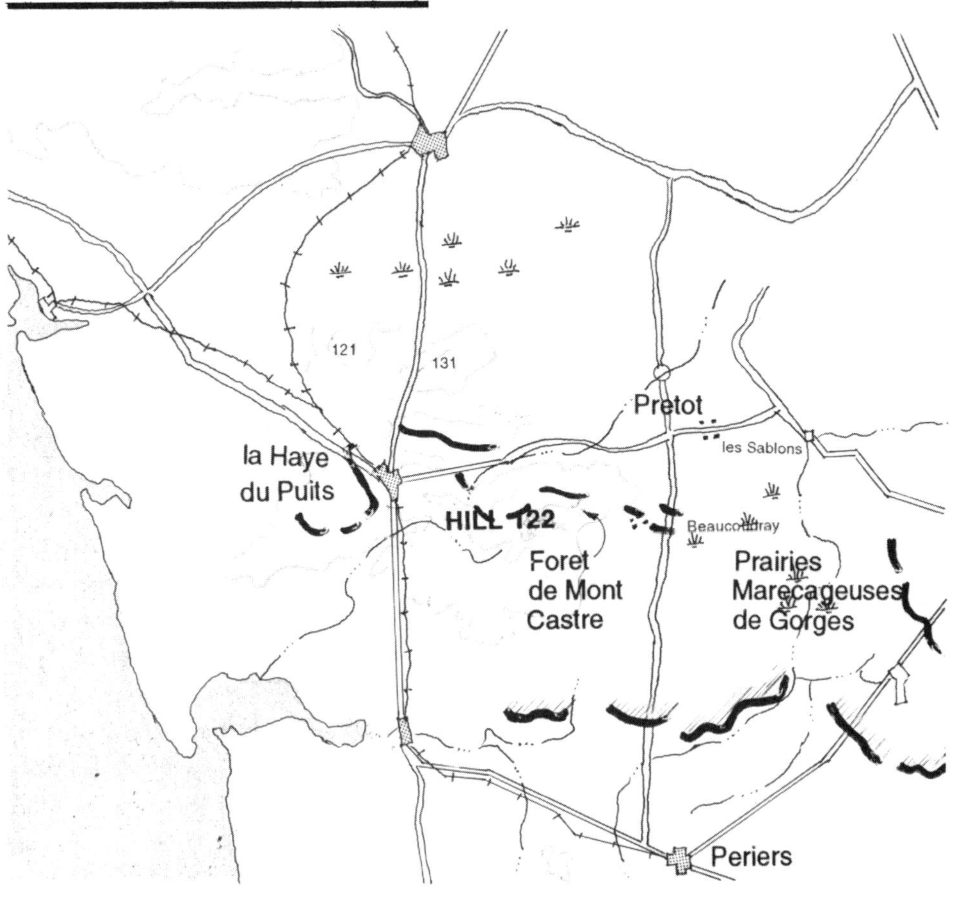

to pull it down a bit and shove it back up, and it wipes the water off of it, but you can't even do that because you're sure enough blind when you pull it down, even if it takes just five seconds.

I started drawing fire on my tanks, and suddenly very close by I saw a bazooka team. The Germans had an anti-tank weapon called a panzerfaust. Up close, it looked like a 16-inch coast artillery piece, although it was really a little over three inches around. Whew, I saw that damn thing pointing at me, and fortunately we were able to get a shot off before he could get us in his sights and squeeze one off.

In the meantime, I've unbuttoned, so that I can stand up on the seat and see what the hell I'm doing.

While we were out there, the stuff that we were going to take out to Pond arrived. They loaded it on the back decks of my tanks. David Hickman, who was a staff officer in Pond's battalion, was going to ride along with us. He had been out there with Pond and had managed to get back, that's how we knew how critical his need was to get some aid out there and get it there in a hurry.

We tried a couple of times that night, but we had to turn back. It was a dark night, and we don't know what the hell is out in front of us, and the Germans are shooting at us. So we turned back because we need more light.

The morning of the Seventh, we tried it again.

Going around that west side of the hill, off on my right front, there's a hedgerow, quite a distance away, and I could see some bushes moving. Bushes and small shrubs, trees, they don't move, but these were moving parallel to that hedgerow. This has got to be a vehicle. So we zeroed in on it and stopped it.

We continued around the road a little bit further and here come a couple of German soldiers walking up the middle of the road. They turned out to be Polish. They had their fingers laced on top of their heads, and they were unarmed.

I don't know what's in front of me, but those boys know. So we turned them around and marched them right back down the road in front of those tanks.

I let them walk in front of my tanks for maybe a hundred yards, and all of a sudden it dawned on me, "Uh, uh, Flowers, you can't do this." I don't know if this is against the Geneva Convention or whether it's against the written law or not, but it's certainly against the moral law to do this. Those kids have surrendered, and here I've placed them in a position to get killed.

So far as those boys were concerned, the war was over. They had surrendered. So I stopped, and they looked back. I motioned for them to come back, and had Ed Dzienis, my loader, who was Polish, tell them to get their butts back up the road and somebody would find them and take care of them.

I went down this road a bit further, and off on the left hand side in front of me I sure enough did see a cannon down there that had a muzzle on it that looked like it was two feet in diameter -- it's an 88 -- but it looked huuugge.

Again, the Lord was on my side. I saw this anti-tank gun dug in on the side of this road, and fortunately, I swung the turret around and had Jim Rothschadl, my gunner, pick him up in his sight and lay one round of high explosive on that gun, and we knocked him out before he could fire a shot at us.

We went on over a distance, four or five hedgerows, and I cut back to the right trying to find Leroy Pond and his battalion, and I ran into some of his boys, led by a captain. I got out of the tank and walked over to him and asked him if he knew where the battalion command post was, and he pointed and said, "I think it's over there somewhere."

Then I said, "You ought to get the hell out of here." He was down in one of these sunken roads, with a hedgerow on either side. "This is not a good place for you to be."

"Oh," he said, "we've got a lot of cover."

I said, "Yeah, you've got the wrong kind of cover. Don't stay in here. I implore you, get the hell out."

I got back in the tank and we went on over to find Pond, and would you believe it wasn't very long after that until the Germans shelled that position where the double hedgerow was and killed that captain and the fellows that were in there with him? If he had only listened and believed me that he was in the wrong place at the wrong time...

When I found Pond, I dispersed my tanks behind his infantry. They took the supplies that I'd brought, and if I'd have been a 20-year-old beautiful blonde he'd probably have kissed me.

They unloaded the stuff and distributed it. He didn't have any orders to move, and I'm certainly not going anywhere without him. Hell, it's his war as much as it is mine.

While we're there, a lieutenant, I think he was with a machine gun platoon of one of their companies, came over and said, "Do you mind taking your tanks out in this field here and seeing if those Germans are still out there?" He said, "I shot at one that raised up out of a foxhole, and I don't know whether I got him or not."

He pointed toward this little clump of shrub or brush growing out in the middle of a field full of weeds.

I got my tank and Judd Wylie's, and we jumped over the hedgerow and went out there, and there was a German soldier down in this big foxhole, the war was over for him. We went on by, and out in front of us we flushed a few Germans out, kind of like flushing quail out of the brush. I use that analogy because of the way these Germans would jump up and run a bit and then fall down so you didn't get a good shot at 'em.

We swung back over in front of the First Battalion's position and saw some soldiers in a ditch over there, and I thought I've come on a bunch of Germans trying to hide from me over there, so I thought, "Boy, this is going to be easy. I'll just pull up to this ditch and I can mow 'em down."

I ran over there, and just as I got up there, why, some lieutenant jumped up and started waving his arms, "Don't shoot! Don't shoot!" An American. He had a patrol out there.

Wylie was coming up on my right side in back of me, and he started shooting. He was too close for me to get him on my radio, so I just swung my turret-mounted .30-caliber around -- I used a .30 instead of a .50 on top of my turret -- I bounced a few rounds off the side of his turret to get his attention, and I gave him a signal to stop firing. I hollered at him -- he was close enough that I could holler and tell him those are American kids over there.

Luckily, he didn't hit any of them.

When we got back to the command post, this lieutenant that had asked me to go out there in the first place says that one of his sergeants had followed my tanks out there, and he says, "He didn't come back. I think that he probably got hit."

Well, I'll go back out and get him. He says, "I'll go with you this time if you don't mind," so, get in, let's go. We took my tank and Wylie's and we went back out there, pulled up on each side of this foxhole, and sure enough, this American soldier was down in it, but he hadn't been hit, he just had been scared half to death. We let him scramble up over the side and get in the tank. I think we put him over in Wylie's tank.

We pulled up a little bit, and a German bazooka team, two men, raised up out of some weeds off to my right. The first inkling I had that there was anything over there at all was I could see this damn rocket coming at me. Head-on, a little to my right. It's unbelievable that you can actually see those things flying through the air, it had a little trail of smoke behind it.

Of course, there's nothing I can do. I saw the thing and saw the soldiers who fired it, and that damn rocket hit on top of my track. I had rubber track blocks, and it hit one of the track connectors.

When that rocket hit, there was a blinding flash of light and I just knew that it was all over. I thought that was the end of it.

I shot at these soldiers and I don't know, maybe we got 'em, maybe we didn't. But when that thing hit that track and didn't come in, and I realized that the damage is outside, I had Horace Gary, my driver, try to move forward slowly to see what happens, and the tank moved. Both sides of it moved. I said well, the track's not completely off.

We went back over a hedgerow, and as we were going over it, half of the turret hatch on Wylie's tank -- the turret hatches are in two pieces, and they fold down -- one of the halves came unlatched and hit Wylie on his fingers, it crushed them.

Wylie didn't want to say anything about it. "Get back, go to the medics," I said.

I had Abraham I. Taylor, my platoon sergeant, take the damaged tank back for repairs, and I sent Wylie back with it.

So we're sitting there with Pond's infantry, and there are still no orders to move. We spent two nights there.

Sometime on the morning of the 10th of July, Jack Sheppard -- Lieutenant Harlo J. Sheppard -- arrived. By then, I needed gasoline for my tanks. I needed ammunition. He brought two trucks up there loaded with jerry cans of gasoline, and some water, and ammunition, and of course, rations, those delicious C rations. I think he had taken command of the company by then, because Jim Cary became a casualty on the Third. He got out of his jeep to open a gate, the gate was boobytrapped, and he picked up some fragments. Sheppard had been the motor officer for C Company, but now he was the company commander.

Sheppard told me that there was an infantry outfit back on Hill 122 -- we're beyond Hill 122 and to the right of it now -- he said there was a battalion of infantry that had been cut off, and they were having a rough go of it.

Well, it looks like they need some help, and they need some help from somebody that's got maximum firepower, and that's my tanks.

In the meantime, the tank that I'd sent back with Taylor had been repaired, so now I've got five tanks.

I went over and asked Captain Pond if he had any orders for us to move, and he said, "Nope, not yet," so I told him about this battalion cut off back there in the woods on Hill 122 and said I ought to go over there and help those people get out of that mess, and he says, "Okay. Now, you will come back?"

I said, "Oh, sure. I don't know how long it'll take. I'll certainly be back before dark."

"Okay," he says. "We need you. 'Bye."

Jack Sheppard

Lieutenant Harlo J. Sheppard, from Tampa, Fla., was the commander of Company C.

There are three presidential unit citations in the 712th. One of them is for the first platoon, C Company. I was with it at the time.

I was taking this tank to Jim Flowers. It was one of his tanks that had been knocked out and we got a replacement for.

We got up on top of the hill and we were going down towards Flowers. I was in a jeep leading the tank, with Jim Bailey as my driver, when a lieutenant colonel stopped me. He said, "I need some tanks down there. I've got a battalion that's surrounded by SS and they need tank support but bad."

I said, "Well, let me see if I can get Flowers released." He was with another infantry battalion, I don't know which.

I called the division commander, and he by voice authorized me, so I called up Flowers, and he came back and joined us.

Jim Flowers

I left Taylor to get the tanks filled with gasoline and stowed with ammunition. Then I took a map and marked it where I wanted, and I said, "You bring the tanks over there. I'm going ahead to take a look," to see what the opposition has in store for us.

I got in the jeep with Sheppard. We went back over on Hill 122, and pulled up over on the west side, I can't remember exactly where but it had to be somewhere between that rock quarry and the heavily wooded area.

I stopped up there because that's where I'd marked for Taylor to bring the tanks, and somebody's got to be there to meet him. So I told Sheppard, you just stay here with Jim Bailey, that was his jeep driver, I said y'all stay here, and when Taylor gets here, why, y'all just wait for me, I'll be back after awhile. If I'm not back within an hour, why, you'll know I'm not coming back.

With that, I walked out in the woods and went in an appreciable distance, and I encountered several Germans. They didn't see me, and I sure wasn't going to cause any trouble for them right then.

I went in maybe two hundred yards, maybe further. I saw enough to know that the going was not going to be real easy but it's not going to be disastrous. There's not all that much stuff out there to stop a tank, not even to slow us down, really. At least I didn't feel like it at the time.

So I went back, and in the meantime Taylor had arrived with my tanks, and I got my tank commanders together.

He didn't get there but with four tanks. One of the tanks, I'll not mention the sergeant's name, that boy died here in the past year or two. It's not important who he was. Somewhere between where they started out and where we were, they, how do you say it, I think he had engine trouble or something, the tank wouldn't run.

We got over to Hill 122 with the tanks, four of them. My Number 1 tank, my Number 2 tank, my Number 4 tank, which was Taylor's tank, and my Number 5 tank. Since Wylie was gone, I needed a tank commander. So I said, "Sheppard, you've never been in a firefight, wouldn't you like to get a little combat experience in a tank?"

I put Sheppard in Taylor's tank so I could communicate with him, and put Taylor in Wylie's tank. Two tanks in the platoon have a two-way radio, the other three only have receivers. Wylie had gone back two days before to get something done about his crushed fingers.

I told the tank commanders what I thought the problem would be that we were going to encounter in the woods, that it's not going to be easy but it's not going to be all that tough. "You got any questions? Then let's mount up and move out."

The driver of the Number 4 tank, that's the one in which I put Sheppard, he wouldn't go. He wouldn't drive that tank. They tell me this happened. I didn't find out about this for probably several years. It might have been twenty years after the war. I often wondered why that man was not in that tank and why Bailey was.

Bailey was Sheppard's jeep driver. But at one time he had been a tank driver, so it wasn't new to him. He volunteered, "Why, I'll take that tank."

Jim Rothschadl

We had backed off the line, and there was a rumor going around that another tank battalion was going to take our place. We pulled our tanks into a little field, and our kitchen trucks were there.

I remember driving into the field, standing up in the turret. Flowers was outside already, talking with somebody in a jeep.

Sergeant Speier, he was the mess sergeant, he knew I liked pork chops. He used to call me Po'k Chop. So all of a sudden I heard, "Hey, Po'k Chop. You hungry?"

I said, "You're god damn right."

And he tossed me up a gallon can of marmalade, and a loaf of bread.

We parked alongside the hedgerow, and somebody came up and said "You can't stand outside. You've got to get underneath the tank," because mortar fire might come in.

There was about two feet under the tank, so we crawled under there, and took this gallon can of marmalade -- we were so damn hungry -- and the loaf of bread. There were four of us, Ed Dzienis, our loader; Gerald Kiballa, the assistant driver; Horace Gary, the driver; and myself. We took a Bowie knife, and we cut open this can of marmalade. And we broke the bread, it wasn't sliced, so we took chunks off, and we scooped out the marmalade with our hands. We ate the whole gallon.

So we're laying there, and Sergeant Speier came over and said, "It'll take about an hour. I've got a hot meal for you." We hadn't had a hot meal since we left England. About that time, a jeep comes racing into this little field with an officer.

One of our tanks was parked about a hundred feet from our tank, and I noticed a commotion over there. Several people were gathered around it, and people were waving arms. So I walked over there to see what was going on.

And here this guy was, he refused to drive. I couldn't believe it. "I'm not gonna go," he was saying. "I'm just not gonna go. The hell with you, I'm not gonna go." And they put him in a jeep, and away they went. We had been told that the rules of war, if you disobey an order on the front, you don't have to be court martialed, they could shoot you right there. They didn't do that. They took him away.

Sergeant Bailey was the communications sergeant, although he knew how to drive a tank, and damned if he didn't volunteer to drive that tank.

Louis Gerrard

My crew at the time was Earl Holman, Abe Taylor was the tank commander, I was the gunner, G.B. Kennedy was the bow gunner, and then we had a driver, his name was L---.

I told Flowers, when I was in Louisville [at the 1988 reunion] -- that's the first time I'd seen Flowers since Europe, since the day we got hit -- I told him the guy, he wouldn't drive the tank, so Bailey says, "Get out, I'll drive the tank."

Jack Sheppard

I said to Flowers, "There's only three men in the tank, you need a driver and you need a commander, so Bailey will take over as driver and I'll take over as commander, but you are the platoon leader, I'm just another tank in your platoon." So he said okay. He said, "You follow behind Taylor." They pulled out in front of me and we pulled along behind them.

Flowers I think fired the machine gun a few times, and all of a sudden we were with this battalion of infantry.

Then we were given orders that we're going to attack across the road. The road went along a big open field with a hedgerow at the far end. Flowers and K Company of the 358th Infantry were going to take that hedgerow. Famous last words.

Jim Flowers

I led the tanks on into the woods and ran the Germans in front of me until I started seeing some of our own infantry, and I asked them where their battalion commander was. It turned out that this was the Third Battalion of the 358th Infantry, and their battalion commander was a man named Jacob Bealke from Sullivan, Missouri, a reserve officer.

When I found Colonel Bealke, he was glad to see me. To say the least, he was glad to see me.

We planned how to get him off of that hill and out of those woods. Some of that brush, it was kind of like a thicket, you couldn't see through it much less walk through it, and they had been catching hell.

They had managed to capture eight of the Germans that I had run down that way, and from them we found out that this is part of the 15th Regiment of the Fifth SS Airborne parachute infantry division. These were fairly clean kids, most of them looked like they might have been in their early to mid-twenties. They had had a bath and a shave recently, and had had something to eat, they had clean uniforms, the whole nine yards. We probably looked like a scurvy bunch of bums by then.

Bealke and I made a plan on how to get out of there. I'd take my tanks and knock this underbrush and thicket down so his infantry could get out. That's one of the reasons they were trapped in there. I'll knock some paths through this stuff so y'all can walk behind me to get out.

So at first, this infantry was walking in front of me, but that didn't last long. We hadn't gone but a short distance and they fell back in line with my tanks. And that didn't last but a few yards, they just couldn't get through that stuff, and there was a heavy concentration of German soldiers. So the infantry walked behind my tanks.

Our plan was to get down the side of the hill, which in some places was pretty steep, and out of the woods onto this hard-surface road that ran on the south side of the hill, and go on out into the fields on the other side of the road and try to get him up on the line with Pond's battalion.

Everything worked out according to plan, except for one thing. His infantry kind of got bogged down.

I ran down the side of the hill, knocked down a bunch of brush and thicket and stuff for 'em, and at first the infantry was right behind me. We got down to the hardtop road, and now I don't know where in the hell the infantry is. I had no idea that the Germans were decimating Bealke's infantry now.

As I come out of the woods and onto that hardtop road, I look both ways and don't see a damn thing, everything looks fine, so I go across the ditch and the hedgerow on the other side, and out into a field.

In front of me was a swampy area. I could tell by the vegetation growing there. I got on the radio and told the other tanks to look out for that as they came across the road. Don't run into that marshy area there and get stuck.

I went around on the right side of this marsh, and as Sheppard came across, why, Bailey ran him out in it and got stuck.

Taylor, who was in Wylie's tank, and Kenneth Titman, who was in the Number 5 tank, they went around on the left side and went on. Then Sheppard got on the radio and said, "Jim, I'm stuck back here."

I thought, "Damn!"

"What do you want me to do now?"

"Well, hell, you've still got your tank gun, your 75. You can support my advance by fire." He can sit there and fire in front of me at any target of opportunity that he can see.

"When I have an opportunity," I said, "I'll get somebody back there to pull you out of that marsh."

I went on, and out in this field there's bushes, weeds and stuff. And there's a hedgerow up there. I don't remember if there's any trees, although there might have been.

The thing that I do remember is that the artillery and mortar fire from the German side was falling in on us kind of like hail or raindrops, boy, there was a lot of it.

I'd run quite a distance across the second field in after I crossed the road, and Taylor's tank and Titman's tank are off on my left, nothing on my right. Sheppard's back stuck in the marsh.

After I'd run quite a distance out into that second field, I recall seeing a blinding flash of light and hearing this big bell ringing.

What had happened, the German had fired an armor-piercing shot from an anti-tank gun and I saw the muzzle flash, and the ringing was that they had bounced this thing off of my turret.

I immediately had Gary stop and back up. I'm sure that I'm in a fire lane that they've cut.

At the same time, I'm on the radio telling the other tanks to look out for that anti-tank gun and gave them the approximate location of it. Let's be careful. So after Gary backed up, I had him pull to the right and then go forward. Hopefully I'm out of this guy's fire line. I'm sure not going to slow down to find out.

As we do that, we hadn't pulled up too far until, I don't know whether it was an armor-piercing shot, it might have been a bazooka, I don't know what it was but it came through the right sponson, where a bunch of ammunition is stored, and ignited the propelling charge in this 75-millimeter ammunition and clipped off my right forefoot, and I suppose that whatever it was probably went out the other side. Instantaneously, the tank is a ball of fire.

Jack Sheppard

We pulled up to the road, all in a line, and fired at the hedgerow with the gun and the machine gun, just raked it, and high explosive, all to hell. Then the platoon leader of the infantry said, "Let's go!" So we all go, tanks and infantry, usually the infantry behind the tanks.

Just after we got across that road, my tank hit a hog wallow, a mud hole, and tipped over. All it would do was that right track would just spin, no traction whatsoever. So we were just sitting there.

I had my head out the turret. You always had your head out unless you were being shot at. I had my head out, my carbine in my hand, in case I saw something.

About that time, the other three tanks disappeared over the hedgerow. Then a round came in from the right and hit the gunner's periscope. It blew up when it hit the periscope, and blasted straight on through to the other side of the tank. A fragment from the shell knocked the gunner's eye out.

My hands were outside the cupola, and it busted the stock of my carbine, and injured me a couple of places on the hand, I don't even remember which hand it was now. It blew my helmet off, knocked my captain bars off of it.

When the shell exploded, it put shrapnel in the radio, shrapnel in the little joe -- that was a generator in the back of the tank, to keep the battery up -- it put holes in the gun recoil mechanism, and oil was leaking out so you couldn't fire the gun. You might fire it one time but it wouldn't stop going back. So we decided to evacuate, real quick. This is a split-second decision, you look around and see all the damage, out you go, because we were expecting another round to come in.

Jim Rothschadl

We were told in training, "Don't freeze." I guess a few guys did. They got so petrified or frightened they just froze. But when we went into combat I kept saying to myself, "Don't freeze. Watch." So I didn't freeze. But I was damn scared. Because you're sitting there without much visibility.

The turret had a toggle switch in it, to traverse the gun, but it also had a little wheel that you could use to traverse it manually. I remember that little wheel very well, because when the tank got hit, that wheel was right in front of me, and it knocked four of my teeth out.

The Germans were dug in on this hill, hundreds of them, close together, in lots of foxholes. And some were on top, working the machine guns.

I was firing the .30 caliber machine gun. I was a little heavy on the trigger, and the barrel was melting. We were told to fire short bursts, or the barrel would get too hot. Dzienis had a pair of big asbestos mittens, and he would screw the barrel off and put on another one. The barrel got so hot that it bent a little bit and the goddamn bullets were falling in front of the tank.

Meanwhile, they were firing at us, with small arms and rifle grenades, which would weld themselves onto the tank and almost go all the way through. They would aim the grenades at the turret circle. If one hit there you couldn't turn the turret.

Then the first big shell hit. It lifted the tank about two feet off the ground.

It was an 88, I'm sure of it. The 88 is a high-velocity shell. And Flowers was looking for it, that 88. He was telling me to traverse from the middle to the right. I quit firing the .30 and switched to the 75.

When the first shell hit, it didn't penetrate the tank. But I remember Horace Gary, the driver, started to swear, "God damn it, let's get out of this sonofabitch! We're sitting ducks. Let's get the hell out of here!" And Flowers told me to traverse to the right a little bit. He was standing right behind me and poking me in the back. I was trying to pick out something through the periscope, but I couldn't see anything clearly. I did see a heat wave, where the blast was from, and I fired one round in there.

Within a few seconds' time, it might have been thirty seconds, the second shell hit. That one came through the turret. There was this god damn humongous explosion and racket, and heat.

The turret was open. It immediately caught fire. And the shell went right on through. Those German 88s were known to be able to hit the front end of a tank and come right out the back. They had double the velocity of our 75s. Double.

I remember I was burning. I was trying to get up from my little seat. I thought just for a moment about unplugging the radio. But the tank was flaming inside. I got out by myself as far as my armpits, and then I fell back in.

Flowers helped me out. I kind of revived and got some air, and I got out of the turret as far as my belly. Then Flowers let himself off because there wasn't enough room for the two of us. I saw him fall backwards onto the ground.

When I finally got myself out I let myself fall head-first onto the ground. My clothes were burning. Now, I had my senses. We had been told, they went all over this in training, you've got to get the fire out. So when I hit the ground I started to roll, and lo and behold, all of a sudden, plunk! I just fell down into a hole. It may have been a bomb crater. The hole was four or five feet deep, and there was a lot of loose dirt. I plunked down in there, and covered myself with dirt.

Jim Flowers

I like to dramatize this a little bit by saying that I'm now standing in the middle of Hell. I get on the intercom and tell the crew, "Let's get the hell out of here," and I reach down and grab Rothschadl, who's sitting in a seat down in front of me. I grab Rothschadl by the shoulders and yank him out of that seat, and start to push him up to get him out of the turret. At this point I don't know I've been hit.

After I pushed Rothschadl out on top, I turned around to climb out myself, and as I stepped up on that ring around where the top and the bottom of the turret are bolted together, when I stepped up on that, why, I didn't have anything to step with. That's when I realized that something is happening.

I fell back down to the bottom of the damn turret basket. To this day I don't know whether I fell or it was Dzienis climbing up my back to get out. It's immaterial anyhow[1].

[1]Jim Rothschadl says he doesn't know how Ed Dzienis got out of the tank, and that for years afterward he thought Dzienis -- who was captured -- had been killed. He believes Dzienis escaped through the hatch on the bottom. It is not uncommon for there to be discrepancies when the same incident is described by more than one person. In most cases, I felt it more important to present the facts the way they are remembered than to try and reconcile the discrepancies.

I crawled, I pulled myself and crawled out onto the turret and jumped down on the ground, and looked down and that's when I saw that I didn't have much of a right foot.

When I climbed out of the tank, I guess it was a reflex, I grabbed my tommy gun and hung it over my shoulder.

The Germans had knocked out all four of my tanks, right then and there. They all went up in balls of fire. Even Sheppard's tank.

Louis Gerrard

We couldn't do anything, we couldn't go anywhere, so Sheppard says, "We'd better bail out." I took my tank helmet off, and put my steel helmet on, and was getting ready to come up, when -- balloom! We got hit right on my side, and I practically flew out of the turret, the helmet went out, and everything.

I got out and laid on the side. While I was laying on the ground, the rest of the crew came around me, and there was a medic. I don't know where he came from, but he was putting sulfa drugs on my arms and everything, and somebody says, "Here comes the Germans," whether it was a patrol or a platoon or whatever, they were coming.

One of the guys started getting his gun, and somebody said, "Oh, whatever you do, don't fire," because they would have mutilated us. It was probably a patrol. There were about fifteen or twenty Germans.

I told the guys, "Get out of here," run away, go on, so they all went, and Bailey got killed getting away. He stayed, he was the last one there, and I kept telling him, "Go, go," and he finally, he got killed getting away. Oh, that was a hell of a mess. I laid there, half-dead. And the Germans took the medic with them.

They took my wristwatch, and my brother Jack had given me a ring. The ring had the word Oran, in Africa. He gave it to me when I was in England, and I wore it all the time. They tried like hell to get that off my finger, they couldn't get it off, so they gave up on that, but they took my watch.

I didn't say anything. The medic told me play dead, don't say a word, don't say nothing, so I was just dead when they came. All I could hear was German, I didn't know what they were talking about, although I could understand the word "eie," they must have been commenting about my eye.

I was thinking I was going to get killed by these Germans coming, and I was thinking about my mother, what would she say? She took it hard when my oldest brother was killed[1], and I thought, now she'll get word another one's killed.

[1]Gerrard learned on June 6 that one of his brothers had been killed in North Africa.

The Germans grabbed me by the heels and put me up on a hill. I think they must have done that so somebody could find me. I don't know what the reason was, but they did that. Then they heard something and they were all in a big rush, they took off real fast. I was expecting a bayonet in the back or the chest or something, or getting shot in the head, I didn't know what the hell the Germans were going to do.

Jack Sheppard

The shrapnel and powder from the bursting shell hit me in the face. I've still got one black spot.

The radio, which was in the back of the turret, was full of holes, and it didn't work. So we had no reason for staying in the tank, and Gerrard was in bad shape. He was not unconscious, but he was in extreme pain. So we all got out and got behind the tank, and they were looking after him, and I had, my face was blasted, I was leaking blood all over my face, and we were trying to figure out what to do.

I said, "Well, I'll tell you what. You all stay here and take care of his wounds, and I'll go back across the road, to see if I can get a stretcher and send it back." I did that. But while I was jogging back, my jaw was flopping up and down.

I didn't know it until I started running, but one large piece of shrapnel, as big as your thumb, hit me in the cheek and went through and knocked a tooth out, and stayed there.

So I pulled it out and put it in my pocket. I was going to keep it, but eventually I threw it away because it was razor sharp.

I found a medic and sent him and a stretcher back up. But before he got there, one of the other guys, well, when one of the guys found me, he said two German SS men had come up and Bailey started to fight with them, and they killed him. I don't know how, but they killed him.

Some infantry men there said, "Hey, didn't you know that they were shooting at you?" They said two rounds, with tracers, went over our head before the third one hit. I never saw them. Never heard them. And then they said, "Did you see those tanks on fire up ahead? The smoke coming up?" That's when I first noticed the three columns of smoke. It might have been four.

Kenneth Titman

Sergeant Kenneth Titman, from Norfolk, Neb., was a tank commander in Jim Flowers' platoon.

We were coming into this open field. Three tanks were together. When we got in there, the German 88s got us. They hit my tank and it exploded, and I hollered "Abandon tank!" The tank was on fire. I looked around and I saw all these tanks running, one tank ran in front of me and hit the tank on the left and both exploded. That's what I saw[1].

I jumped out of the turret, and hit the back deck. Blood was coming out of the top of my combat boot, and I knew I was hit.

When I got down off the tank and looked up, I saw the loader coming out of the turret, and he was on fire when he hit the ground.

I knew Cohron [Kenneth Cohron], my gunner, didn't come out because the 88 hit him directly and I had some of his flesh on my helmet.

Morrison [Clarence Morrison], the driver, put the tank in reverse. The assistant driver dropped the escape hatch, and the tank had power enough to back off, and the two of them got out from under the tank. I don't know where they went after that.

When I got out, I went for a slit trench, and when I got in it, here comes a bunch of Germans and they stuck a gun at me.

I said "Alles kaput," and they saw my leg was all shot up. They put me on a litter, and took me back to the rear.

Jim Rothschadl

I lay there for quite a while. My hands were all burned, and my face. I stuck my hands into the dirt.

Meanwhile, the god damn devils were firing at us. I could see tracers going over the top of the hole.

After awhile the firing stopped, to almost nothing. By that time it was almost dusk. Flowers had crawled from where he was laying by the tank to a hedgerow that was about 25 feet away. There was a hole in the hedgerow that was made by a bomb or something. Flowers crawled through there, and lay down on the other side.

Then he began calling my name. I could hear him plaintively. He usually called me Corporal Rothschadl, but several of the times he said "Jim. Jim, please come over here. Please come over HERE. Corporal Rothschadl," he said it many times, at least a dozen times, by the time I crawled through there.

In addition to my burns, the tendon on my right foot was cut. I don't know if it was a gunshot or a shrapnel wound, but it cut the tendon. I could take my foot and pull it up until my toe touched the leg.

And it didn't hurt. Anyway, I crawled over there. I was kind of dazed, but I had my faculties. I kept following his voice. I came through this hole in the hedgerow and there he was, laying flat on his back.

[1]This might explain why Sheppard is unsure whether he saw three or four columns of smoke.

Jim Flowers

After we got on the ground, there were a few infantry soldiers and a few of the tankers. We can't stay where we are, with these burning tanks and the Germans over on the other side of that hedgerow shooting at us. The only thing we can do is get over on that side of the hedgerow with them. So I gathered up whatever we had, and we attacked that hedgerow, and got over on the other side. It was messy, but it didn't last long.

We ran the Germans off, and then we moved over a distance and got into a field on the right side of where my tanks were burning, and that's as far as we're going.

By now, the blood is squirting out of my foot, and my face and hands are burned, all the skin is falling off my hands. So I had Gary, my driver, help me get my belt off. I had coveralls on over an o.d. [olive drab] uniform. I got my belt off and put it around my right leg above my knee, and picked up a stick, and we twisted the stick to make an improvised tourniquet.

After we got that done, I had him reach in my coverall breast pocket and get out my package of morphine syrettes.

There also was an infantry soldier with us who had been hit real hard in both legs.

Jim Rothschadl

On that side of the hedgerow was a pie-shaped field, about four acres in size. We were laying there, it was still daylight, and there were some infantry boys with us. And then god damn, they started firing at some Germans that were coming across a hedgerow on the other side of this field. There was a hell of a firefight going on.

Pretty soon things quieted down, though, and by now it was getting dark. Flowers told everybody who could walk to try to go find help.

Jim Flowers

I had Gary use a syrette on each one of us -- Rothschadl, the infantry soldier and me. He took a pocket knife and cut a hole through our clothing. Then I told him, everybody that you can find that's ambulatory, get them the hell out of here.

That left Rothschadl and this infantry soldier and me out there on the ground. Rothschadl had been burned in the face, he could hardly see, his eyes were swollen shut.

I had no idea what the situation was back there with Bealke and his boys, but I said to the others, go back and as soon as you can, get an aid man and a couple of litter teams out here to pick us up and get us out of here.

So Gary took my morphine syrettes that were left and stuck 'em in his pocket, and got the guys that were still around, gathered them up and started back. On the way back, that's where Gerald Kiballa, who was my assistant driver, got killed.

By now it's getting late in the day. Sometime that night, I heard something moving down on the other side of the hedgerow, which was over where my tanks were burning, they had exploded in the meantime.

I listened, and it wasn't coming from the right direction. It was coming from behind me, back where the Germans were. So I crawled up on the hedgerow and with the few rounds of ammunition I had left in that magazine, I sprayed in the direction that I could hear these boys coming from. I don't know whether I hit any of them or whether they knew where the firing was coming from. But they didn't bother me.

I crawled back down the hedgerow where I'd been laying and waited and waited, and sometime during the dark hours, I heard somebody coming up on the same side of the hedgerow that I'm on.

I told this infantry kid and Rothschadl, don't move, don't make a sound, don't even breathe deeply. But these guys were coming right to us. And in a little bit, the one that was in front stopped and looked, and he said something in German to the fellow behind him. They were in file, and they just walked around us. I don't know whether they thought we were dead or what. They could see that if we weren't dead, well, we weren't long for this world. But the last man, or one of the last men, in that little column stopped and came over to us, and he had a red cross on his arm.

That boy came over, and he looked at us, and he checked my tourniquet. The bleeding had long since stopped. He checked it to be sure that I had released the tension on it. And he opened his first aid kit, which was a canvas bag, and he got out a gauze roller bandage. My combat jacket had knit cuffs, he pushed those cuffs on this jacket back up. I had a wristwatch on my left arm and an identification bracelet on my right, he just slid them up as much as he could to expose these burned hands, and he went to work bandaging each finger individually, and then my whole hand up to a point above where the burns were. He had dry bandage. Each one of my fingers, and he looked at my burned face. Of course there's nothing he could do about that.

I asked the man for water, and he didn't give me any. It's possible he didn't understand, but I think he did. The German word for water is Wasser. He couldn't have misunderstood, so he probably just didn't have any water.

Then he went over and bandaged Rothschadl. And he looked at the infantry soldier. I don't know what he did for him, he wasn't burned, so I don't think he put any bandage on him.

That's the night of the Tenth. I don't know how many German soldiers moved through. I thought for a while it was a whole German army, but it was probably a patrol, it might have been a squad. I would rather suspect that it was twelve, fifteen, maybe twenty men.

They moved on up, and they didn't come back.

Jim Rothschadl

Later that night these Germans walked up to us. One of them stopped and knelt down alongside of me, and I could see a red cross on his arm. The swelling in my face had closed my eyes, but I could see if I pulled the skin down below my right eye. And I was so god damn thirsty, so thirsty. I said "Wasser," I could speak a little German, my dad could speak German. I looked up and he was kneeling down, and he pulled out a canteen. I saw this canteen and I thought, "Jesus Christ, he's going to give me some water!" And he took the cap off, I can still see that, he took the cap off and tipped it upside down. He didn't have any water. But he bandaged my hands, he put some gauze on them. Then he did something with Jim, and there was an infantry boy that was laying there, too, who was still alive.

The infantry boy was moaning. He was trying to talk. He was in really bad shape. He was wounded in both legs, and he had a bad wound in the stomach.

Jim had five morphine syrettes. He gave me a shot early on, while I was still in a state of shock, you know when you get hurt real bad you go into shock. He gave me a shot of morphine, and that lasted about three hours. And I guess he gave himself some, and he gave the infantry boy some. And that was it. I got one shot, I might have had two, I don't know.

The next morning, we were still laying there. We didn't sleep much. The Germans set up their line right there, and they were walking back and forth past us all the time.

I can't figure out why they didn't kill us. They must have thought we looked so damn horrible that we weren't gonna hurt anybody. So they just left us.

That day, our people -- we must have been quite a ways out there from our lines because they put artillery in, and they don't put artillery in at close range. The Germans were lined up there where our tanks were burned out, and our people knew they were lined up there. So they laid a hell of an artillery barrage, not knowing that we were there. Even if they had known they would have done it.

It just practically plowed up that field. And one of them landed between Jim and the infantry boy. I heard Jim scream. He let out a hell of a scream. And I looked over there and Jesus Christ, his other leg was gone.

Somehow he managed to get a tourniquet on it. It's Sunday night now, we were out there the night of the 10th, and this is the night of the 11th.

During that night, the Germans did what they did many other times, they picked up their stuff in the night and moved back a few hedgerows.

Jim Flowers

Sometime on the 11th, our artillery shelled that position, and they ended the war for some of the German kids because I could hear them screaming. And one of the shells -- several of them landed nearby, as a matter of fact I was almost covered by dirt, these things would hit and explode and throw dirt out -- one of them landed just right to hit the infantry boy. Shell fragments from it hit the infantry soldier and me, and did an almost complete traumatic amputation of my left leg this time, about seven inches below my knee.

I had to get this belt off of my right leg and over to my left one, because I haven't got all that much blood left, especially since I'm pretty well dehydrated.

I took the belt off of my right leg and put it on the left, then pulled it up as tightly as I could, twisted the stick, and slowed the blood down. Then I checked Rothschadl, he didn't get any shell fragments.

The infantry boy had been hit, he'd been hit hard.

I crawled, pulled myself over on my elbows over to him, and he's a bloody damn mess. I can't just lay there calmly and let this boy join his ancestors. So with whatever mobility I had left in my bandaged hands, I managed to tear some of his clothing off of him and get it ripped up into strips to put some compresses over the places where he's bleeding badly.

We made it through the rest of the day, and then that night, this is the night of the 11th now, I couldn't tell you whether it's a full moon, whether it's dark or not, I don't remember. The Germans evacuated that position, and in the meantime, our artillery had stopped trying to kill me. There's a boy named Frank Norris who was a lieutenant colonel commanding a field artillery battalion in the 90th Infantry Division, and who became a major general after the war. I've accused Frank of trying to kill me. He said hell, he didn't even know me.

We laugh about it, and he admits that it could have been his battalion that was firing on that position.

Louis Gerrard

I laid there all night [of the 10th], and then this artillery opened up, and the dirt and cinders and everything, stones were coming off the road, they were hitting me on the head and all, I said, boy, I've got to get the heck out of here, so I crawled back up the hill, and I heard this one guy say, "Get the hell over here." There were some GIs in a big slit trench. So I got into that, and I think I must have practically been exhausted. Then they called for a stretcher.

They took care of my wounds and put me on the stretcher, and put the stretcher on a jeep. They had another soldier on the other side, two of us going down a big narrow road, Christ, I could hear the small arms fire, I thought I was going to get killed before I got back to the beach.

Jim Flowers

Sometime on the morning of the 12th, this infantry soldier told me he wasn't gonna make it, and he asked me to administer the last rites to him. I said, hell, I don't know whether I told him but I'm not a Catholic boy, I'm a Baptist. I don't understand anything about the last rites of the Catholic church, but I can pray, that was one thing I can do. So I crawled over and did the best I could, but at the same time, I admonished this boy for even thinking about dying, and asked him to just hang on a while longer, they'll be here eventually to get us.

He didn't make it.

Jim Rothschadl

When morning came, the 12th, it was a quiet, early dawn. Everything was quiet, you couldn't hear a shot. In fact I heard birds singing. I was laying there, and I was really feeling bad. I was feeling so bad that I thought about dying. I wanted to.

Then Jim said, "Give me a cigarette."

I had cigarettes, but my hands, you'd be surprised how a fellow swells up. My hands were huge from the swelling. I couldn't get in my pocket. I remember trying to get in my pocket because the cigarettes were there, and I wanted a cigarette, too.

The next thing he said, he swore a little bit, he said, "Jesus Christ, Jim, you'd better go get some help."

I said, "Why?"

"I'm getting gangrene in my legs. I'm getting gangrene." He said, "Can you see a little bit?"

It was hard to talk because I'd swelled up so much. But I knew what he said. I was desperate myself. And everything was quiet. So when he told me about this gangrene, I crawled out through the hole in the hedgerow. But I turned the wrong way. I was confused somewhat, in terms of directions. The tanks were there, they were still smoldering. So I put my left shoulder to the hedgerow and was crawling along, blind, then I'd stop once in a while and I'd look. And I was trying to call for medics. I don't know if I got any noise out or not. And I don't know how far I crawled. It might have been three hundred feet, or it might have been more, but all of a sudden I heard this awful kind of a laugh. And I stopped. There I was sitting in front of a German machine gun nest. There were three guys behind it. It was a water-cooled machine gun, because it had the big casing on the barrel. And they were looking at me. They were saying something and they laughed. And I thought, "Well, okay, shoot me. Go ahead." I didn't give a damn.

They must have thought I looked awful. My clothes were burned, I suppose, and I was all puffed up.

After a few seconds, I turned around. I put my right shoulder to the hedgerow and I crawled back. I came back to the hole and continued on past it, and I'd stop every once in a while and try to call for medics. I could hear. There was nothing wrong with my hearing. And I heard a little noise. So I opened my eye up, and there was a GI. He must have been down on his hands and knees because I saw the helmet down toward the ground, and a head, and even though I couldn't see that well I immediately recognized that it was a GI helmet. So I must have hollered or something, and pretty soon about three or four of them came from around a corner in the hedgerow.

They picked me up and carried me some distance. It wasn't too far. They were going through water. I could hear water. I was so god damn thirsty. I was so thirsty. They laid me down, and I was begging for water. And I heard one of the guys say to the other fellow, "Just give him a little bit now." I could have drank a barrel. "Just a little bit. Don't give him much, now. Just a little bit." And I was angry about that, because I was so thirsty.

I got that water down. Then I was telling these guys -- by that time there were about eight or nine of them -- I was telling them my lieutenant is laying back there. I begged for them to go back there and get him.

So they left. They came back in a few minutes and said, "Well, he's dead."

I tried to get up, and I said, "No, no." I was begging and begging, and they went back again. Then they brought Jim and laid him down alongside of me, and they sent for some people with stretchers.

They carried us on stretchers until they came to a jeep, and they laid us both on the hood of the jeep, crossways. The jeep took us to an aid station, and then they put us on the hood of a different jeep, which took us down to the beach.

In the meantime they had given us some shots.

They took us down to the beach, and this jeep went right into the water, and took us to an LST. And it was full. They left space for walking, but the LST was full.

Jim Flowers

Sometime that morning, I heard some noise coming in my direction.

The first clear recollection I have is hearing this voice say, "Well, here's some more of 'em." Then he said, "Wait, here's another one." This is coming my way. When they got up close to me, why, one of these boys says, "I think these are still alive."

I heard these boys coming in my direction, "Here's one I think is still alive." He came over and looked, after I assured him that I was still with it. The boy came over with a lieutenant, and it turned out that this is G Company of the 357th Infantry, and this lieutenant was a boy from the western part of Texas, his name is Claude Lovett.

Claude looked at me, and I asked him for a drink of water, so he gave me some water out of his canteen. He got on his radio and called back and told them to get some litters up there, and a jeep, put the litters out over the hood of it, get us out of there.

Jim Rothschadl

When we got to the hospital in Southampton, Jim and I were still together. I was on a gurney and he was laying over to my right.

Some doctors and nurses came over, and they were looking at me, and one of the nurses hollered, "Jesus, come and look at this guy. They must be using gas over there." And then the chaplain came in. A Catholic chaplain. I happen to be Catholic. It shows on your dogtags. And he was gonna give me the last rites. He did. I didn't want him to. I said "Damn!" I swore at him, and told him to get the hell away from me. I made it this far I'm gonna make it. I don't need no last rites. I was really angry. But he went through the procedure.

Jim was still nearby, and I heard him talking. I knew his voice, being with him so long. The last words he said before we were separated, he said, "God damn it," I'm quoting now. He's talking to the nurses or the doctors. He said, real loud, "God damn it. Take good care of that corporal. He's the best god damn gunner in the United States Army."

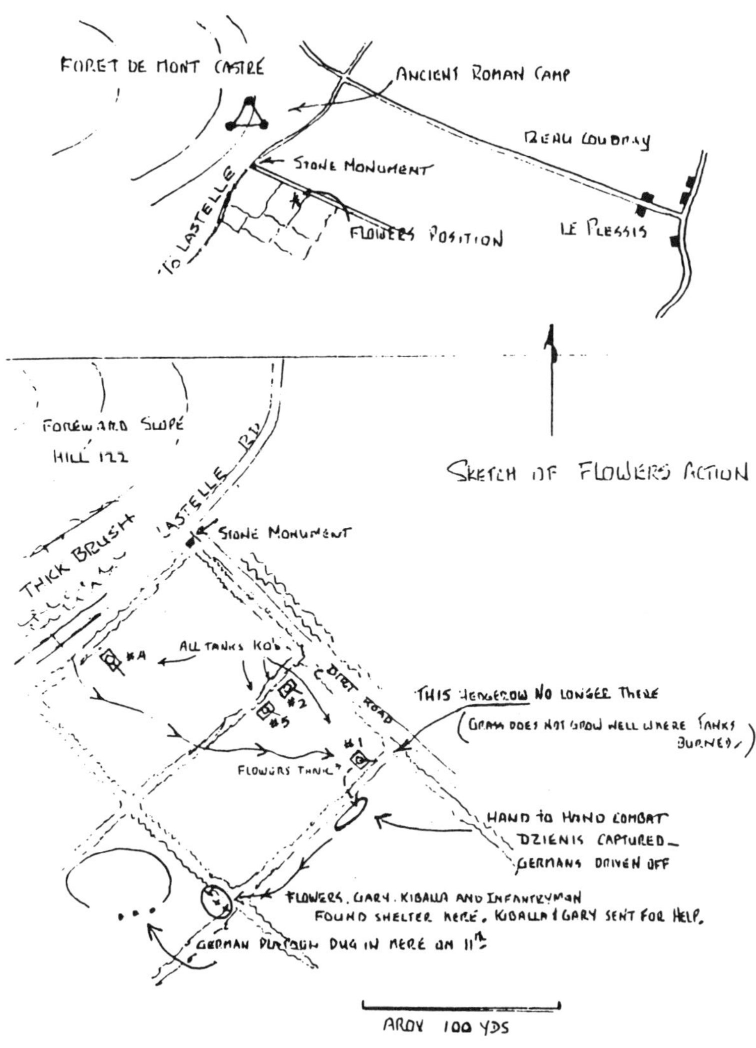

SKETCHED BY EAMES L. YATES

REPRINTED WITH PERMISSION FROM "WAR FROM THE GROUND UP" BY JOHN COLBY

CHAPTER 4

The Frying Pan

Ruby Goldstein

One time when we were on maneuvers in Tennessee, my tank was guarding a road -- this was all simulation -- and the water in our five-gallon can was awful. You couldn't drink it.

There was a farmhouse by the road, so I went and knocked on the door. A woman answered, and I asked her if she had any fresh water.

She said yes, so I went back to the tank and dumped the five gallons of water out -- I wasn't gonna do it in front of her house -- and when I returned with the empty can, she took me to a cave in the side of a mountain. There were rocks inside, and water was coming down from somewhere in the mountain.

It was crystal-clear water. I took a drink with my canteen cup. Never in my life did I taste water that delicious.

So I filled the five-gallon can to bring back to my crew. Then the woman says, "Are you fellows hungry?"

"Well, kind of."

You know what she did? She went out, and she had some fresh-killed chickens. She took the chickens, she had them all cleaned up and ready, and we had southern fried chicken, and she made biscuits for us, we were there for quite awhile.

Tony D'Arpino

You know, I've thought of this many times, if I knew then what I know now, I'd have kept a diary. With names of towns. I can remember when our company took Reims, where they make champagne.

Now, the first tank we had, behind the driver and the assistant driver there was a cubbyhole for shells for the 75-millimeter gun. But every time you wanted one of them, you'd skin your knuckles trying to get them out of there, so we never used it. Instead we would pile the extra ammunition on the turret floor. So when we got to Reims, ol' Tony got the bright idea, pink champagne. I had every one of those cubbyholes filled with pink champagne. I was drinking pink champagne for breakfast, dinner and supper.

Ed Spahr

Ed Spahr joined the 712th as a replacement in Normandy. He was a loader, and then a gunner, in C Company.

We used to have an old frying pan hanging on the back of the tank. We never washed it in water. The exhaust fumes would blow on it.

We'd stop if we saw something. One time we caught a rabbit. The rabbits were large over there, and we had chicken and rabbit at the same time. Now we were out in the field, so no one knew about us eating this wild stuff.

This pan would be so dirty, and we had a bucket hanging on the back of the tank as well, we used to brew coffee in it. That bucket was so black, you'd swear it was blacker than the coffee. Every time we'd get ready to eat, we'd make coffee in this, and we would say, "Well, if the meat is contaminated, if the chicken is contaminated and the rabbit is contaminated and the water around here is contaminated, these pans can't be contaminated because there's nothing on them but road dust and exhaust fumes," and we'd eat like kings.

We'd all joke and josh about things like that, and somebody would make some remark like, "Well, overeating with poisonous food is better than dying with a bullet."

Ruby Goldstein

We didn't have the kitchen trucks very often, so whatever you could scrounge you scrounged. We would get these big cans, put a little hole on each side, and put a piece of wire through the holes. And we built a fire. We put dirt in the bottom, made holes in the bottom, put some gasoline on it, and put a smaller can on top of it, with a little bit of water. Then we went scrounging for vegetables.

One day we hit a potato field. So if you hold your lever and you gun the engine, the tank turns, one tread's stopped and you're turning. And what are you digging up? Potatoes.

We'd peel the potatoes, chunk it up, throw it in. We had cans of English style stew. And we'd throw in whatever vegetables we could find. And you know something? It was the best thing you ever tasted.

Tony D'Arpino

I can't remember who thought of the idea first, but you get an empty five-gallon can with a handle on it, something like painters use; you put gravel on the bottom, about six inches, and then you put some potatoes. Then you put about six more inches of gravel on top. And you tie it underneath -- the tank had two exhausts coming out, you tie it to that. And after running all day long, the potatoes are baked. We put the gravel on it so we can't get the smell. We used to have baked potatoes all the time.

Dick Greca

Sergeant Richard Greca was part of a maintenance crew.

In Service Company, we'd go fishing with hand grenades.

Throw 'em in the river, and fish would come up, big German brown trout, and we'd pick 'em up.

Then one day I was in a little rowboat and I dropped one off the side of it, that's the last time I did that, because I discovered that the water wasn't too deep.

One night we went up to check the tanks, and the crew heard us talking, and they got scared and thought it was the Germans out there, so they threw a hand grenade out. Two of us got hit, but not serious.

I jumped under the tank, so I wouldn't get the shrapnel, and then the doggone tank started to move. I said, "Now what?" I got out of there real quick.

George Bussell

One day Eugene Crawford said we were gonna get some eggs.

I said "How the hell are we gonna get eggs? We can't speak French."

He said, "I know how to ask for eggs. You go up and knock on the door, and when they come to the door, you say, 'Avez vous des erf.'"

I said "Is that right?"

He said "Sure."

That's all he knew how to say. So he walks in there, he knocks on the door, and this woman comes out, and he says, "Avez vous des erf?" And she shook her head no, and he says, "Well where in the hell can I get some?"

Ruby Goldstein

One day when I was in the replacement depot waiting to rejoin the battalion, we were getting hungry. It was after breakfast, and it's getting close to noontime, and who knows when the heck you're gonna get chow, or what you're gonna get.

So this fellow and I, we take a walk, and we get to a farmhouse, where we get some eggs. But we bought 'em. The Germans wouldn't buy them. They'd take what they want. I had some francs in my pocket, I said "Give me six eggs."

I put 'em in my field jacket, three in one pocket, three in another. We go along, go into another farmhouse, and I want some more eggs.

The woman in the house could understand what I wanted. She goes out to get the eggs, and I go to sit down...forget it! I made a mistake. I crushed the six eggs in my pockets. What a mess I had.

I got the other six eggs. I cleaned up as best I could. I cleaned out my pockets. Then I said, if she had a rabbit we could buy a rabbit. So it cost me, I think it was ten francs, it's two cents a franc, twenty cents, and I got a rabbit. It was a nice, big, fat one.

We get back to camp, we said, "How the hell are we gonna kill this and cook it?" So this one kid from down South, I don't remember his name, he says, "I'll show you how we do it."

He takes the rabbit by the hind legs, on the tree, Bam! Hits the head right on the tree, holds the hind legs, puts the rabbit on the ground, puts his foot under the neck, and pulls his head right off. Then he takes a knife and guts it.

We got a couple of branches from a tree, and two forks, cleaned them off, dug a little pit, and started a fire. I got some salt from a guy, and we poured it all inside of the rabbit to clean it out, we didn't have any water. We poured all the salt, and we're scraping it with knives to clean it out, and everybody, their mouths were getting full of saliva, you know, we're gonna have something to eat.

We turned that thing, and we're turning it and turning, it should be done by now. We break a piece off and go to eat it.

Did you ever eat shoe leather? You started chewing, you figured look, it's better than nothing. You spit it out, you couldn't eat it.

CHAPTER 5

Hill 122
(continued)

Jack Sheppard

After the infantry took the area, I went up, me and the first sergeant, and we looked in the tanks, and there's nothing in the tanks but ashes down on the bottom.

Right next to one tank was a foxhole, and in it was Abraham Taylor. He had a rifle leaning over the edge, and he was dead. He had been shot through the head. Quick. But he was the only one I knew for sure was dead. All the rest you wondered about. Did they get out and were taken prisoner, or what?

After that, we were down to seven [out of an original 17] tanks, and not many men. When the first replacements came on, we weren't wearing any insignias, because the snipers would use them as targets, and the only way you could identify an officer was I had a white stripe, about an inch and a half long and about four inches wide down the back of the helmet. If it was up and down it was an officer, if it was sideways it was a sergeant, so you knew who the command was.

These recruits walked up to us and we're all just standing there, and one of them looks at me and says, "Hey, Mac, what in the hell happened to you?" And the first sergeant says, "Shut your mouth, that's a company commander." That must have made their day. If a company commander can get looking like that, what's going to happen to them? I still had my combat jacket, and it had bloodstains on it. And my face was bandaged, my hand was bandaged, and I still had two of the most glorious black eyes from the concussion.

Kenneth Titman

After they got me back, the Germans took me to an interrogating officer. And he said, "You know, your battle is over. You're going back to the rear."

And I said "Oh?"

And he said "Yep. The war's over for you. What outfit are you from?"

I wouldn't tell him.

Then he said, "How many men are back there in that tank?"

I said, "I don't know."

I was sitting there, and while this guy was asking me all those questions, they opened up one of those burp guns. And I said, "What was that?"

He said "That's somebody wouldn't talk."

Well, I figured that's just a gimmick. So I said, "I'm not telling you nothing." Well, the Germans to me, a soldier's just like a doctor or a lawyer or anything like that, that's their profession. That's the way they think. And they appreciate somebody who doesn't tell them information.

He said, "We're gonna take you back to Rennes, to the hospital, and when we get there you're gonna have good care." Well, they put me in a meatwagon and they took me back down the road, we had artillery falling all around us, our own artillery, and they took us to this hospital. They put me in a bed there, and my leg was so bad, it was full of shrapnel and infection was setting in. The French nurses came around with these sticks, when the wound's all opened up, they put the sticks on there to heal, to try to burn the pus and everything off. That kind of hurt a little bit, and she said, "Well, just take it easy, because we might get liberated."

They put a big red cross on top of the hospital. We didn't have anything to eat. All we had was peaberry coffee and moldy bread. When I got liberated I weighed 110 pounds. And Dr. Powell, my doctor, told me when I got liberated and they took me down to the field hospital, he said, "If you'd have been there ten more hours you'd have lost your right leg."

They put me on a plane and took us over to Swindon, England -- that got me, because Swindon is where we were before we made the invasion. Dr. Powell looked at my leg, and he said, "Well, we're gonna open your leg up. You've got a piece of shrapnel up next to your bone and one back behind it. We're gonna cut that leg open, and we'll give you a spinal shot, to deaden it. You're not gonna feel a thing. I want you to keep your head, lay down and don't move." And he opened my leg up and took out two big pieces of shrapnel from my tank. About as big as my thumb.

Jim Gifford

When I got into the 712th, they told me to go over to where Jim Flowers' tanks were. That was my first contact with the 712th, to go to Jim's platoon, which had just been knocked out.

There were four tanks on that road, and there were two or three on the south side of the hill, or the north side. The Germans were buried into that hill, and they waited for those four tanks to make their turn, and then they knocked them out one at a time, and killed almost everybody in the tanks, they really hit 'em good.

I had the shitty job of going back to those four tanks and getting the dog tags of those that had died. We made up a little box. If you found anybody's remains, you always put their dog tags in that box. It went with the body.

I had to get in the tank and dig these, look for the...well, these guys had all been incinerated, because these tanks were like a furnace. It was like getting into a furnace after something's been destroyed. So I had to dig around. I'd go where the tank driver was supposed to be sitting and I'd find a dog tag. I wouldn't even find the body. This is the way it was. It was a very horrible experience, especially when you're gonna get in a tank yourself the next day.

I don't remember any of the names. I just found the dog tags. They were all our crews, I could look up the names. There was just one tank in particular that, one guy, a gunner had survived a little bit, but it's a gruesome story, I probably don't even want to tell it to you. He was still sitting in the gunner's seat. There was nothing left of him but maybe his hips. And when I was looking for the dog tags I pushed this thing, I thought it was a piece of the machinery, and it was, a piece of it came off like a turkey, like the skin on a turkey came off, this big black crust, and then I realized it was what was left of him.

Those guys never knew what hit them. Those tanks exploded. You've got all that hundred-octane gasoline, nobody had a chance.

Nine members of the first platoon, C Company -- James A. Bailey, Kenneth R. Cohron, Paul A. Farrell, Harold A. Gentle, Gerald A. Kiballa, Laverne Patton, Eugene Tannler, Abraham I. Taylor, and Stephen J. Wojtilla -- were killed on Hill 122.

CHAPTER 6

Tarr's Platoon

At the first reunion I attended, I learned that the officer my father replaced was Lieutenant George C. Tarr, whose death was described earlier by Jim Flowers.

Jule Braatz

Jule Braatz, from Beaver Dam, Wis., was a platoon sergeant, and later a lieutenant, in A Company.

A platoon was made up of five tanks. There were five men in a tank -- the driver and the assistant driver, and then up in the turret were the loader and the gunner, and behind the gunner stood the tank commander. There were five tanks like that in a platoon, and there were three platoons to a company.

Our first day in action, we left our bivouac area to report to the 82nd Airborne regimental headquarters. From there, one of their runners directed us up to where they wanted us.

We moved out from our bivouac area and we got to someplace. I was platoon sergeant, I ride the fourth tank; the lieutenant was in the first tank. It was raining. In Normandy there's a lot of sunken roads, and we went down this little dirt road and we stopped. I don't know what happened, and all of a sudden the corporal was calling me on the radio, and he said, "Lieutenant Tarr has been hit."

I finally found him, because they were around a bend, or on another road. He had been to the headquarters there, and he was coming back to the tank and some German artillery fire came in and killed him.

Then I, as platoon sergeant, I'm supposed to take over, so I went into his tank, and got orders from headquarters. They told me where to go, to go right down this road.

In the meantime, one of the tanks in front of the tank that I'd normally be in got stuck, so consequently the last two tanks couldn't come through, so then I just had two tanks.

We moved up the road and we met this infantry company that we were supposed to work with. Then this tank that I was in got hit by a mine, blew it up, killed one of the guys. So I took the other tank, basically, we went down the road. That was around La Haye du Puits.

I can't remember how many days it would be, but we had sort of been put into an immobile situation for a while. We were sitting in reserve there, waiting for a call, when your father came and joined our company. Battalion headquarters would assign replacements, and at that time I was the only one that had lost an officer, so they assigned him to my platoon.

Lieutenant Howard brought him over and introduced him to me and said, "This is your new lieutenant." Your dad was very candid and said, "Hell, I don't belong here. I'm an infantry officer, I don't know anything about tanks." And I said, "Well, I'm gonna start to teach you." So we got up on a tank and we got inside and I showed him this and that, and we got out, and we walked down the front of the tank, and I said, "Now, be careful when you jump off of these things, because you don't have a flat space, and you could jump off and twist your ankle." And so help me God, he did. So then, we took him over to the medics. The battalion had two doctors.

I have no idea how long it was, but in that length of time we got orders to move out, so we moved out.

From there on, it's more or less hearsay, or secondhand information, in that he came back and we were gone, and instead of maybe waiting, he was anxious to get up there. So about that time the first platoon got orders to move, and he went with the first platoon tanks because he figured he'd be up somewhere where we are, and then he could join us.

He rode in what they called the bog, or the assistant driver's seat down front. The driver was Pine Valley Bynum [Quentin Bynum], who later was killed. And the story is, your father wanted to get out of the tank to look for his platoon, and Bynum kept telling him no, because they were getting a lot of mortar fire, but he insisted. So he got out. Bynum says he hardly was out and Bang! A round came in and some of the shrapnel from it hit him.

Clifford Merrill

Captain Clifford Merrill, from Springfield, Me., was a company commander with the 712th. He spent 32 years in the military and retired as a colonel.

I was the commander of A Company, which was assigned to the 82nd Airborne Division in Normandy. The rest of the battalion went to the 90th Infantry Division. I worked with the 82nd until the 8th of July, when the 82nd was replaced by the 8th Infantry Division.

They had to break those people in. It was tough, they'd shoot you as quick as they would the Germans. They were scared. I was, too.

They didn't advance much. In fact, they lost ground.

I had one platoon leader who was extremely good, a chap named Ed Forrest. I talked to Ed, and the artillery commander of the 8th Division, and we decided that we'd stir things up a bit. So I had Ed's platoon advance. In the meantime, Ed had a small receiving set in his tank and he was in contact with a spotter plane.

He made an advance, I guess about two and a half miles, knocked out a couple of tanks. Reuben Goldstein was in that platoon.

One place -- the story was told to me, at that point I wasn't there -- one of the tanks came around this turn in the road, and there's a bunch of Krauts, they had a hogshead of cider, that's about 20 barrels of cider in one huge container. They hit the hogshead of cider, and the Krauts as well.

Hundreds of gallons of cider, it was too bad to spill all that. But Normandy had lots of cider, and Calvados.

I was back and forth across that front line all the time. Hell, I never got to sleep. I'd go to sleep standing up. I traveled in a jeep mostly. I'd have a tank following me.

One of the leading infantry battalions that was supposed to have been engaged with the enemy lost an assistant division commander, he got killed trying to lead a platoon. Imagine a brigadier general leading a platoon. He went out where he shouldn't have been. He got hit, heck, the Germans laid down such fire that the other members of that platoon, nobody could break him out. He bled to death.[1] So the next day I went up in that area, and one of the first people I came across was this battalion commander digging a hole.

I said, "What are you doing?" I was standing up.

He said, "We're being fired on."

I said, "They're not hitting me." Oh, you could hear bullets, but that was everywhere you'd hear them. If they hit a tree thirty feet over your head you'd hear the snap. I didn't pay any attention to those.

I said, "I don't see any Krauts around. Let's see what's going on." So I left him and I went along the front-line hedgerow. Everybody was hiding down behind the hedgerow, and I said, "What goes?"

Well, the Germans are right over there, at the next hedgerow. And someone said there's a machine gun on the other side.

There was a captain there, I asked him about it, and he explained where the machine gun was, and I said, "Well, I'll go have a look at it." I had a tank with me, it had a 105-millimeter gun on it.

I went on foot up this little trail, armed with a tommy gun. I went up there and I couldn't see anything. I got down and kind of crawled along, and I looked up, and there was this damn Kraut looking right at me. To this day, I don't think he saw me. There was no look of surprise or nothing. He didn't do anything.

[1]Brigadier General Nelson M. Walker of the 8th Infantry Division, to which A Company of the 712th was briefly assigned, was killed attempting to organize an infantry battalion for an attack.

Instinctively, I brought that tommy gun up, and I ripped him up. Then I heard the machine gun. I could see where the muzzle blast was moving the bushes, and I said, "Well, I found the machine gun. I guess I'll get the hell out of here." I started back, and they dropped either mortar or grenades, I'm not sure, and the first one caught me right in the back, knocked me down, and as I was laying down another one went off and got my right leg. I had a broken back and two inches knocked out of the small bone in my leg.

After awhile, somebody came up and put a patch on me. I made believe I was out. It was a German medic.

I waited. They left. The tommy gun was laying in the leaves, they hadn't seen it, and I had a pistol inside my shirt in a shoulder holster, they didn't find that either, but they put a patch on my back. They figured I wasn't going to go anywhere. They jabbered awhile, and then they left.

I picked up my tommy gun. Hell, I could walk, I hobbled a little but I didn't realize I had a broken leg, and my back didn't hurt. I walked a couple hundred yards back to the front lines. Then the medics took over.

I saw the tank commander of the tank that followed me up there, and I told him what to do. I heard him shooting after that.

I gave him my tommy gun, too. I said, "Take it into Berlin."

That was the 13th of July. That was all the combat for me.

Morse Johnson

Morse Johnson, from Cincinnati, was a tank commander in Headquarters Company. He later transferred to A Company, and received a battlefield commission.

I was the tank commander to whom Captain Merrill said "Take it into Berlin." I don't recall firing after that, but he might have heard fighting, because we were in the hedgerows.

One time when we were with the 82nd Airborne, there wasn't much going on, it was a stable place, and I walked over and was talking to Sam MacFarland and a couple of his men, and a couple of 82nd Airborne infantry people were there, we were talking to them, there was really sort of dead silence, and one of them said, "Hey, I think we'd better..." and the other said, "I think so." About three minutes later, they started to shell. And it shows, they'd been there for twenty days before we got there, how you get to sense what might be happening. You can feel it.

Clifford Merrill

While I was in the hospital I got several letters from my first sergeant, Charlie Vinson. I've kept them all. He told me all about who was wounded and this and that.

The way he got around the censors, the first man in the battalion to be killed was a lieutenant, George Tarr, Charlie would say so-and-so joined Tarr's platoon. He couldn't come out and say somebody got killed, they'd cut the letters, or black it out.

We were going down this hill. The Krauts had been shelling this area periodically, interdiction fire I guess you'd call it, and then something happened, George got down off his tank for some reason. I don't know why, I wasn't talking to him then on the radio. He was curious about something, I guess. But he didn't get down all the way. A shell hit on the deck, knocked him down, and then another shell went close to him. He just had a brand new baby. A little boy.

I couldn't write that letter. I think I let Ellsworth Howard take care of it, or maybe Vinson did, because I knew him well. A nice guy. Methodical. And slow. He'd do anything you told him, do anything for you.

In fact, Ellsworth Howard and I were talking about George the other day. What we commented about was a train ride from Fort Jackson up to Camp Myles Standish. We had old George all excited about keeping track of the troops. We said, "George, go count noses." Howard, his nickname was the Gremlin, he was a real needler that guy, still is, but he was worse then. He'd say, "George, get up there and count noses," and George said, "Well, I did that just about an hour ago," and Howard said, "Yeah, but you know, we're going to combat, and you never know when one of these guys might just take it into his head and jump off this train." We wanted to get him doing something, rather than worrying about his kid, his wife.

"Okay," he said, "I'll go count noses." Well, he got it organized, he got it down by car, the number of soldiers in each car. Lord, I laughed about that. I didn't interfere, because Ellsworth Howard was the executive officer, let him go ahead and take care of things. I can still hear him, "George, go count noses."

CHAPTER 7

"Ballgame's Over"
(The Falaise Gap)

August 6-20, 1944

Jim Gifford has a photo that he took on a trip to Europe in 1953. He used a Polaroid camera, and the picture has faded around the edges. It is not a dramatic shot. In fact, all it shows is an open gate in a hedgerow and two bare trees.

In an old battalion newsletter, Tony D'Arpino has a reproduction of another photo taken several years after the war. It, too, is a not-very-dramatic shot, of an intersection in a road just south of Le Mans.

In both cases, you have to use your imagination.

"That's the tree that the sheep was in," Gifford says, pointing to a scraggly two-pronged tree just to the right of the gate.

"I was in a tank in back of Lieutenant Lombardi's tank as we were going through a hedgerow," Gifford had said before removing a cigar box full of photographs from a filing cabinet. "Tony D'Arpino was driving Lombardi's tank. No, he wasn't. Another man was driving it, I can't think of his name. Sawyer. Tony was the assistant driver.

"As they were heading towards this gate in the hedgerow, I saw a sheep up in a tree.

"I said, 'Oh, shit, Lombardi, don't go' -- I'm calling on the radio -- 'don't go through that gate because there's a sheep in a tree. There must be a mine there.'

"Lombardi kept going, and all of a sudden there was a big black explosion, his tank was obliterated for a minute, and the next thing Lombardi comes stumbling out of the smoke. He had been hurt a bit, but he was all right.

"I set him down. He was pretty well shook up. Then I ran to the tank, and Sawyer was just sitting there in the driver's seat. He was stunned. He lost his hearing, and was evacuated. He's probably deaf today."

"The first tank I was in hit a mine," D'Arpino said when I interviewed him at his home in Milton, Mass.

"The night before, they shot everything they had at us. That meant either they were counterattacking or they were moving and didn't want to take all this ammunition with them.

"So we knew the area was mined. I can still see a cow pasture, with a gate, and it was open. Lieutenant Lombardi figured we can go through that gate. And I don't know what made him do it, but just before we got to the gate -- I was the assistant driver, and this guy named Cardis Sawyer from Texas was the driver, Klapkowski was the gunner, and La Mar [Grayson C. La Mar] was the loader -- just before we got to the gate, Lombardi told Sawyer to stop, and he said, 'Open hatches.' And we all opened our hatches. Then he said, 'Proceed through the gate.'

"That's the last thing I remember for a while, because Boom! Shit flying all over the place. My helmet was gone. I could feel something hot running down my left leg, I thought my leg was blown off.

"The three guys in the turret, they got right out. Sawyer and I stayed in the tank, and I was stone deaf. When the stuff cleared and I looked down, I saw the transmission had a crack in it, and the hot oil was running down my pant leg and inside my shoe.

"There was an aid station down the road. So Sawyer and I went down there. Sawyer went in first. I heard him scream. I said, 'The hell with this,' and went back to the tank. I never saw Sawyer again.

"Afterward," D'Arpino said, "I had this constant ringing in my ears.

"Now they made me a driver," he said. "I told Lombardi, 'You know, you ought to keep me out of that driver's seat. I want to stay in the tank, but give me another job, because I can't hear. You might tell me to stop and I'll keep on going.'"

There's a building in the photo of the intersection. The building wasn't there in 1944. D'Arpino had only recently taken over as driver when his tank approached the intersection. He looked to his left and saw the lead vehicle of a German column approaching. He didn't know it, but the column was three miles long. He looked to his right and saw open road. Then he heard Lieutenant Lombardi.

"Turn left."

D'Arpino was sure the concussion had affected his hearing.

"What did you say?" he shouted.

"I said turn left."

As soon as he made the turn, D'Arpino says, Stanley Klapkowski fired a round of high explosive ammunition into the lead German vehicle, knocking it out and blocking the road. The column disappeared over a rise in the road, but Klapkowski would fire, elevate the gun a little, and fire again. Then a squadron of P-47s appeared overhead, knocking out the vehicles in the rear, and bombing and strafing the German column.

D'Arpino says Klapkowski got a Silver Star for the action, and was credited with knocking out something like 37 vehicles.

Ray Griffin, in a memoir he compiled for his grandchildren, says that after hearing the firing from a distance, he called Lieutenant Lombardi on the radio, and "Lom told me that I'd have to come back and look or I wouldn't believe him."

This was early in August. D'Arpino, Griffin, Lombardi, Gifford, none of them had any idea that the scene of the wrecked German column would pale in comparison to the apocalyptic vision of destruction that would confront them within the next two weeks.

Jim Gifford

All of the tanks in my platoon went in different directions one day, and we were supposed to come back to a checkpoint, but one of the tanks didn't return. Nobody knew what happened to it.

So just before dark, I went out on foot looking for it. I had a couple of grenades with me, and a tommy gun. I went through some woods and followed this road -- carefully, naturally, because I don't know what the hell is out there because we're behind the German lines.

I came to a crossroads, and there was a house there with a little woodpile in front of it. It was almost dark now, so I settled down for the night right there. I didn't want to go walking in the dark back towards our line, I'd get my ass shot off by friendly fire if not by the Germans, so I slept in that woodpile, and I'll never forget, a cat came up and meowed, and sat with me. He stayed there most of the night with me.

Just before daylight, I saw a column coming down the side road, and they stopped. There were about twelve, fifteen of them, they walked right by me. But there was no point in my shooting at them, they were a point, out reconnoitering like I was doing, and eventually they would go back to their own line. So it would have been just plain suicide to throw, what did I have, two hand grenades and a tommy gun? So I let them go by me.

When daylight came, I went further along the road, and then I crossed it, and I came to a hedgerow. I walked along that hedgerow, came to the opening in it -- it was a high hedgerow, seven or eight feet high, and about five feet thick -- and I turned to go into the next field, which was a wheatfield. As I did so, I found myself face to face with a German point man, and he had a tommy gun too, a Schmauser we called them.

Behind him, there were about fifteen guys, all loaded for bear. They had bandoliers of ammunition hanging around their necks, they had big machine guns, a whole goddamn line of them.

I stood there. I froze. I knew if I raised my gun I was going to get a thousand bullets in me. I didn't know what the hell to do. And the guy looks at me. We're only two feet from each other.

The guy was clean-shaven and he was about my age, and he had on his German helmet and a gray uniform, he must have been a fresh recruit, because his uniform was pretty clean. But he was so startled to see me that he didn't know what the hell to do. He had to make a fast decision, too.

As a matter of fact, the guys with him made the decision for him. They realized that maybe I was the lead man of another bunch. Lucky for me they didn't come into my field before I went into theirs, or they would have realized I was alone, they would have probably slaughtered me. But they weren't sure how much was behind me and I just stood there. I didn't raise my gun.

The last guy in their line turned and started running into the wheatfield, and Jesus, they all turned. I guess they figured I had about a hundred guys behind me. I never raised that goddamn gun. I just held it. And the other guy backs away from me, and he starts turning, and he goes down through the wheatfield and way the hell over in the corner of it and disappears.

I went along the wheatfield following them, to see where the hell they're going, and still looking for the tank. It was a risky business, but I don't know, you do these things and afterward you figure, now what a stupid thing to do, but you do them, you can't explain these things. And then, in the leaves, I saw something glisten. I went over and they had thrown all their guns down and covered them with leaves, but they didn't have enough leaves to cover them. And then I saw down there, in this little wooded ravine, there was a stream, and there was a little vacant field, and there in the middle of that field was our tank, close to the stream, sunk below the tracks. It had gotten stuck in the mud, and the Germans were all standing there with their hands on their heads, they had surrendered to the crew.

Another time, right after Lombardi's tank went over the mine, I got out of my tank and went over the hedgerow to reconnoiter. Before you pull tanks up into an unknown area you go up ahead and look around, if possible. So I was creeping up ahead, jumping behind this tree and that tree, going through a field, and now I'm up ahead maybe four or five hundred yards. The tanks are waiting to see what I've got to say when I come back.

While I was out there, I came across a dead German soldier. I jumped over a hedgerow and the guy's laying there on his back in a foxhole. I looked around, I didn't see anyone else, so I picked up his tunic and put my hand under it to see if he had a luger, but he didn't have one.

Then I went on up ahead towards this house. I'm looking through my field glasses now, and I don't see anything out there, I said Jesus, they must have pulled out.

So I go back to tell the outfit, and as I come by this German soldier, he's gone. The sonofabitch was alive all that time, and he must have played dead when he saw me coming. I don't know where the hell he went. That was a thrill. I thought Holy shit, I don't believe this.

At the same time, I found an American soldier that somebody had sniped, he was laying in the bushes. He was about 18 years old. I picked him up, he didn't weigh 120 pounds, and I carried him over about three fields, heading back towards the tanks, until I got to a road, and then I laid him down in the road.

Then I radioed back to the tanks, and I said, "There's nothing up here, they've withdrawn."

Lester Suter

One night, after we had advanced about 12 miles, I was put on guard duty. It was midnight, and there was a dense fog. I had to stay from midnight till four in the morning.

So I'm there, and I'm standing guard, all of a sudden I hear sounds. I thought, "Jesus Christ, don't tell me they're sneaking up on me." And I hear these sounds, and oh, boy, am I scared, because any minute they're gonna rush at me. So I got against a tree there, put my back against a tree, I says, "Well, they're gonna have to get me from the front, not from the back," and so I kept hearing this, and I says, "Why the hell don't they come faster? The sonofabitches, they know I'm here, so why not get it over with?"

And it still got closer and closer, and man, I had my gun cocked and everything, I was ready to fire, and all of a sudden, out of this fog steps a big cow. Oooooh boy, there were about three cows eating the grass, and I thought they were Germans sneaking up on me!

Jim Gifford

We got orders to head towards Caen. The tanks gathered together, and suddenly we found out we were assigned to an outfit called Task Force Weaver. That was an armored outfit that was going to break out of Normandy, and that's what we did. We went through Caen, to St. Lo.

We got to one town, I don't remember its name, we pulled into an apple orchard, and they had dropped gasoline off. How they got it there I don't know.

So we spread our tanks around, and they told us to dig a foxhole, everybody, they said dig foxholes.

I said, "What the hell are we going to do with a foxhole?" You know, we're moving all the time. But they told us we'll be here all night, dig a foxhole.

The next morning we're putting more gas in the tanks and getting replenished, and suddenly I see these airplanes going over, and I'll never forget, I was counting them, I counted 37 Messerschmitt 109s, those are German fighter planes. First I saw the cross, I hollered to the guys, I said "Geez, look at the French crosses." And then we looked again and shit, those are German crosses. The French had a similar cross, the Cross of Lorraine it looked like way up in the air.

We watched them go out of sight. What we didn't know was that they were looking for us, and they found us. So the next thing I know, Geez, the shells are firing, bullets are flying all through everything, and we all ran for our foxhole, and when I dove in the foxhole, Geez, there were two guys under me. There were three of us in that hole. And we came out, and all they hit was one armored vehicle which they set on fire.

Then we continued into a town called Mayenne. We took the town, and at night we straddled the road with our tanks. And then during the night we hear these trucks coming. So we go out by the edge of the road, and Jesus, here's a whole column of German soldiers and trucks coming through the night, they're about fifty feet apart. And they're barreling down the road in the dark. They go right by us, of course we're keeping low, it's dark, they can't see us, but they're looking for us.

They go down into the town, in Mayenne. It was an old medieval town, it had a river, and they crossed the bridges and reached the town square. Then they turned around, you could hear their transmissions shifting gears, and the next thing they start coming back out. There were maybe four, five, six trucks. And as they went by us, we're waiting for 'em. We started to slam 'em with everything we've got, and blew them all up.

We let the last truck go through and then we hit them, so that we got them all. They were a mixture of infantry and air force men, because on some of their lapels we found air force emblems. We wiped them out. Whether anybody captured any of them I don't know.

One guy came running at me. I was right by the hedgerow, and he and a couple of the other guys jumped into a gully to the right of me. I threw a grenade in at them. I didn't know whether I'd hit them or not, but when I looked the next morning they were in there, and that's when I saw the lapels.

And the one guy -- it's a funny thing how honest you can be at a time like that -- one guy, I picked him up, lifted him up to look for a luger. We were always looking for lugers, because you could trade them for something. So when I picked him up, his tunic broke open, and he had a wallet which was thick with this white French currency, I don't know what it was but it's like instead of having a ten-dollar bill if you had a thousand-dollar bill you'd get white currency. It was all wrapped up with rubber bands in this wallet, and I felt bad. Oh shit, this was this guy, his parents or whoever his heirs are back home should get this, I don't want it. And I put it back in his tunic.

About an hour later I thought about it, I said, "Shit, his family's never gonna get that," so I went back, but somebody had already beat me to it.

Forrest Dixon

When they made this advance towards Le Mans, they left half the trains back in Mayenne. The trains had ammunition and gasoline. Well, we got into a little firefight on the way, and we were using more gas and ammunition than we thought.

So Colonel Randolph and General Weaver[1] called me over, and Colonel Randolph says, "Captain Dixon, you and Major Caffery [Clegg "Doc" Caffery] go back to Mayenne and get the trains."

I couldn't understand why he wanted me up there, but I thought, well, I originally was a tanker, maybe he's going to give us a few light tanks or something. It was midnight, and we had to go through sixty kilometers of no man's land.

"Yes sir," I said. "What are we going to take back for protection?"

"Oh, I think you and Major Caffery would be better alone." So all we had was a jeep.

The most eerie part of that was Colonel Randolph and General Weaver held out their hands, and General Weaver said, "Hope to see you tomorrow."

I sure hoped so! That's the first time I ever shook hands with a general. "Hope to see you tomorrow, boys."

Jim Gifford

After Mayenne we started swinging toward the north. We swung around and we headed toward the Falaise Gap. We didn't know it, but we were making a big circle.

It was a bright, sunny day. We came out on a hill, and you could see this valley out in front of you. Across the valley you could see cliffs. This was the Falaise Gap, which was a famous old gap that went back to medieval days. William the Conqueror's castle was in the Falaise Gap. The villages go back to his time.

That was an area, that gap, where armies came and went for generations.

We were on a hill on the east side of the gap. As darkness started to fall, we started to disperse our tanks down on the hill, and our A and B Company and the 773rd Antitank Battalion were out into the flatland. I was with C Company up on this ridge. So our whole Task Force Weaver column was building up.

We made a circle of our tanks, just like the covered wagons, because we were behind the lines, we don't know what the hell's gonna be there when daylight comes, so we're always ready for an attack.

The next morning, it was just daylight, I took my field glasses and I went back up the hill so I could see out over this valley. I'm looking down in the valley in the early sun and

[1] Brigadier General William G. Weaver

I see all these little sparkles, little sparks all over the valley, what the hell is that? I looked through the field glasses and I'm telling you, I couldn't believe the sight I saw. It was thousands of bayonets flashing in the early morning sun. These guys, these infantry guys, were walking toward us, now they're about three miles away up that valley, and they're dispersed among hundreds of tanks moving along. Holy shit, I saw this, this was coming toward us, this is it. So I ran down, I got on the radio and I started hollering over the radio what's coming. And it wasn't twenty minutes later a bunch of our P-47 Thunderbolts were flying in towards them, at treetop level, those guys were our saviors, they were our angels up there, they were there all the time so we felt secure. They used to run in groups of four, and they came flying in one group after another. They'd go and the next thing there'd be some more of them coming, they were knocking the shit out of them, and shells started flying over us, big shells. Part of Task Force Weaver behind us -- we're in the lead because we're tanks -- so all that task force that was behind us were dropping their blades, what they call blades on these big guns, and firing from wherever they are back there. They had their Pipers, little airplanes, Piper Cubs, they were painted grey and sort of a greenish color, they were flying over us directing the artillery fire.

Well, these poor bastards out there three miles away, they were catching bloody hell, I'll tell you, they were getting it. We were firing at them from a mile or two away. We weren't waiting 'til they got to us, we were blasting away at 'em. And our A and B Company were spread out across the valley and the 773rd Antitank Battalion, they were spread out. And this monolith, whatever you want to call it, was slowly rolling, with all the destruction that was going on, it was coming right along by us -- and Jesus, it wasn't stopping -- and we were hitting everything. They had hundreds of horses drawing artillery. And instead of turning and coming up the hill toward us, they continued to head toward the gap with our A, B and 773rd Antitank Battalion dispersed there, and those two companies were catching hell because the Germans started rolling through them. And when they hit these two companies plus the 773rd they started piling up, and the next thing they turned and they started to go back and started running into themselves.

When the whole thing started, over on the cliffs across from us tanks were shooting, and we thought they were Germans, so we were shooting at them for almost an hour, until we were told those are British and Canadian tanks, stop shooting at them.

From what I understand, about 50,000 Germans actually got through us, but the other 200,000 piled up. By 2 o'clock in the afternoon, airplanes had been flying over dropping leaflets, they were all over, I've even got some of those leaflets, I have them somewhere in my stuff here, saying surrender, wave the leaflet, you'll be okay. And we got orders, they kept coming over the radio, stop firing at 2 o'clock. Stop firing at 2 o'clock. But you could fire at anything, you wanted to shoot at a tank, you could shoot at a tank. Anything you wanted to shoot at, there it was, it was a slaughter, and most guys were just shooting without even looking, it was that bad.

Then at 2 o'clock it stopped, and they started coming up, out of the gap. Their equipment was burning all over the place, as far as you could see, burning equipment, it must have been as bad as that situation in Iraq. It must have looked the same. There was so much equipment, for miles it was burning all over the place, and these guys were coming out waving flags and waving papers. By the time they got up to us on this ridge -- we were alongside of a dirt road which wound behind us -- there were hundreds of them. They were coming past the tank.

I looked down from the tank, and these guys were all dusty, dirty and filthy, and tired. They were a bedraggled army, it was a defeated army. They were just so goddamn glad to just be alive. They kept looking back at the carnage and shaking their heads just like we were, lucky they weren't back there.

I remember one guy, there were about five or six, young guys they were, carrying a wounded soldier who also looked young. He was on a makeshift stretcher, and a halftrack of ours was going back. I stopped the halftrack and I told them, I said bring him up here and put him on the canvas which was laying on the halftrack. So they put him up on there, and then the five or six guys with him, they were all Germans, got on the halftrack to go with him, and I figured let 'em go, they ain't gonna do harm, they're glad to be out of this battle.

You know, it's a funny thing, there's almost like a signal, somebody blew a whistle and the ballgame's over. They weren't trying to shoot us anymore or anything, they were just glad to be surrendered. For hours they were coming up out of there, going back down the road.

Ruby Goldstein

We had a driver in my platoon, Duane Minor, he was from Minneapolis, Minnesota, I think. He was married, tall, a handsome looking kid.

In back of the driver, up above, in the turret, you've got your 75-millimeter, you've got your gunner, tank commander, and your loader. Sometimes the machine gun would get so hot from firing that if you don't open up the cover, she's gonna keep firing. And he's sitting down below, he got up, opened up the hatch, and someone left the cover on the machine gun in the tank behind him, and it fired. It killed him. That's how accidents happen.

We had another kid, at the Falaise Gap. A Company was closing the gap. And everything was quiet. In the distance was the woods out there. We didn't know what was in the woods. But we knew that it was our job to encircle and we had to close this gap.

We got out of the tank, and took a little Coleman stove we had, put it in back of the tank. You light it up, take your cup, put some water in it, heat it up for coffee. A mortar shell lands, beeko, he's gone. Just for nothing. Out of the blue. That was the only one that landed at that time, the first one.

Then, after we jumped back in the tank, all hell broke loose. That's when I caught shrapnel in the neck.

I took out my handkerchief, and I held it up against my neck. I jumped down, and a jeep came by, and they had a stretcher with a fellow on it, and one in the back seat, and the driver. I got in the front, and we went to a first aid hospital. It was in back of a huge building, like a castle, but we went around the back, underground, to the cellar like, and they had all the guys who were wounded, everybody in line, waiting their turn to get treated.

Finally, I was next. There was a kitchen table, a white porcelain table. Strip to the waist, lay down. He's got a flashlight, he's lookin' at it, and he says, "Oh, that's nothing. A little bit more and I wouldn't even have to do this." I said, "Thanks."

Then he had a pail there, and he dug a knife, scalpel, who the hell knows what the heck he had there, he went in and dug it out and I hear "clunk." I said, "What was that?" He said, "Ahh, you don't want to see it." But I looked. It had flesh on it, and it was bloody, with dirt on it. He dug out another piece, and that was it. He couldn't get it all, because it had already gone in. I still have it in my back, small pieces. And then somebody put sulfanilamide, they bandaged my neck, that's it.

And you know something funny? It didn't hurt much. When you get hurt, the shock is so great that you don't even feel the pain. In fact, if somebody came in and stuck a knife in you and it was unexpected, you wouldn't feel it right away. It's afterwards that you start feeling the pain.

Then I went to a replacement depot, and from there they sent me to another replacement depot in the woods, and I rode in a truck all day long to catch up with the outfit. And when I left, they don't know what happened to me, nobody does. They don't know if you're alive or dead or nothing, you disappear. If somebody close to you knows that you got hurt, that's all they know.

Sam Cropanese

Sam Cropanese, from West Paterson, N.J., was a gunner in A Company.

I was wounded at the Falaise Gap. But there were many battles before that. A lot of battles. The first one was at St. Lo. I never knew what a hedgerow was. When I saw those hedgerows, I said, "My god, no wonder nobody can see anything." They were taller than the one-story houses, and the hedges were so close together that you couldn't see nothing. My god, traveling down those roads, all of a sudden, Bam! A shell would smack one of the lead tanks, and the lead tank would pull back, sometimes it would just knock it right out.

The first one that I heard was killed was Lieutenant Tarr. I think it was Braatz that came back and said, "We lost one of our lieutenants."

And we said, "Who is it?"

"Lieutenant Tarr." Ohh, boy. I knew Lieutenant Tarr very well. Lieutenant Tarr was one hell of a nice man. Slow talking. Tall, heavy. I can still see him. They told me that he had come out of the tank, and they told him to get back in because there was a lot of firing, a lot of stuff coming in. And he started running up to the tank, he got up to the tank, he got on the track, was just ready to step into the tank, when a shell hit right there and just blew him right off. He was gone instantly. And Braatz came back and said he was on the side of the road, we just left him there.

When I first went overseas I wasn't too scared, but when I heard that Lieutenant Tarr got it, now this is only one, I started getting scared, too. I said, Geez, he got it already, we're all gonna get it.

Then we started with one battle after another. Some battles we were in! One, in Avranches, we pulled in about 12 o'clock at night, and all of a sudden, the whole sky lit up. They were dropping flares down. And I heard over the radio, get up against the buildings, hurry up, don't stay out in the open. Get up against the buildings. So all the tanks went up against the buildings, and all of a sudden the bombs came down. They bombed the hell out of us. We heard the bricks and everything coming down on top of the tanks. I remember, I was crying in the tank, Eugene Crawford, he was crying in the tank, we were praying and crying, oh, I'm telling you, what a feeling that is! We thought we were gone. All those shells are hitting next to you, hitting the brick houses and raining bricks on top of us. Every time a bomb would go off, the tank would shake all over the place, but we wouldn't dare move, because if we did, the planes up on top would see the lights of the tank, the flames shooting out from the motors, and they would sure as hell hit us. So none of us dared move until it was all over, and they took off and went away.

Then we dug out of the bricks, opened up the hatches and looked around and said, "My god, how lucky can you get?"

Red Rose

Sergeant Walter F. Rose, from Jonesville, N.C., was a member of Service Company.

I was never seriously wounded. I've seen the shells coming in, and went rolling and tumbling. The only time I was ever wounded, we were being strafed one night and I hit a clothesline in a yard. That's the only blood I ever drew.

They hollered, "Let's get the medics up here, Rose is wounded." I mean, the blood was flowing. I said, "No, I'm not, I'm just skinned."

It was night. It was in the village at Avranches, and I was running through the dark, around behind the houses trying to get away from that highway because I knew the flares were down there and they're coming in, they're strafing down on that road, and you got out of your vehicle trying to get away from there.

They told me I could have a Purple Heart because the plane was strafing. I turned it down.

Steve Krysko

Steve Krysko, from Scranton, Pa., was a gunner in A Company.

During the battle of the Falaise-Argentan Gap, I was firing 75-millimeter shells into a wooded area as fast as my loader could ram them into the gun's breach. Suddenly, a running, hand-waving infantryman materialized in my periscope. I reached up, grabbed onto the hatch rim and hoisted myself into a standing position in front of the lieutenant. Even now, the infantryman's words have a disquieting effect as I recall the moment: "Stop! You're killing our own men!"

I fell back onto the gunner's seat, laid my head on my arms, and cried. As far as I was concerned, the war was over for me. It hit me that not only was I killing human beings, which, in itself, is traumatic, but I was killing our own men.

I refused to fight on, and had to be sent back to A Company's rear "safety zone." I crawled under a disabled tank and lay there for the rest of the day. No one said anything to me. I tried to convince myself that I was "Section 8" -- mentally disturbed -- and would be sent back to the States because of "battle fatigue." By dusk, however, I realized that faking a mental breakdown is something I couldn't do. The next day, when I learned that my tank commander had screwed up orders, I refused to go into battle with him. He had been told "Don't fire on the left," but inadvertently he heard, "Fire on the left."

Sam Cropanese

One time, it was in the daytime, and I heard German planes coming over. Then I saw one stray American plane, with the double fuselage, a P-38. He came out of nowhere, and he chased one of these German planes. I was watching them, but they were firing, so I got scared, I dove under the tank and I stayed there, and I'm watching from under the tank. What a dogfight. I'd never seen a dogfight. They were chasing each other. All of a sudden, the P-38 hit the German plane. The German plane was smoking like crazy, it went into the clouds and just disappeared. The P-38 turned off and went away.

Another time we got called out by the 359th Infantry Regiment of the 90th Division. They got hit with a lot of tanks, and they were stuck. Panzers and all kinds. They were knocking the hell out of them. So they called two platoons in, we were one, we went in with five tanks, and another went in with five tanks.

As soon as we got there, we heard these 88s going under us, and on the side, and smacking the tank and glancing off. Luckily they didn't hit my tank, but I could hear them just banging and going under, there were so many 88s firing at us, it was crazy. All of a sudden I heard the lead tank say, "Let's get the hell out of here!" So we backed up the tanks and we got out fast, and they called in the TDs, the tank destroyers, to take care of them. We got out of that battle there, it was bad. We didn't know where the firing was coming from, and we were right in the middle of it.

We had so many battles. Mayenne, Ste. Mere Eglise, Avranches, St. Lo.

Finally, we got to the Falaise Gap. We were bivouacked in the area, and it was early in the morning, about 5:30 or 6 o'clock. I was outside. I had my little stove out. We were making coffee. All of a sudden, a treeburst came down, it hit the trees and it just rained on us. It was an 88 shell. The first one that hit was the one that got me. It hit me, spun me around, threw me right on the ground. Infantry men were all around, and the tankers and everybody, I heard crying and moaning, oh my god, I wouldn't want to hear that again. There were so many people hurt with that one shell that burst out, and after that it was coming in from all over.

I got hit in the face. The left side of my lip was hanging down, and my nose was split open. A piece of shrapnel about an inch and a half hit me. It went in through the jaw, busted the jaw, and stayed right in the bottom, just missing the jugular vein.

I got into a ditch, and I must have been there about three hours. A medic got to me before that, and I still remember, he got a needle and thread, and he hooked the piece of lip that was hanging, he hooked it back on, put a couple of threads in it, he put a bandage on it with that sulfa, and he said, "Now you stay here until they come and get you."

When the jeep came and got me out, I still heard firing going on all over the place. We drove out of there fast and went back to where the tanks were, and Eugene Crawford, who was in my tank crew, got into the jeep. He grabbed ahold of me and said, "Hang on, Sam, hang on. We're going down to the aid station, and they'll take care of you there."

Right where the tanks were, they gave me plasma. They hooked it up on the jeep, and Eugene was holding it up, he was holding me, and we went down to the first aid hospital. Eugene got out and he said, "Sam, take care of yourself, you'll be all right, don't worry, you'll be okay," and I was saying, "Gene, I feel myself going, I'm going, I'm not gonna make it, I'm not gonna make it," and he was crying, he was saying, "Sam, you're gonna make it, you're gonna make it, don't worry, don't worry." Then he left, and I went in the ambulance, they took me to Le Mans. And in Le Mans they operated, they took the piece of shrapnel out, and they gave it to me. I still have the piece of shrapnel.

While I was in the hospital in Le Mans, my head was all bandaged up, and I was on a stretcher. There were no tables or anything, the stretchers were all on the ground. I'm on the ground, and I'm looking up, and I see someone that I know, and I says, holy Geez, could it be? It was Joe Bernardino, who was in my tank. So I hollered out to him -- I couldn't call out too much, because my jaw was wired shut -- so I was trying to say "jo...jo...jo." He looked over, and he didn't recognize me. So he came close to me, he says, "Holy Jesus, is that you, Sam?" I says, "Yes, yes it's me." We started talking there, and he told me that when the shell came in that hit me, he was in the tank. He had gone in to get some sugar, and he had his gun, I don't know what he was doing with it, but he had his gun out, and when the shell hit, it shook the tank, the gun went off, it ricocheted and hit him in the face. How do you like that action?

Jim Gifford

The next day it started to drizzle, and we organized a whole bunch of guys, and their job was to just go down into the Falaise Gap and shoot wounded horses. The Germans were using horses to draw their caissons, these towed guns, and these poor horses were catching hell from all this slaughter.

Some of them died instantly, some of them were injured, and some of them were just laying down with their heads up. It killed me to see that. I remember one horse, he had a shell in his shoulder, it was sticking out, a big, round shell, it was about ten inches long, and four or five inches of it were sticking out of his shoulder, and he's standing there, he had a shattered leg, and he's eating the grass. He's not even jumping around or anything, he's just standing there, poor sonofabitch.

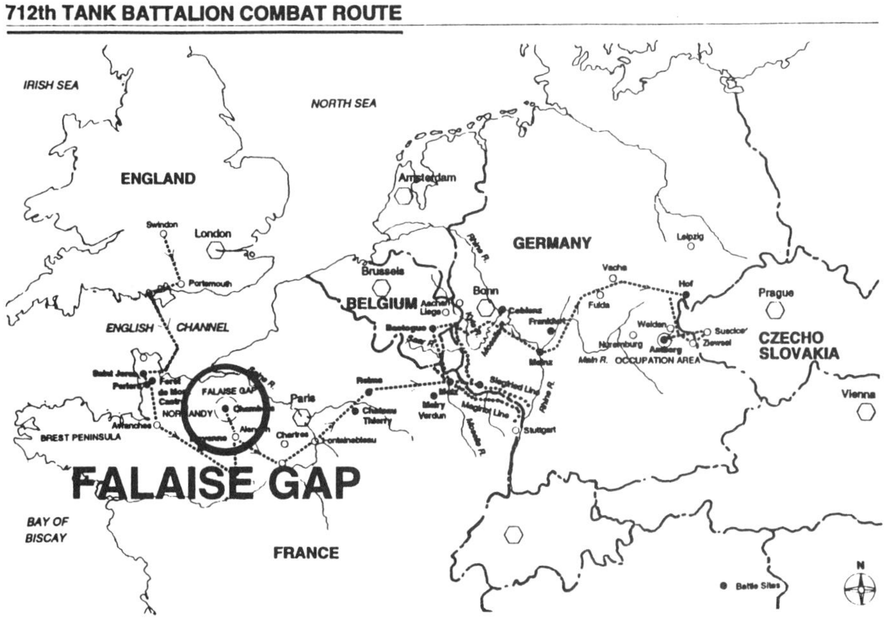

CHAPTER 8

Mairy

Sept. 8, 1944

By the beginning of September, "we were moving, moving, moving," says Jim Gifford.

Task Force Weaver, a column of armor and infantry, was penetrating deep into France, and by now was in the vicinity of the World War I battlegrounds of Verdun and the Argonne Forest.

Nobody was getting much sleep, least of all Forrest Dixon. By the time the task force pulled out of Avranches, each of the three tank recovery vehicles and two ten-ton wreckers under his command was towing a disabled tank.

"I told the colonel," Dixon says, "'If we lose one more tank' -- this was from engine trouble -- 'We're gonna have to destroy it, because I'm towing all the tanks I can tow.'

"And he said, 'How long will it take you to change a motor?'

"I said 'Three hours.'

"He said, 'Are you sure?'

"'Yes sir, I can get it done in three hours.'

"He said, 'The next time we stop, I'll get word to you, and if we have to pull out before you get the tank done, you destroy it and you stay with us, because it isn't safe unless you stay with the column.'"

At daybreak on Sept. 8, one of Dixon's maintenance crews began changing the engine in a tank. There had been a great deal of firing in the middle of the night, but things had calmed down. Nearby, in the Service Company area, were stacks of five-gallon jerry cans of gasoline and piles of ammunition.

The crew had the engine out of a medium tank and was working on it when a pair of German Mark IV tanks suddenly appeared.

I had heard several accounts of the battle at Mairy before realizing the speakers were talking about the same event. They were ahead of the lines. They were behind the lines. The fighting broke out in the middle of the night. It took place first thing in the morning. The moon was out. The sky was cloudy. Somehow, all of the above seems to be true.

TANKS FOR THE MEMORIES

At the 1993 reunion of the 90th Infantry Division in Louisville, I was speaking with a veteran who had just returned from a visit to the Patton Museum. He had a glazed look, as if he had seen a ghost.

What he had seen was a German tiger tank, one of the museum's prize exhibits.

"No wonder one of those looked so big from three feet away," he said.

The tank he was reminded of, part of the newly equipped 106th Panzer Brigade, had stopped just outside the soldier's foxhole at 1:45 a.m. on Sept. 8, 1944.

It stopped so that the tank commander could take a closer look at a large panel, on which a sign was painted directing all and sundry to the 90th Division artillery command post.

George Bussell

I was across the street from my tank, standing guard, about 2 in the morning, and I heard this stuff coming down the road. I could tell by the tracks it wasn't ours. The noise was altogether different. They had steel tracks, and we had rubber.

I just squatted down there by a tree, and this outfit came down the road, and they stopped. And this lieutenant or whoever it was, the commander, he was leaning way out of the hatch.

The 90th Division had a sign down there, Christ, as big as the wall of my living room. Red, white and all that crap. It said "90th Division artillery C.P.," And that's what the tank stopped and was looking at. And I was squatting there.

Then some doughboy, I don't know who he was, took a rifle and he took a shot at this guy in the tank, but he missed him. And boy, when he missed him, hell broke loose and tanks started rolling in. But we were all camouflaged. Hell, those tanks came right up to me and never did see me, and I sure as hell didn't uncover till after they were gone. Then after they were gone, I was outside by the road trying to dig a foxhole and that dirt was as hard as a rock. Man, I'd have dug a foxhole if I could've. Finally I made it up to the command post, which was on a hill.

The German tanks were down below, and there was a two and a half ton truck coming along there just like nobody's business. A German tank comes out, Pow! He blew that truck all to hell. Where we sat, they had tow mounted tank destroyers. When daylight came they stuck the tow mounts in on the German tanks, and knocked quite a few of them out. Then our tanks came in.

That was a hairy time. Man, I could see myself going and everything else.

Doc Reiff

Captain Jack Reiff was the head of the battalion's Medical Company.

I rarely went back to the rear. I just stayed right with the headquarters company and the mortar platoon, an assault gun platoon, and the medics, and usually there were maintenance people around.

My men were out with the different companies. They would be assigned with the different infantry regiments, and they'd take an ambulance and a halftrack with them.

I can't remember why, but I went from where our battalion was back to the division headquarters, to turn in a report or something, and I reported to the division surgeon. Of course, I looked like Willie and Joe, I mean I was covered with mud and dirt.

I went back to the division surgeon, and he said, "Where's your battalion?"

And I said, "Well, the companies are out with infantry regiments."

And he said, "Where's the battalion headquarters?"

So I pointed to the map and said, "Right there."

He said, "Oh, no, you couldn't be there. That's in enemy territory."

I said, "Colonel, I've been in a tank battalion for nearly a year now, and if I couldn't read a map I'd be dead."

And he said, "But that's all enemy territory."

So I said, "Let's go in and look at the operations map." The division headquarters map was about eight feet tall, with red marks for the enemy and blue marks for the Allies, everybody's all dressed up, and here I was looking like I just got out of a foxhole.

So we did look at the map and sure enough, over there it was red, red, red. So the division surgeon says, "Let's go and look at the G-2 map," that's intelligence, they're a little bit more savvy about where the enemy was, and the same thing.

So I left, and went back to battalion headquarters, and sure enough, they were right.

Jim Gifford

During the afternoon of Sept. 7, we were in a column, and we were told don't use the radios, we were trying to be quiet. And a little Messerschmitt 109 comes by, about 200 feet off the ground, right alongside of us. I can see the pilot now looking at us, and he went whipping off, nobody fired at him. That was about 3 o'clock in the afternoon.

Then we dispersed the tanks around this town called Mairy, and we were in the woods on both sides of the highway. In the meantime, I went up ahead to reconnoiter with a jeep. There were some infantry guys at a crossroads about a mile up the road, and I sat and had some coffee with them. Then I said "Well, I'm gonna go on back."

I returned to the tanks. And then during the night, Jesus, a German column comes down the road. They didn't know where we were, and they stopped.

I ran up to the road with Scott [E.L. Scott]. I told him to grab a bazooka, and he and I ran up to the edge of the road. We didn't want to fire our guns because they'd know where we were. So with the bazooka I figured I'd catch that first tank, and the son of a bitch stopped up there, he turns that gun, and boom, he hits George Peck's tank, and he turns and he hits another tank, and the guys are sleeping on the ground next to it. And one shell, it bounced off the tank and went right straight through this guy that was sleeping, he was a lieutenant from one of the other companies. The next day I went over to see what happened, and he was still in his sleeping bag, and I pulled it back, and the damn round, he had a hole in his back, he never knew what hit him.

This must have been about four in the morning, because all of a sudden it started getting daylight, and then we started shooting the shit out of them, and the whole column fell apart.

A couple of the German tanks went over to the left down through a field, and we had one tank pull up alongside, I don't know whose it was, and he fired, he knocked it out, and the crew piled out, and they started running up the road towards us. So we threw a machine gun up on top of the bank, took it off the jeep, and as they came toward us, they gave up.

Then another tank started down behind them, and he stopped his tank, and the crew got out, they didn't fire, they came over towards us and gave up.

John McDaniel

John H. McDaniel, from Paragould, Ark., was a member of A Company.

Lieutenant Bell [Harry Bell] used to get on me all the time because I wouldn't sleep with my shoes on. For one reason or another I just couldn't sleep with them on, and he'd say "We're gonna get into it, we're gonna get attacked sometime, and you're not gonna have your shoes on."

I said, "I'll put 'em right here," beside me, and I can put my shoes on in a hurry, I don't have to lace them up. So he got to the point where he pulled his shoes off, too.

When they woke us up that night -- what happened, one of the kitchen people from this little command post fired on these tanks, and when he did, boy, there was just a terrible commotion, and it woke us all up -- I couldn't find my shoes. I reached for them where they ought to be and they weren't there. So I got in the tank just like I would have with my shoes unlaced, I just got in it barefoot. I was the assistant driver, Swartzmiller [William Swartzmiller] was the driver.

We all got in the tank, and the first thing Bell did was call Lester O'Riley, who was the company commander. And Lester said, "Are you sure it's not our people?"

And Bell said, "No, I can read on the tank. They're German."

And Lester said, "You're sure they're German?"

Bell said, "Yeah."

And Les said, "Give 'em hell."

When he said that, old Bell told Swartzmiller, "Fire it up," and boy, when he fired that tank up -- now, we had an advantage in that we had an electrical turret, and they had to traverse theirs by hand, but they were facing right straight toward us so they didn't have much turning to do. And boy, they fired on us, and hit us in our suspension system.

After that we couldn't move the tank, and Bell said, "Bail out!" so everybody bailed out.

When we abandoned the tank, I took off across the field because I knew about where Lester was.

Somebody hollered at me and said, "Are you American?"

I said "Yes," and he said, "Come over here," to the wooded area. So I ran out of the open field into the wooded area and it was General Devine[1]. He had his colonel with him.

I said, "My company commander's right up here," where I was going.

He said, "You just stay here with me."

Then he and the colonel were talking. He said, "When I woke up, I reached to wake up my driver, and he wouldn't move. He was dead." As soon as it got light I went over there, and that boy was laying there just like he was asleep. He had a little hole right in his forehead, there was no more blood than there'd be on the end of your little finger. I guess that hot shrapnel pierced his skull and seared that blood. He looked like he wasn't 20 years old.

I had heard General Devine tell his colonel about the driver. So I stayed with Devine, and boy, when you get in combat like that it will really work on your nervous system and your stomach, too. I told him, "I've got to use the bathroom," and he said, "Go right back over here," and he said there's some digging equipment. So I went over and dug a place, and used it, covered it, and came back.

I stayed with him till it got light, and when it did, I asked him, "You reckon we're gonna get out of here?"

It was cloudy at that time. He said, "Just as soon as these clouds clear out, we'll get 'em." He said don't worry about it. He was so cool and calm, I was really surprised. And his colonel seemed to be in good shape, too.

After it got daylight, I started toward the tank and I met old Bell. I said, "I couldn't find my shoes this morning." He said "These are not mine I've got on."

I said "They're mine! I thought they looked like 'em." And he pulled them off and gave 'em to me, and then he went barefoot.

[1]Brigadier General John Devine

MAIRY

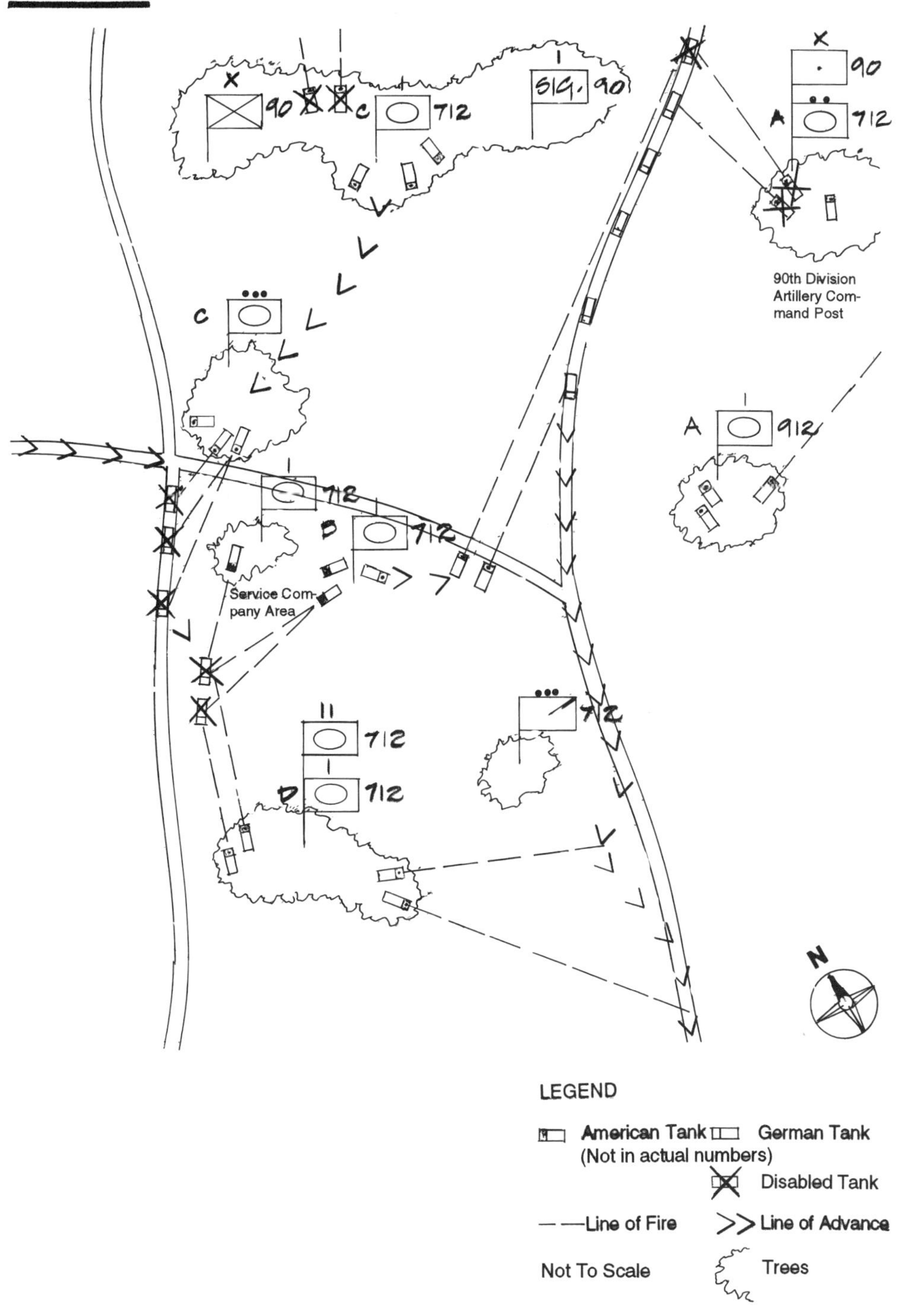

90th Division Artillery Command Post
Service Company Area
LEGEND
American Tank
German Tank
(Not in actual numbers)
Disabled Tank
Line of Fire
Line of Advance
Not To Scale
Trees
N

Doc Caffery

Major Clegg "Doc" Caffery was a member of Headquarters Company.

Mairy was a little crossroad in France. We went into a bivouac there one afternoon, the artillery c.p. was about two miles to the north of us, and they had two tank companies protecting them. We were in a wooded area.

Early that morning, about 3 o'clock, I heard a 75-millimeter go off. And minutes later, Les O'Riley comes on the tank radio, telling Colonel Randolph that he is firing on a German armored column.

Things quieted down, and then at daybreak, two of these German vehicles, they were light tanks, Mark IVs, came into our area. I was in the wooded area with the headquarters vehicles, and Dickie [Forrest Dixon] was not too far away, with Service Company.

I was hiding behind a tree, and I saw Dickie climb into this inoperable tank with no engine, and with battery power, he knocks off one of these tanks.

Forrest Dixon

Service Company always bivouacked in the center of the battalion when we were on the road, because our people were service troops, and we had all the gasoline and the ammunition with us, and we needed the protection.

The shooting started about 2 o'clock. Of course, we were all alert, and wondering what was going to happen. I don't remember why but the Service Company boys were just very, very excited and it looked like they just didn't know what was going on, and they didn't know what they should do. I had been awake for two days practically, and I thought, "Well, I'm gonna just put my bedroll down by the halftrack where the radio is and see if I can't get some sleep," and maybe that would at least quiet them down a little bit.

This was probably 4 o'clock. The shooting had stopped -- nobody knew there were other tanks in the area. So I got my bedroll and told the sergeant in charge of the radio, "If anything happens you wake me up quick." He said okay. And nothing happened. I got up the next morning, I think it was about breakfast time.

One crew was working on a tank -- they had the motor out -- when someone yelled "German tanks!" and everybody took off. I can't blame them for that.

I thought, "Oh, shit." I had been up for I guess 48 hours, and had barely had any sleep, and I was too goddamn tired to run. So I got in the tank.

Besides, all the gasoline and ammunition was in our area, and I guess I might have been thinking about that.

One boy stayed with me, I don't know who it was, but he was next to me and I said, "Do you know how to load a gun?"

He said, "I think so."

And I said, "Well, you get the gun loaded and I'll see if we can't get one of those tanks."

There was one round of ammunition in the ready rack, and he couldn't get it out. I said "Let me try." So he took off.

I put the round in the gun, and then I thought, "I won't be able to turn the turret." Because the boys were supposed to disconnect the electric when they took out an engine. When I hit that traversing box I didn't expect to hear it groan. You know, it kind of groans when the gun turns. I was a little bit surprised. I thought my boys obeyed me better than that. But I'm glad they didn't. It takes a few minutes to disconnect the electrical system, and they were trying to save time.

"I had the round of ammunition in, and the turret turned, and then I got to thinking, "I'll bet the sight isn't lined up with the barrel," so I thought I'd just better wait. I kept it pointed at the lead tank, and when it got about 50 yards from me, that's when he saw me and began to turn to get his gun in my direction, and I let him have it.

Then I grabbed the radio and I hollered, "Sam, I need your help!" That was Sam Adair, he had the assault guns, and I knew that the assault guns were just up a little ways. So I didn't get out of the damn thing. The Germans saw the assault guns coming, and they stopped right quick and everybody got out with their hands up. I stayed right inside the tank. I didn't want them to know I was the only damn fool there.

Doc Reiff

They just came attacking right across a field. And there was a tank sitting there. Dixon jumped in this tank, and he starts shooting this German tank.

So the German lieutenant gets out, one of his arms was badly injured. In the first place, it was a great insult to call a German officer "Leutnant," that's a second lieutenant. "Oberleutnant" was the first lieutenant, they were very touchy about that.

So this kid comes out, and I'm speaking to him in broken German, I said, "Alles kaput," and he said, "Nein, nein, nein, nein." So I said, "You're kaput." We're still speaking in broken German. I said, "Well, you're certainly out of action."

And he said, "Which bone is it, Doctor, the radius or the ulna?"

Thirty German tanks, 60 halftracks and over 100 miscellaneous vehicles were captured or knocked out, and 764 prisoners taken at Mairy, according to the battalion's unit history.

CHAPTER 9

Maizieres Le Metz

October, November 1944

Jim Gifford

That next day, we licked our wounds, and then we progressed towards Hayange. We were close to the Moselle River, and this town is on its west bank. As we came into the town, now we've got a lot of infantry, we're a big task force. The infantry was sitting along the road, just waiting to move up, and there was a farmhouse there.

I went in the farmhouse; they were trying a German colonel. He was an SS colonel, and there was a bunch of officers in there trying him. He had ordered the execution of a whole bunch of people in that village, and he got himself caught. I didn't understand the details of the trial, but he was being tried by a military court there. And they had French people there, there was quite a group.

I was waiting to move up, and in the meantime, they brought this guy out. There was an old stone house and it had apple trees in the yard, and this big old stone fence went around the house, supporting the apple orchard away from the road.

They walked this guy over, and put a rope around him, and tied him to the apple tree, put the rope around the center of him. And they put this firing squad together, it was the first time I ever saw a firing squad. They brought about six or seven guys off the road. They blindfolded him, and he stood there, and Jesus, they shot him. I don't know what the hell he did, but they said he ordered the execution of a whole bunch of people in the village.

From there, we moved towards the Maginot Line, and we got up to near the Moselle. Some of our outfit had gone into the Maginot Line and then we were told to pull back, and to hold up in this area, because we were out of gas. So this whole massive force stopped, and we all picked areas for ourselves.

We dispersed ourselves around that area, and while we were waiting for gas to come up, we didn't move for almost three weeks. We could have walked in through the Maginot Line, but they came back into it, and later it had to be taken.

While we were waiting there, things got kind of hot. It was all small stuff, nothing big happened. At least we had a chance to rest a little bit and lick our wounds, so to speak.

When we started out again, our particular unit had to go down with the 357th Infantry to take a town called Maizieres le Metz, which was by the Moselle River, and this is when the whole thing started up again.

We came down into that town. It was a railroad center, with four or five tracks going through it. The town straddled the railroad tracks, and there was a slag pile there.

We were there for over two weeks, and we had a lot of action going on. Every day it was something. That's where I was walking across a field with this infantry officer, and he looked at me and said, "I think I've been shot." So we both ran over this ridge, and we got on the other side of the ridge, his jacket had a hole in the right shoulder, a small hole, like a pencil hole. And I pushed his jacket up and there was a bullet that had gone in his back, right there, but that's the reaction, he didn't get knocked down, he just said, "I think I've been shot." There was a jeep on the road, I flagged it down and told the jeep to take him back, and I never saw him again. We never heard a thing. We were just walking across the field towards this slag pile when he looked at me, startled like, and said, "I think I've been shot." Sometimes a bullet will enter you, it comes in so fast I guess you don't realize it.

I got the Bronze Star at Maizieres. We were getting ready for an attack to take the town, and the infantry was there. The morning of the attack Colonel Barth, Major Henry and myself were standing by the side of my tank, and as we were going to move out, we didn't realize it but the Germans had moved in during the night. Now it was daylight, it was just about time to move out, all of a sudden this German soldier crossed the railroad track and threw a hand grenade at us. I got hit in the left leg, but I had a very small wound, it wasn't much. Colonel Barth got hurt bad, and Major Henry, a piece of shrapnel went through his legs, and he died a little later.

Then Colonel Mason took over from Colonel Barth. He was an infantry colonel. So I had to deal with him, and he was a very, very qualified guy, he was really a good line officer, he knew everything that was going on. I told him we could still do the attack, because we were lined up all night getting ready. So he said okay.

So then we started out with the tanks, and we headed out across the railroad tracks, and we made our turn to go up the main street.

The houses were all old cement houses, they go back probably a hundred years, and they're right next to each other. So we were going up the main street, there are no alleys, and they're usually two stories high. Tony D'Arpino was the driver at the time, and I think Ed Spahr was the assistant driver. I'm not sure who the gunner was.

As we drove down the street, the shell fire was real heavy. They were dropping everything at us, and the whole street was boiling with dust and explosions. The shell fire was blinding the driver, and he went up on the sidewalk and started grinding the side of a building.

So the next thing, I'm looking up ahead, and there was a fork in the road, and there's a hotel, and in the lobby of the hotel, it had windows, there was a gun firing at us. So I hollered to the gunner to put white phosphorous in, and he put the white phosphorous in, and then I took control. You can take control away from the gunner if you see something that you can't take the time to tell the gunner, so I took control away and I aimed it for that lobby and fired, and it blew up in the lobby. Later, after we took the town, I went in that lobby, and Jesus, the gun was there, and there had been a guy behind it and there was nothing left but his boots, that white phosphorous wiped him right off the face of the earth.

Immediately after I fired the gun, we were still on the sidewalk grinding up against the building, something made me look to my right. I'm up in the turret, and level with the second story of the building. I look, and here's a guy with a rifle pointed right at my face, and he fires. I looked at him, he looked at me, and he fired the gun but it missed me.

It was such a surprise. I just saw this guy shooting at me, and I just didn't have a chance to do anything, it happened that fast. He fired and he was gone into the room, disappeared immediately.

By this time, Tony's got the tank straightened out and he's pushing the tank out into the street. Then we continued up to the end of the street.

We got towards the end of the town, and we stopped up there and reconnoitered, and the infantry came behind us, and we took the whole town. Everything happened quickly. So we took that town, and held it, and in the meantime, we got orders to move further to the north, I forget where the next town was.

The Bronze Star was because Mason wanted to take the town with infantry, but I offered him tank support and he really appreciated it, so I led the attack into the town.

Tony D'Arpino

We were there for almost a month at Maizieres le Metz.
They had schoolhouses where one room were Americans, the next room were Germans, there were tunnels under them.

Our tank stayed in the same position for three weeks. We were guarding a couple of roads, and I can remember, they used to drop off the rations in the center of the town. They had five sets of railroad tracks, and the Germans had that place zeroed in, so the jeep could only come down so far with the supplies. They'd dump them there, and then we'd have to go get them and lug them back to the tank. And I've got a five-gallon can of water on my shoulder and Klapkowski's got chickens and stuff, frozen chickens, it was some holiday, and we had a few other rations. And I dropped that can of water so many times, I'd hear "ding," and I'd drop the goddamn can and hit the ground. Finally, when I got back down to the house where our tank was at the corner, there was no roof on the house, it was blown off -- down in the cellar was a bin full of potatoes. So I told Lieutenant Lombardi, "This is it. You guys want to eat, you go up there and get the goddamn rations. I'm not going up there no more." I said, "I'll eat the potatoes down in the bin."

But that place was really something. They had it zeroed in. I can see the slag piles all across the way there. And down at the end of the street was a pasture, and the cows were dead.

As a matter of fact, I was driving the first tank, when we first got into position down there, I was just easing into position, and I shouted, "There's a gun pointing at us down there! There's a gun pointing at us." I didn't know at the time it was the leg of a cow. So we put one round into this dead cow.

While we were in Maizieres, we were sent some chicken, and Klapkowski wanted to fry it.

All the stuff was in the house where we were staying. As a matter of fact, they had a lot of dishes, beautiful dishes.

So Klapkowski is looking for flour, he wants to roll this chicken and fry it. And he starts a fire in the stove. I said, "There's smoke going up the chimney. For Chrissakes, they can see us."

"Awww," he says, "they know we're here anyway. We've been here so long, they know we're here."

He goes down in the cellar -- there was some stuff stored there -- and he gets this bag, it had some German writing on it. He says, "Is this flour?"

I felt it, and said, "No. That feels like plaster of paris."

He said, "No, that's flour."

So he rolls the chicken in this stuff. And he's saved the bacon fat from the 10-in-1 rations, whenever he fried anything, like potatoes and stuff, he'd use this.

He fried the chicken, and it came out the prettiest golden brown you'd ever want to see. But you couldn't eat it. It was tough. So he just banged it against the wall and knocked the plaster off. The plaster came off in one piece, and the chicken underneath was cooked.

Then he set the table. He got the tablecloth, and set it with five dishes. Afterward, he said, "Okay fellas, time to do the dishes." And he opened the window, tablecloth, dishes and everything else, out the window. I don't know how many plates we broke in that house.

CHAPTER 10

Dillingen

Dec. 1-17, 1944

"The next I heard about your father," Jule Braatz said, "was that he had come back to the battalion sometime in December."

I was speaking with Braatz at the 1987 reunion, before I began collecting stories for this book. I have not seen him since.

"We were across the Saar River," Braatz said. "We were across without a bridge and we were floating stuff over. We were being supplied by, you might almost say porter service. In other words, the colonel of our battalion had gathered up headquarters and service company people, and they would come down to the river, and they'd go across, and they would carry ammunition and rations and gasoline into town.

"So your father must have come back to the battalion, and Colonel Randolph, who was just crazy -- and I don't mean that he was crazy in that sense, he was the bravest man I ever saw. He had no fear whatsoever. But a good commander, a great commander. He was very sincere. He thought of his men. But I don't think he had any fear. He didn't have to be where he was, but he was always around looking into the welfare of the different companies.

"He told your father to take charge of this ammunition detail, or supply detail. I don't know if he had been back to the battalion one day or two days. All I know is what I heard then, that he had led a supply unit over, and he got hit with a machine gun. They opened on him from the pillboxes. I don't think that he was with the battalion much more than two days' total time.

"Randolph always felt that we get the stuff up to the boys in the front, so I don't think he'd have let your father sit around the battalion headquarters doing nothing for very long."

That was the last I was to learn about my father's experiences until the 1993 reunion in Orlando, Fla. Caesar Tucci, the battalion association president, had been a sergeant in D Company, and mentioned that he had a copy of his company log.

The next day, during a quiet moment, I began skimming through the D Company log. I turned to the section on Dillingen, and there, under the entry for December 10 (which happens to be my birthday), I encountered the following:

"10 December 1944 -- The 357th Inf. Regt. had crossed the Saar River and had penetrated into the enemy lines. Their position was rather precarious due to enemy forces and pillboxes to their direct front and on both flanks. All their available manpower was needed to hold the ground they had.

"Supplies were needed very badly, so 40 men were called from the Battalion to act as the carrying party. Ten men and one officer were chosen from the Company and included 1st Lt. Hiatt, 1st Sgt. Thompson, Sgt. Kwiatkowski, Tec. 5 Roderick, Pfc's Sparks, Vincent, and Pvt's Kittelson, W. Doyle, Murray, and McLesky.

"The carrying party left the Company area at 1830, proceeded to the "C" Company area near Buren, picked up the men from that Company, and parked at a chateau about 1/2 mile west of there. A guide was picked up and the party was marched to the river and to the row boats stowed with the food, ammunition, and medical supplies needed by the Regt.

"Great care had to be exercised in making the crossing because of the nearness of the enemy, and very swift current. The boats were rowed by our men because there was also a shortage of engineers. The supplies were unloaded on the beach, and the 40 men started carrying them to a large chateau located about 1 1/2 miles west. The terrain between the two points was low and marshy, and was covered on the right flank by two German machine gun nests located in the outskirts of the town of Pachten.

"Guided by the fire from the partially burning chateau and by following the railroad tracks for part of the way, the party reached the chateau and dumped the first load after being subjected to heavy searching mortar fire. The time was now about 2400.

"The return trip was made without event except that the point was missed by about 1/2 mile to the left. A wet and heavy snow began to fall that made traveling conditions even worse. A group, consisting of Kwiatkowski, Sparks, Mallak, Kittelson, Roderick, Doyle, Murray, Vincent, and twelve others, formed a party to carry bundles of litters, two men for each bundle of litters. About eight minutes after the party left, Vincent reported back to the 1st Sgt. after his partner was unable to continue from exhaustion. The balance of the men from the group reached the chateau with the litters.

"An enemy pillbox had been captured several days before and was being used as a forward medical station. The position had become too hard to hold with the available forces and that section was forced to retreat. There were 25 litter patients in the pillbox that would have to be left behind to be captured by the Germans unless evacuated by forces other than the holding forces. The litter carrying group at the chateau was asked to, and agreed to, try to evacuate these patients.

"Each man took a litter, and, placed under the command of Lt. Elson [this was my father], they started toward the pillbox around 0300, taking cover advantage of trenches wherever possible. Heavy artillery, mortar, and small arms fire was encountered all along the way.

"While crossing a road, Lt. Elson was hit three times by small arms fire believed to come from our own troops[1]. The group was ordered to drop the litters and return to the chateau to check on our own firing and to wait until the enemy fire moderated. Again the group started for the pillbox, recovered the abandoned litters, and proceeded slowly onwards. Progress was very slow, due to the extreme darkness, thick woods, mud, rough terrain, and still heavy enemy mortar and artillery fire.

"The pillbox was reached about 0700. The litters were loaded and the trip back started with the litter patients, about 40 wounded that were able to walk, the small group of medics, and the holding force that amounted to about 15 soldiers.

"It was soon discovered that the group was heading in a slightly wrong direction and Pfc. Sparks volunteered to carry the Red Cross flag and try to lead the group back to the proper place. He hid his weapon in the folds of a blanket and set off on a new course, waving the flag as he went. Fortunately the Germans respected the flag and ceased small arms fire, but the men were still subjected to air and tree burst from artillery. A German machine gun nest was passed that had just been knocked out by the infantry. This nest was passed on the way up to the pillbox and must have been in operation at that time. The chateau, or forward C.P. of the 357th Infantry, was reached with the 25 litter patients. The time was about 1030. This group was released, but had to remain at this C.P. until the river could be crossed under the cover of night."

Caesar Tucci

Caesar Tucci, from Buffalo, N.Y., was a sergeant in D Company.

Around the first of December, they requested volunteers to man gun positions on the Saar River to kind of make a fake for the Germans, to make them feel that we were coming across in strength. So there was a lot of firing to be built up, and I volunteered. They said this would be a mission of two or three days. So I went down and manned a .50-caliber machine gun at that position.

We had .50-caliber machine guns and mortars that we set up inside the houses and various areas on the west side of the Saar River to fire across at the pillboxes of the Siegfried Line.

I traveled light, because they said it would be two or three days. I didn't even take shaving equipment.

To get down to the firing position, we had to reach the top of a hill, and then the halftrack had to make a mad dash because it was exposed to direct fire from the Germans

[1]This would be what he had described as a German machine gun. I found myself wondering if he knew of this possibility.

on the other side of the river. It was like going through a gantlet. They were firing at us, but we beat it, we got into the town, and then we were out of their view.

We set up our headquarters in a brick apartment building. My partner and I sandbagged the machine gun in a German home on a porcelain kitchen table and had it fixed to shoot out the back window of the kitchen across the river.

The fire missions would be announced to us on the radio. When we were told to start a fire mission, we would run across the street, put the back plate on the machine gun -- we'd never leave the back plate there because German patrols would come through the town at night -- and when they gave us the word to fire, everybody, mortars, 50-calibers, everything, they'd fire across that river, to give a real show of force. That would go on for four or five minutes, and the gun would get real hot, so that when the fire mission stopped, I had to reach out with an asbestos glove, take the barrel off, ram an oil patch through it right away, and then take the back plate off the machine gun and beat it across the street back into the building.

That two- or three-day fire mission lasted two weeks. We were relieved from that position on my birthday, the 16th of December.

Jim Gifford

When we got up to the Saar River, we took this little village, it wasn't even a town. I went into a house there. I went downstairs in the cellar, and there was a pile of coal there. I saw something sticking out of the coal and I kicked it, and these people had put a lot of their private things there -- an accordion, and their silverware and stuff which meant nothing to us but the accordion did, because we had a guy, Snuffy Fuller, who was a lieutenant in my outfit who could play the accordion, so I pulled it out, and I told one of the guys, "Take it over and give it to Snuffy." So Snuffy kept that accordion, he used to play it a lot.

Then I decided, well, this is a good chance to take a bath. So I started to heat some water up, and I filled the bathtub. The tub had a window alongside it, and you could look out through the garden, you could look down the slope all the way to the Saar River.

Now I'm just settled in to take my bath and soak, when all of a sudden I see a shell burst down by the riverbank. When a shell goes off, you always watch to see where the next one's coming. You walk these shells. We got so used to being hit with shells that we knew what they were gonna do. So I watch to see where the next one's gonna hit. The next one hit closer to the house. Oh shit, they're coming this way. The next one came down right below that field. So I grabbed my nose and slid down into the water. The next thing, "Boom!" Right in the garden. Knocked the goddamn window frame and the glass and everything out.

When the smoke cleared, I came up out of the water. The goddamn window was gone, and the glass and the frame and everything was in the water with me.

The next shell -- I'm still waiting to see where the next one's going -- went over the house and landed across the road. Then I got up out of the tub and that was it. That was my bath. I made sure I didn't cut myself, and I dried myself off and got the hell dressed.

Bob "Big Andy" Anderson

Sergeant Robert Anderson, from Prophetstown, Ill., was a tank driver in A Company.

I got my first Bronze Star in Dillingen. I was the first tank across. The engineers had laid down our bridge, and we were sitting on the bank waiting to go across, and they came back and they said "Now, when you go across, go slow." Well, you can imagine how it is with a 33-ton tank going across water. I was probably three-quarters of the way across, when two German planes came in and started strafing across the river. And if you've ever seen a tank go at full speed, you ought to have seen me go across the river.

We got all five tanks of our platoon [Third Platoon, A Company] across, but two of them got mired down out in the mud. We had cables that were 15 or 20 feet long. I hooked three of them together and dragged them back there in the mire, and then I went and got back in my tank, and I pulled the two tanks out. That's what I got the Bronze Star for.

Forrest Dixon

We were listening to the BBC on the night of the 16th, and we heard that the Germans had broken through with ten thousand men at Aachen or someplace. So Colonel Randolph called General Stillwell and said, "Is it true that just north of us they broke through with ten thousand men?" And Stillwell gets on the telephone and says, "It's true all right, but it isn't ten thousand men. It's ten divisions."

Then Colonel Randolph says, "What do we do?"

"Sit." That was the night of the 16th. And I don't think we got back across till the 20th or the 21st.

At first, the engineers had put a bridge across, and it was covered by a smokescreen. And I'll never forget, we put a tank destroyer platoon across the bridge. And the next group to go across was the first platoon of A Company, and Sergeant Bussell, who was my driver back when I was in D Company, yelled at me. I recognized him. I said, "Be careful." He was a good driver, but careless. So I said "Be careful."

One tank would be leaving the bridge, one tank in the middle, and one tank going on. And just about then, the wind changed direction, and the smokescreen cleared, and the bridge was wide open.

I heard about three shots from the Germans, and all of a sudden, my god, right behind Bussell's tank, the bridge was cut. I picked up the mike, and I said, "Bussell, give her hell or you'll drown." And his tank started to sink. Then he gave her the gas, and he went across the rest of the river at a 45-degree angle. But he got across.

After we lost the bridge, they set up a ferry.

Jim Gifford

The Bulge started on the 17th of December, when we were in Dillingen. We had just gotten across the Saar River, we had pontoon bridges, we got into Dillingen to start a beachhead there, and then, all of a sudden, they were telling us to pull back. We didn't know why. They were saying, "Pull out of Dillingen, get back across the river." And we were all pissed off. We had taken all this risk getting in there, and what the hell are you telling us to come back for? It's ours, this town is ours. We didn't know that there was this big Bulge rolling. So we started pulling all of our vehicles back.

What we also didn't know was that there was a whole German army out there in front of us. And they were ignoring us. They were going by us, but they had enough of their men that were also containing us and watching us, and they were going to wipe us right out. And we were so pissed, because it was quiet in Dillingen. We were getting small shell fire, but we took the town, and we were saying "Hey, let's go," but if we went much further, we would have run right into that juggernaut.

Ed Spahr

We kept one tank as an outpost. It was almost three-quarters of a mile outside of town, set up overlooking the Siegfried Line. We would take turns manning the tank in case the Germans would come back through there. We'd go back into town to eat, but always, night and day, there was a whole crew in the tank.

To get to the tank, we had to cross a zigzag trench that the Germans had built. Well, one day I was going up -- we'd rotate people one at a time; we didn't rotate the whole crew, so there would be one fresh man there all of the time -- I was going up through this open field, and I thought I heard something going past, close to me, it just sounded like somebody snapped their fingers. I couldn't figure out just what this was because you could see all around and I couldn't see anything.

The second or third time I heard this, it seemed like it was getting closer, something just snapping going past my head, and all at once I realized that somebody was shooting at me, because after I'd hear this snap, a second or two later I could hear a rifle crack. It wasn't loud. It was way off. I'd say he was a thousand or more yards away, but he was shooting at me.

When I realized this, I made a leap, rolled through the grass, I came to this trench, and I dropped down in it. I didn't know which way I fell, or landed, and I didn't know which direction to go in.

The trench leaned a little bit towards the tank on one end and away from it on the other. So I thought, "Well, I'll go down through these zigzags here a little ways one way, and then I'll look out, and if I can't see the tank I'll go in the other direction." I should have been within sight of the tank. I was maybe 300 yards away from it.

As I came around one of the zigs in the trench, I just happened to glance ahead of me and I saw a German soldier, sitting down, and he had a ... we called them burp guns ... he had a machine pistol laying across him. The first thing that came to my mind was, he had that gun aiming at me. I didn't take time to check it out, whether the gun was really pointed at me or not. I had a Thompson submachine gun with the stock cut off, slung on my shoulder, and I had about a 15-round clip in it. We had 15- and 30-round clips, and I think I was carrying a 15-round clip because being in a tank it wasn't so bulky, and I just swung around and I pulled the trigger on it, and I could see the dust flying out of his uniform, and I just emptied that clip.

I stood still a little bit and didn't move. I thought he should fall over. He never moved. I put another clip in, and I eased up to him. I kicked his foot. He never moved. Nothing moved. I discovered that he had probably been dead for two or three days or longer, he was stiff as a board. I have to laugh at myself ... I've only told one or two guys about this, me shooting the hell out of a dead soldier.

Lieutenant Jim Flowers and his wife, Jeanette, at the 1993 reunion of the 90th Infantry Division in Louisville, Ky. Below, Jim and Elizabeth Rothschadl at their home in Waubun, Minn.

Robert Levine of River Edge, N.J., a veteran of the 90th Infantry Division, was behind Jim Flowers' tanks when they were ambushed on Hill 122. Here Levine, who was captured and lost a leg as a result of his wounds, retraces the route taken by Flowers' tanks on July 10, 1944.

The monument on Hill 122 dedicated to First Platoon, Company C of the 712th. James A. Bailey, Kenneth R. Cohron, Paul B. Farrell (spelled Farrel on the monument), Harold Gentle, Gerald Kiballa, Laverne Patton, Eugene Tannler, Abraham I. Taylor, and Stephen J. Wojtilla were killed, and four tanks incinerated in the attack. Lieutenant Jim Flowers, who survived but lost both legs, was awarded the Distinguished Service Cross, and the platoon received a Presidential Unit Citation.

Forrest Dixon in the Michigan State University ROTC at Fort Custer, Mich., in 1937. At left, Dixon in 1993. Below, Dixon and Fred Lemm beside the Mark IV tank Dixon knocked out at Mairy.

PHOTO BY JACK ROLAND

The "dragon's teeth," anti-tank obstacles that were a key element of the Siegfried Line. The 712th and the 90th Infantry Division were probing the line at Dillingen when they were pulled back across the Saar River and sent north to join in the Battle of the Bulge. Later the battalion played a key role in breaking through the Siegfried Line.

From left, former crewmates Ed Spahr, Jim Gifford, Tony D'Arpino, and Bob Rossi at the 1992 reunion in Harrisburg, Pa. Gifford was wounded when their tank was hit.

Gifford at Kirschnaumen in 1944.

Gifford's tank on Jan. 7, 1945, three days before it was hit. Silhouetted are Stanley Klapkowski, upper left; Rossi, upper right; and Spahr, standing.

Clockwise from top left: Ed "Smoky Stuever" and his sister-in-law, Catherine; Joe Fetsch, who drove a gasoline truck for the battalion; Forrest Dixon and Helen Johnson; Lester and Ruth O'Riley; Clegg "Doc" Caffery; Clifford and Jan Merrill; and George Bussell.

Upper left: Bob Rossi, right, and his brother, Johnny, who was in the 4th Armored Division. The two were reunited when the 4th and the 712th crossed paths during the drive through Germany. The markings indicate the tank was one of the more heavily armored 43-ton models that the battalion got a limited number of late in the war. Above, Jim Gifford inspecting the tank in which Lieutenant Henry Duval was badly wounded on July 7, 1944, at La Haye du Puits, in Normandy. Shells penetrated the tank below where Gifford's right foot is, and about an inch to the right of where his left foot is. At right, a smoke pot used for providing cover.

Bob "Big Andy" Anderson at his home in Prophetstown, Ill. Below, Big Andy butchering a cow that had to be destroyed because it had a broken leg. Almost 50 years later, Anderson says: "That cow's leg was no more broken than yours or mine!" With him are Private John C. Owen of Montgomery, Ala.; Corporal Daniel T. McCaffery of Pittsburgh, and Private Ted Duskin of Charleston, W. Va.

Clockwise from upper left: Pfc. Billy P. Wolfe of Edinburg, Va., who was killed at Pfaffenheck, Germany, on March 16, 1945; Lieutenant Francis "Snuffy" Fuller, who was Wolfe's platoon leader; the monument that includes Wolfe's name among the county's war dead; Billy's sisters, Maxine Wolfe Zirkle, left, and Madeline Wolfe Litten.

A tank trap in Germany. Right, the day President Roosevelt died. Below, my father, Maurice Elson.

The remains of a German tank near Mairy, France, on Sept. 8, 1944. Where the arrows intersect was a slit trench, from which two 90th Division infantrymen fired a bazooka, hitting the tank. The tank fired back, severely wounding both men, before it burst into flames and then exploded. Below, General John Devine's "peep," which was hit at Mairy. Devine's driver was killed.

Clockwise from upper left: Otha Martin; Russell Loop (next to photo of himself in uniform); Jim Gifford and Ruby Goldstein; Les Suter; Tony and Mary D'Arpino with their daughter, Ann; Jim Cary making a presentation to Carl and Tim Kaye, whose father, Colonel Vladimir Kedrosky, recently passed away; Wanda O'Kelly and her mother, Lillian Howell, whose husband, Richard, was killed when Wanda was 2 years old; Grayson and Arlene La Mar; and Wayne and Barbara Hissong.

From left, Leroy Campbell, John Zimmer, Lloyd Seal, and Clarence Rosen. At right, John and Sylvia Zimmer at the 1992 reunion. Below, a souvenir that Zimmer has had signed by many of the battalion members.

The Merkers Salt Mine (inset: Jack Sheppard with souvenir). Below, Frances Griffin at the Plainsman Museum in Aurora, Neb., with some of Ray Griffin's memorabilia.

The former dry goods store in Argos, Ind., where Wayne Hissong, right, visited the mother of a friend who was killed. Below, the German P-38 Hissong threw away before he was captured; it was later recovered and returned to him.

The photos on this and the next three pages were "liberated" by Jim Gifford from a headquarters that was captured "as the Germans were going out the back." Above, a horse-drawn column. Below, unfortunate but all-too-frequent victims of war.

Above, a German tank firing (note the puff of smoke at the left of the picture). Below, Fieldmarschall Erwin Rommel in a photo probably taken in North Africa.

A German military ceremony. Below, a scene at headquarters in Berlin.

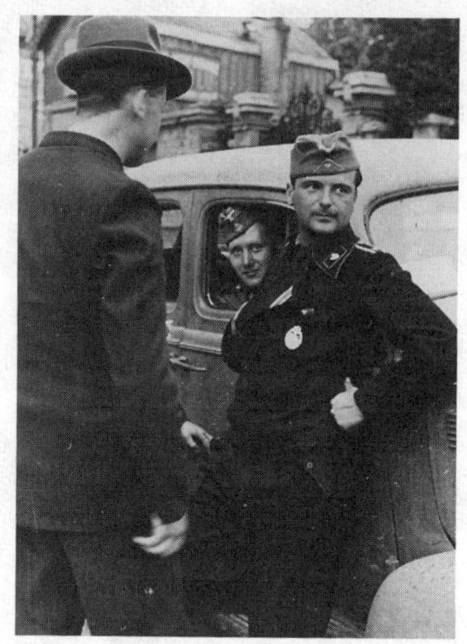

Clockwise from upper left: young German soldiers; an SS Panzer officer; a towed 88-millimeter gun; the dragon's teeth of the Siegfried Line; a typical road block erected to slow the Allies; members of the German People's Army.

An unidentified member of Service Company standing in a crater made by a shell from a railroad gun at Hof, Germany. None of the 32 men sleeping in the building immediately behind the crater were injured. Below, a platoon of tanks in formation.

Clockwise from top left: bombed German vehicles, possibly at the Falaise Gap; the road to the Bulge; a German tank at Mairy; a 357th Infantry Regiment maintenance truck destroyed by a mine near Mairy; the wreckage at Heimboldhausen, Germany, after a bomb landed in a carload of black powder, destroying A Company's headquarters on April 3, 1945.

PHOTO BY JACK ROLAND

This photo was taken at Habscheid, Germany, on Feb. 8, 1945.

From left, Lieutenant Colonel George B. Randolph, Captain Vladimir B. Kedrosky, Captain Jack Sheppard, and Lieutenant Ray Griffin at Kirschnaumen, France, in 1944. Colonel Randolph was killed on Jan. 9, 1945, at Nothum, Belgium.

Lieutenant Ed Forrest of Stockbridge, Mass. Forrest, one of the most proficient officers in A Company, was killed at Heimboldhausen, Germany, on April 3, 1945.

From left, Lieutenant Sam MacFarland, Captain Kedrosky, and Lieutenants Dale Albee and Hank Schneider in Trois Vierges, Luxembourg. Schneider was killed later that day.

The entrance to the crematorium at the Flossenburg concentration camp. At right, Jim Gifford beside one of the ovens. The battalion helped free 1,100 inmates, and later caught up with others being marched away.

At left, Gifford in an aircraft factory manned by slave labor from Flossenburg. Above, Hitler's house in Regensburg. The house was razed so it couldn't become a monument.

An M4A3 tank at the Patton Museum. Below, the monument to the 712th. Opposite page: Inscriptions containing the names of 97 battalion members killed in action. It was recently discovered that one member, Lieutenant Chancy Miller, was omitted.

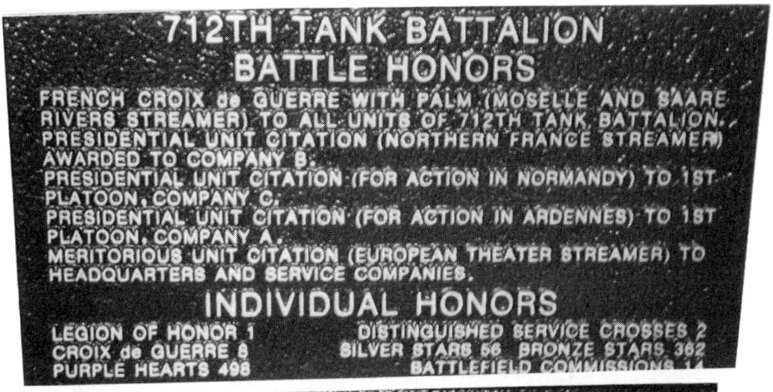

712TH TANK BATTALION
BATTLE HONORS

FRENCH CROIX de GUERRE WITH PALM (MOSELLE AND SAARE RIVERS STREAMER) TO ALL UNITS OF 712TH TANK BATTALION.
PRESIDENTIAL UNIT CITATION (NORTHERN FRANCE STREAMER) AWARDED TO COMPANY B.
PRESIDENTIAL UNIT CITATION (FOR ACTION IN NORMANDY) TO 1ST PLATOON, COMPANY C.
PRESIDENTIAL UNIT CITATION (FOR ACTION IN ARDENNES) TO 1ST PLATOON, COMPANY A.
MERITORIOUS UNIT CITATION (EUROPEAN THEATER STREAMER) TO HEADQUARTERS AND SERVICE COMPANIES.

INDIVIDUAL HONORS

LEGION OF HONOR 1
CROIX de GUERRE 8
PURPLE HEARTS 498
DISTINGUISHED SERVICE CROSSES 2
SILVER STARS 56 BRONZE STARS 362
BATTLEFIELD COMMISSIONS 14

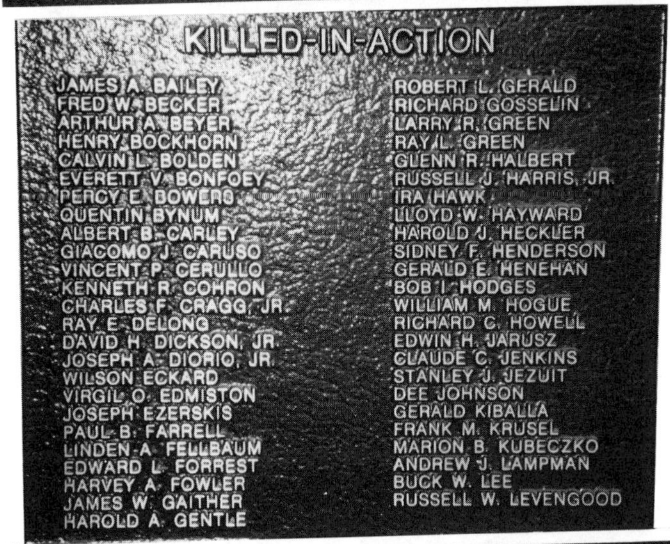

KILLED-IN-ACTION

JAMES A. BAILEY
FRED W. BECKER
ARTHUR A. BEYER
HENRY BOCKHORN
CALVIN L. BOLDEN
EVERETT V. BONFOEY
PERCY E. BOWERS
QUENTIN BYNUM
ALBERT B. CARLEY
GIACOMO J. CARUSO
VINCENT P. CERULLO
KENNETH R. COHRON
CHARLES F. CRAGG, JR.
RAY E. DELONG
DAVID H. DICKSON, JR.
JOSEPH A. DIORIO, JR.
WILSON ECKARD
VIRGIL O. EDMISTON
JOSEPH EZERSKIS
PAUL B. FARRELL
LINDEN A. FELLBAUM
EDWARD L. FORREST
HARVEY A. FOWLER
JAMES W. GAITHER
HAROLD A. GENTLE
ROBERT L. GERALD
RICHARD GOSSELIN
LARRY R. GREEN
RAY L. GREEN
GLENN R. HALBERT
RUSSELL J. HARRIS, JR.
IRA HAWK
LLOYD W. HAYWARD
HAROLD J. HECKLER
SIDNEY F. HENDERSON
GERALD E. HENEHAN
BOB I. HODGES
WILLIAM M. HOGUE
RICHARD C. HOWELL
EDWIN H. JARUSZ
CLAUDE C. JENKINS
STANLEY J. JEZUIT
DEE JOHNSON
GERALD KIBALLA
FRANK M. KRUSEL
MARION B. KUBECZKO
ANDREW J. LAMPMAN
BUCK W. LEE
RUSSELL W. LEVENGOOD

KILLED-IN-ACTION

WALLACE LIPPINCOTT, JR.
WESLEY E. LOCHARD
FRED LOCKHART
ARNOLD L. LUND
DALE F. McGEE
ALFRED M. McLAUGHLIN
EVERETT F. McNULTY
JACK MANTELL
TULLIO MICALONI
NICHOLAS MILCZAKOWSKI
LEE N. MILLER
DUANE A. MINER
JOHN C. MITCHELL
JAMES N. MOLONY
PHILIP L. MONROE
STANLEY J. MUHICH
RICHARD A. NEWCOMB
LAVERNE PATTON
WILLIAM PERNA
EDMUND PILZ
FRED R. PUTNAM
GEORGE B. RANDOLPH
THOMAS J. REILLY, JR.
CHARLES RICHARDSON
ARTHUR ROSELLE
GEORGE A. SAVIO
WILLIAM J. SCHMIDT
HENRY SCHNEIDER
PHILIP L. SCHROMM
FRANK L. SHAGONABE
PAUL SHANNON
ROY SHARPTON
RONALD W. SLICK
REX SMALLWOOD
DOYE E. SMITH
JOHN L. SMITH
EUGENE TANNLER
GEORGE C. TARR
ABRAHAM I. TAYLOR
GERALD E. THOMAS
ERVIN ULRICH
PAUL J. VETRONE
MARSHALL T. WARFIELD, JR.
ZIGMUND J. WESOLOWSKI
JOHN R. WILLIAMS
WARREN B. WILLINGER
BERNARD A. WINGERTER
STEPHEN J. WOJTILLA
BILLY P. WOLFE

CHAPTER 11

Kirschnaumen

Dec. 25, 1944

Howard Olsen

Howard Olsen, from South Bend, Ind., was a sergeant, and later a lieutenant, in A Company.

One of our lieutenants got a combat pass, and he went back to Paris, and a pilot came up and asked him, "Are you from the 712th?"

And he said, "Yeah."

The pilot said, "Well, we got word to watch out for you guys because you're out in front too far."

When we were on the way to the Bulge, we stopped in this one town, and I went to the command post for something, and all of a sudden I heard machine gun fire. And they said an American plane was strafing one of our jeeps. They said there was a German in the plane. I could hear it strafing, but I couldn't see it. There was a wall between me and the road.

Jim Gifford

We were in Kirschnaumen on Christmas day. It was a small village alongside the road. The houses were close together. The road split, and there was a church in the middle of the road. So we all went to Mass that morning.

The church was full. The townspeople were there, and we were all in there. About 10 o'clock, we came out of the church and went back toward the houses where our tanks were tied up. And the next thing an American fighter plane comes down about 100 feet off the damn roadway shooting the hell out of everything, and he knocked that church apart. And everybody had just left. Then, Jesus, he came back down again, doing the same thing, and he came down again doing the same thing.

There was a ridge on the right, there was a long field, and there were woods at the top of it, so we backed some tanks up there along the woods, about three or four of them, and we waited for that sonofabitch. We knew it was an American plane, but we had been alerted to look out for Germans using American equipment.

About 2 o'clock in the afternoon he came down again, about 100 feet off the ground, and we could look right into the plane. I was on the .50 shooting at it, and I could see the bullets go straight into the fuselage, right along the side of the plane. They didn't hit the pilot.

There was a low ceiling at the time. The plane smoked and started to turn over and headed right up out of sight into the clouds, and the next thing we saw was a parachute coming down out of the clouds.

The guys jumped in the jeep and went to pick up the pilot, and I'll be damned, it was an American major who thought that we were Germans because he couldn't see the Saar River up ahead. He had crossed another river and thought that he had crossed the Saar, so he was shooting the hell out of us. He was lucky he wasn't hurt.

Friendly fire killed a lot of guys. Today they call it friendly fire. Back then I guess we called it accidents.

CHAPTER 12

"He Liked His Tea"

Bob Rossi

One of the real characters of the third platoon was Sergeant Jim Warren. He was a career Army man.

Just prior to the Bulge, we were staying in this house in Kirschnaumen. There was a GI blanket covering a hole in the wall where a shell had hit, and it was pretty cold.

We were standing around kibbitzing one evening. There was a kerosene lantern hanging down from the ceiling on a cord. And Jim Warren, he always had half a load on, he's shadowboxing the lantern. We're laughing. He's playing around, he's boxing the lantern. He throws a haymaker at the lantern, misses, and hits me. I go flying across the room. I come up with the biggest lip you ever saw. This was late at night. The next morning, as we're getting up, I could hear him saying to somebody, "I never touched the kid." And I went over and showed him the lip. He believed it then.

Tony D'Arpino

When we were on the Siegfried Line and we were waiting for gas, we had our tanks scattered, and the civilians used to come and ask for food. One day there was this blondish woman, and I look, and I see Sergeant Warren go into the tank first in the driver's hatch, then she went in there. All you could see was her head.

So I went around, I got all the guys in the tanks, and we made a circle around this tank. When the blond climbed out, she was smiling from ear to ear, and when Sergeant Warren came out, he looked around, and he said, "You sonofabitch, Tony!"

I told that story several times, and nobody remembered it. Then the first time I saw Buck Hardee at a reunion, he said to me, "Do you remember the time down at the Siegfried Line with Sergeant Warren?"

"Yeah," I said. "I've been telling that story and nobody believes me."

Bob Rossi

Sergeant Warren told us he was in the Marines first. He was getting discharged, and his records were being sent to San Diego. But in the meantime, he had knocked up a Hawaiian girl, and the sheriff of the island was gonna come to grab him. Now Warren technically was a civilian, and the only way he could beat the rap was if he joined the Army. So he stayed in the islands with a searchlight outfit.

Tony D'Arpino

Sergeant Warren was part-Indian. He'd been in the Army for years, as first sergeant, busted, he was a buck sergeant when he came to us as a replacement. He told me he was on his third or fourth wife, she was about 18 years old.

He had scars on his face, and he could remember when MacArthur was a major. At that time he was in the field artillery. He had charge of some field guns, and he said MacArthur was going to pull an inspection. He said they scrounged some paint, and they painted the guns all up, they had all old equipment, and they had it looking beautiful.

He said when they pulled the inspection, MacArthur told Sergeant Warren and his crew to take off their shoes and socks. He wanted to see if they had cut their toenails square.

Bob Rossi

Sergeant Warren said they spent weeks polishing up the equipment, painting this and painting that. Now here comes MacArthur, and he says, "Ten-hut." Warren said he gave him the biggest highball [salute] you could ever give an officer. MacArthur says, "Sergeant, how do you cut your toenails?"

Warren says he was mystified.

MacArthur says, "Show me how you cut your toenails." He made him sit down on the parade ground, take his shoes and socks off, and as he's sitting there, he made the whole battery crowd around Warren, and says, "Now this man is going to suffer from ingrown toenails, because he doesn't cut his toenails properly." And Warren's sitting on the ground, everybody's razzing him, he took some razzing for weeks. He hated MacArthur for making a fool out of him.

Tony D'Arpino

Sergeant Warren took over the No. 2 tank, and when Lieutenant Lombardi said "Cover me," Jesus, his gun was practically touching the back of our turret, that's how close he was. He was really there.

Sergeant Warren had one problem. He liked his tea. Lombardi used to get his liquor rations -- all the officers had liquor rations -- and anything he didn't like, he would give to Warren.

One time we were waiting for our flanks to catch up, and Warren was drunk. He'd drunk the last of Lombardi's beer and whatever else was around.

So all of a sudden, there's a counterattack, and we've got to move out. And Sergeant Warren said to Lombardi, "I've got to have a drink."

Lombardi said, "I ain't got nothing."

Warren said, "I've got to have a drink."

Lombardi said, "Mount the tank and let's go. We've got to move out."

Oh boy, then I hear clunk-clunk. Now Lombardi never buttoned up, never. He might duck down inside the turret, but he never closed the hatch. Then I hear on the radio, "That sonofabitch is shootin' at me."

And we all said, "Who? Who?"

It was Sergeant Warren. He had his .45 out, of course you couldn't hurt the tank and all, he had his .45 out and he was hitting the turret because Lombardi wouldn't give him any booze.

Warren had a smile from ear to ear. But he was a good man in combat.

I remember one time I was driving Warren's tank, and the same thing, there was a little counterattack, and I can still see it: There was a little lake or a pond, and there was a little road alongside of it. We were supposed to guard that road, and Warren was standing in front of the tank, guiding me into position.

Now he's behind this little scrub brush tree, and he's telling me, "Go on." I don't want to go, though, because I'm gonna hit that tree and knock it over on him.

So I'm motioning to him, I'm pointing at the tree.

"You guinea son of a bitch," he says. So I says, all right, and I gunned the engine. I got right to the tree, I pulled back the levers, I snapped that sonofabitch off, and it comes down and knocks him out cold.

He never said a word to me about that afterward.

But all his tank crew liked him. He took care of his tank crew, and he made sure that they didn't do anything crazy.

Bob Rossi

In the spring of 1945, we were traveling down this road and we came upon this horse-drawn artillery blocking the road. One horse was dead and the other was just standing there.

Warren got out of his tank and borrowed a 7.65 millimeter gun from someone and started to shoot the horse in the head. The first shot made the horse stagger a little, then he just kept on firing until the horse fell. All he had to do was cut the harnesses and let the living horse go. The gun he used was too small a caliber. With so much death and destruction around us, it was such a senseless killing. He had half a load on as usual, and I'm sure if he weren't drunk he might not have killed the horse. He then had his driver push the two horses and the artillery piece to the side of the road.

A few years ago I got one of the newsletters, and it said that Milford Anderson and Warren had died about the same time. I just filled up. These are the guys I was in combat with, they're both dead. I wrote to Anderson's wife, and I think I sent her a picture. And I wrote to Warren's wife, and I told her what a great guy he was. In combat, he was the type of man that you wanted behind you, because he was right there. He drank a lot, but he was a good soldier.

I wrote to his wife and I told her about the incident where he gave me a shot in the mouth.

CHAPTER 13

The Battle of the Bulge

January 1945

In one of the magazines of the era, either the Saturday Evening Post or Collier's, Forrest Dixon said, there was an article that showed a picture of a tank, and it said, "Here lies a colonel beside his tank, dead."

"I had that magazine for the longest time," Dixon said, "and then I don't know what happened to it. That was our colonel, Colonel Randolph. The issue was probably around the 10th or 15th of January, 1945."

It probably would have been later. The photograph was taken on Jan. 9, 1945, moments after Colonel Randolph was killed by an artillery shell in Nothum, Belgium.

The code word for "killed" was "kitten." Captain Jim Cary, who had recovered from his wounds in Normandy and was now the commander of B Company, radioed back to Captain Vladimir Kedrosky: "George kitten. Do you understand me? George kitten."

Kedrosky, who was about to take over as commanding officer, said he understood.

"This was the beginning of relieving the boys in Bastogne," Dixon said. "The 4th Armored went by road with their tanks, and we and the 90th Infantry Division, and some tank destroyers, headed for Bastogne across country. The 4th Armored got there first."

After being pulled back across the Saar, the 712th had been kept in reserve for several days, and then was sent north, covering between 60 and 75 miles in one night, on icy, mountainous roads.

During the night march, many tanks were slipping and sliding off the road. One tank came within a few feet of slamming into Jack Sheppard's jeep. Jim Gifford had one of the newer 43-ton tanks with a 76-millimeter gun, and when it started going down one steep hill it wouldn't stop. Gifford told D'Arpino to head for the telephone poles along the side of the road, and the tank began snapping the poles as if they were matchsticks until the tank was so tangled in cables that it finally came to a halt.

At the bottom of the hill, Gifford recalls, "we went into a village, and it was so icy that Tony couldn't maneuver the tank through the square, and he slid right through a house."

As they neared the Bulge, Gifford says, "you could see the dead Americans all over the place, burned American vehicles we were going in and out of. And we tried to avoid the dead bodies that were in the road. Once or twice we had to stop and pull them out of the way. I remember one guy, I picked him up, he was like a statue. When I tipped him over to get him out of the way, he just stuck in the snow like a frozen statue. The dead along the road, there were so many, so many that you just had to ignore it almost, you take it like it's normal. There's really nothing you could do for them."

In addition to an enemy that would engage virtually every unit of the 712th Tank Battalion in the fiercest fighting they had encountered since the hedgerows of Normandy, the tankers faced a new enemy: cold so bitter that ice would form on the inside of the tanks, the men would have to use blowtorches to warm up the engine before starting it, and frostbite would join the trenchfoot from the mud of Dillingen in claiming a large number of casualties.

Tony D'Arpino

I always said, the Air Force had it rough, but when they got through with their mission they went back to a nice barracks, hot meals, showers and everything else. The Navy, the same way. They're on the ship. They have their battles and then you've got a bunk to sleep in, they've got cooks cooking for 'em.

Us guys, we had no heat in the tanks in the goddamn winter. I remember digging out snow, putting branches down on a blanket, and a blanket on me; when I woke up in the morning I had about twelve inches of snow on me.

We had a rotation plan in our tank. The engine compartment, that stayed hot almost all night. We used to take turns, one night apiece, sleeping on the engine compartment.

You can just imagine, it's raining, you're soaking wet and you get cold, in that goddamn piece of steel. There were no fans even. When they fired the big gun, the smoke and everything else, you've got nothing to suck that out. Today everything is different, but they didn't have none of that stuff. And those tanks were cold.

Ruby Coldstein

I had a pair of green knit gloves. And a leather glove over it. When I'd post the guard outside on the tanks, I had my boots and overshoes on top of the boots. It was so cold I used to take my gloves off and suck my fingers, I'd have the fingers in my mouth and suck them so that I wouldn't freeze.

And you didn't stand. You were scared, you didn't know what to do. As you stand still, you're not moving. You're not circulating. And you didn't know whether you should move or not, because your ears have got to be wide open to hear things. And if you were having perimeter, you have a section, you stay there, you don't go traveling because you're gonna get killed, whether it was by friendly fire or enemy fire. So you stayed in that area. But it was cold.

George Bussell

You could take your finger and scrape the frost off the inside of the tanks, because they didn't have any heat. I had an assistant driver, Johnny, from Tennessee, I forget his last name[1]. He told me, "George, if I get home, and it's in the middle of July, and I think how cold I was, I'm gonna build a damn fire."

Tony D'Arpino

I used to have a ritual when I was on guard duty. You're scared, I don't give a goddamn what anybody says, I mean, it's one thing being scared and another being yellow. And you're scared. And I used to have a ritual. I'd be alert, but it kind of occupied my mind. I'm the only boy in my family, I have five sisters, and when I was on guard duty, I'd start with my oldest sister, and picture her in my mind, her name and everything else, then I'd go down to the next one, and the next one, and the next one, and the next one. And this kept me going. Then my mother and father. Then I'd think of my uncles. And by the time the two hours was up, you went through the whole family. But it kept your senses.

We had these knit hats in the winter. Your hair, it hurt just to touch it, and the guys used to joke, "Well, I guess I'll comb my hair," and they'd take the hat and screw it around a couple of times, and it looked like they'd stuck their finger in a socket.

O.J. Brock

O.J. Brock, from Corbin, Ky., joined A Company as a replacement during the Battle of the Bulge.

I had a birthday on the Queen Mary. My birthday is the 27th of December, so I was a young kid of 19. When I got to France, I went to a repo depot, and got the assignment to go to the headquarters of the 712th.

[1] This may have been John Owen of Montgomery, Ala.

They had about eight or ten of us at that time, replacements, I think three of us went to A Company, and some to C, and some went to Service Company.

That was certainly an overwhelming experience. I was assigned as an assistant driver during the Battle of the Bulge. It was winter and there was snow on the ground. I'd look out, and I'd wonder why they hadn't picked up the dead Germans. Some of them had their helmets laying beside them, and all the dead, the artillery was horse-drawn, and the dead cattle and the horse-drawn artillery was on the side of the road.

It's rather shocking to a young kid to see all that, the war zone, that fast. You go in and you get off the trucks and go into combat in days. It was certainly an awakening experience.

I was in combat less than a week after I was brought in from headquarters. That's why I say it was certainly an unusual experience for a young kid. I guess you mature very rapidly as you go along, however. I talked to the old-timers, and they'd been there for months and months.

They just said "Welcome to the best tank battalion in the world," and they told me that the past record was certainly unique in the European theater, that they had quite a few accomplishments, a lot of successes. Of course, they had a lot of people killed and wounded, and we know that's part of war, but the morale was certainly excellent. People talked about family life. Most of the guys were talking about getting home and getting back to their families. A lot of them weren't married. Most of them were younger, and had girlfriends. They had plans. They had goals.

They answered my questions, although I didn't have too many. I looked around and right away I could see that they were certainly excellent soldiers, and I knew then that they'd been through a lot of combat.

The first person I saw get killed was in my tank. I was the assistant driver, and we had a rendezvous in this town, I don't remember the village. It was a small, rural community, and Hank Schneider -- we called him Hank, he was a lieutenant, he had gotten a battlefield commission. He had the maps and things, and they were making plans for the next few days. We were attached to a regiment of the 90th Infantry Division. We didn't have any infantry people with us at that time.

As we approached this objective -- it was a small community, with some churches and small storefronts -- Peter Charapko, he was in the third or fourth tank and I was in the lieutenant's tank, he said, "Hank, we've got snipers all around. You'd better button your hatch."

It wasn't five minutes later that Hank was hit in the head with a sniper's bullet, and he fell down through the top of the tank. We radioed back, and the gunner said turn around, and told us where the aid station was, but Hank was dead immediately, shot through the head.

We stayed back in headquarters for a couple of days. We had to clean the tank out, all the blood and stuff. But that was certainly a shocking experience. I didn't know the people too well, but still it's certainly a heart-wrenching experience to lose some of your friends and comrades.

Ruby Goldstein

Hank Schneider got shot by a sniper, between the eyes. He was warning everybody to keep their head down. And I heard pop-pop. Bingo, he got it, warning somebody else.

Morse Johnson and Bob Hagerty made the arrangements for the 1988 reunion in Louisville, and Hank's son came to the reunion. I had gone to the chapel in Fort Benning when Hank got married. His wife came from Chicago, that's where he was from.

She had the baby when we were overseas, so I don't know if he got a picture of the baby or not at the time.

After Hank got killed, she remarried, and the husband adopted the child. Then the husband died, and she married another fellow, and they moved. And Ray Griffin, I don't know who told him or how he did it, but he finally located the son. Maybe the son was trying also to locate somebody, but anyway, they made the connection, and he came to the reunion.

None of us had ever seen him, so we didn't know what to expect. I don't know if it was Merrill or Charlie Vinson said to me, "That's Hank's son." So I went over to him, introduced myself, and got to talking to him. And he, like yourself, wanted to find anything, he never saw his father outside a picture. Morse and Hagerty were on the podium, and the son asked if he could speak to the battalion, and everything right from the heart. And I'm telling you, you really got a chill.

Ed Spahr

I was wounded on the inside of my left arm. Our tank got knocked out, and luckily, we all got out. They hit us somewhere in the track, and busted it, so that if we kept going we'd have just gone around in a circle.

After we got hit, Lieutenant Gifford stuck his head out, and a machine gun bullet struck him around one eye. He had blood all over. Well, when he got out of the tank, I don't think he thought he was hurt as bad as he was, and he stepped behind the tank, away from the incoming. When we got behind the tank, Lieutenant Gifford tossed me his camera, and said: "Take a picture of me."

So I'm standing there with my hands up taking the picture, that's the only way I could have gotten hit in a spot like that, I had to have my arms up. It just felt like a bee sting.

It was no big deal to me. I really didn't think I was hit until the medic asked to see my hand because when I dropped my arm the blood would drop off my fingers, and he wiped it off and said, "I can't see where the blood's coming from." And then, all at once, he said, "It's coming down your arm. Take off your shirt." And there it was, I was bleeding like a stuck pig.

Bob Rossi

Just prior to the Battle of the Bulge, Jim Gifford was brought in as our new tank commander. He was our tank commander and platoon leader. We were staying in a hayloft in the town of Berle, in Belgium. We wondered where Lieutenant Gifford was all day, and he came up the footladder and said, "Come here, I want to show you something." He had draped the tank in white sheets.

Jim Gifford

In Berle, I went around to the houses -- we didn't have white paint yet, they finally brought up some white paint, but we didn't have it, so I went around to all the houses and took all the white sheets they had. People didn't appreciate that, but I brought them back and handed them out to guys to cover our tanks with, because that airplane coming down there got me to realize that they could see us in the road. It had started to snow a lot. By the time we got up to where we were running into the enemy in force, some of the tanks had white paint on them, some of them didn't. I don't remember whether the paint was on our tank or not when we got hit that day.

Bob Rossi

Lieutenant Gifford had gotten a package from home, and I can remember he had some canned chicken. He shared his package with all of us.

I can recall vividly, we were talking about home and everything, and he said to us, "You know, I'd rather lose an arm or a leg than lose my eyesight." He said, "There's too much to see in this world." And the next day when he got hit, he got hit in the eye.

Tony D'Arpino

They said that there was a small pocket of Germans, it was holding the infantry down. They just wanted one section of tanks, us and Jim Warren's tank, to clean it out. It was just supposed to be a small pocket. And it turned out to be a little more than that.

Bob Rossi

There was concentrated machine gun fire. Lieutenant Gifford got hit in the right eye, the bullet lodged in his cheek. I thought he might jump out of the tank, and I yelled to him to keep down or they would blow his head off.

He said, "I don't want to jump out, I want Warren to come forward to help us." Then he said to me, "Rossi, how bad am I hit?" And I lied, I said, "You don't look bad, Lieutenant," but he looked like somebody hit him in the face with a sledgehammer.

So he says to me, "Fire the smoke mortar." And in my excitement, I forgot to knock the cap out, and when I fired the first mortar it went up and just missed coming straight down on top of us. Then I fired some subsequent mortars to give us a smoke-screen.

As we were abandoning tank, Lieutenant Gifford was firing his .45 and pulling Spahr out by one of his arms. Spahr's leg was locked. Spahr was the assistant driver, and his machine gun was firing by itself it was so hot. And I said, "Twist the belt, twist the belt," so he could stop the bullets from feeding into the machine gun.

Jim Gifford

It was a strange thing. They would fire at us, and you could hear like rain on a tin roof. As soon as we were hit, they were spraying the tank so we couldn't get out of it.

I reached up, and I fired the .50-caliber into the front, and the firing stopped. Then, when I stopped firing the .50, it started up again. So I told the guys, "Fire your guns." I said, "I'll fire the .50, and Tony, you get out." Tony was helpless down there, he's no use to anybody because he's the driver, so there's no point in him staying. So we fired the guns, and all the firing at the tank stopped, and Tony went out the hatch. We kept it up until he got around the corner.

I just had my arm out, just so I could reach the gun, because I had already been shot being up there, so I knew they were going to try to pick me off.

Then Klapkowski got out, and Rossi was the next one, he went out. Then I told Spahr. Spahr was down inside. He had the .30-caliber machine gun. He would fire the .30 in one direction and I was firing the .50 in the other direction, and while we were firing, it was amazing, they laid low. They could see us, but they didn't want to get hit. And that fourteen, fifteen seconds between the time we would stop firing and they'd start hitting the tank again with their machine gun fire, that was when we had an opportunity to do things. It gave us about ten seconds.

So I said, "All right, Spahr, you fire, and then you stop firing, and then when you hear my gun stop, get your ass out of there." So that's what we did.

Then out he came. He stopped firing. I fired and I stopped. I jumped out. And Jesus, he's back there trying to get something inside the tank, and he was sort of stuck, and I reached up and I'm grabbing him to pull him out of the hatch, and it turns out he's trying to get his duffel bag. I said "Leave the goddamn thing in there, what are you, kidding?" And he said, "I've got all my stuff in there." And I said, "Forget about it," and I pulled him off the tank, and then we both ran back, and we got behind Warren's tank.

Bob Rossi

After we got out of the tank, Klapkowski and I were running in a zigzag, we could see the snow being kicked up around us. There was an armored recon truck coming toward us, and as we were running, Lieutenant Gifford said, "Fire that .50 and protect these boys." And the guy in the truck yelled out, "It's our last box of .50." He says, "Fire it anyway, you son of a bitch!" And that's when they started firing the .50 to give us cover.

As we got out of the line of fire, Lieutenant Gifford handed his .45 to me, he says, "Hold this for me 'til I get back." And with that, he said, "Take my picture."

I said, "Lieutenant, I can't take your picture." So he gave the camera to Spahr. And there he was, having his picture taken. He had gotten a Bronze Star that morning, he had the ribbon, his face all puffed up, blood all over his combat jacket, he says, "Take my picture."

CHAPTER 14

"We're Gonna Burn"

Ed Spahr

When they stopped you, you got out of that tank as quickly as possible. We carried almost 200 gallons of high octane gasoline, 102 octane I think it was, and it didn't take long to burn. The gas tank was on the side, toward the rear of the tank, on each side of the engine.

Usually the tank commander, if he wasn't disabled, he was the first one out. The gunner usually was second, and his loader would be third. The assistant driver and the driver, they had their own hatches to come out. Now, they would have no problem getting out unless the gunner left the gun barrel over the top of one of their hatches, then they couldn't open that hatch. They would have to crawl across the transmission and get out the other side, which, if they took that long to get out, a lot of them didn't get out, because the ammunition burning, the gasoline burning, it didn't take long -- seconds -- until that tank was completely involved in flames, same as an airplane. It was so quick.

Tony D'Arpino

I'll say one thing: We had the best working escape hatch of anybody in the platoon. I used to oil that thing up good, so that when you touched the lever it would really fall out.

Sometimes that was the only way of escape. If you're inside the tank and the hatches are down and the gun was traversed over your hatch, you can't open it to get out, you have to go out the other way.

I can remember always telling Klapkowski, "You son of a bitch, if we ever get knocked out, make sure that gun's in the center, because if I can't get out because you've got the gun traversed over my hatch," I says, "I'll haunt you. I'll come and pull the sheets off of your bed."

Bob Rossi

They said there was no reason for the 75s not to fire, that all the powder would burn. We found out differently. One time I went to put a round in the breach, and it hung up there. Some of the powder was frozen, and didn't fully burn. I didn't know that, and after I went to throw the next round in, Klapkowski and Gramari had to go out of the tank and knock the round out of the breach with the rammer staff.

Tony D'Arpino

Klapkowski, he was crazy as a bedbug. He was one of the best gunners in the company, but he had other -- he probably thought I had faults, too, I don't know -- but anyway, we had Gramari as a loader, Klapkowski's the gunner, and a round jammed after he fired. So Klapkowski got Gramari out there, and they're hitting the front of the shell with the ramrod, which is a long wooden pole with a bell-shape at the end of it, and Klapkowski says, "Gramari, here's the secret of this." He says, "Don't hold the ramrod tight, hold it loose."

And Gramari says, "What do you hold it loose for?"

"Oh," Klapkowski says. "In case the round goes off while you're standing in front of the barrel, you won't get splinters."

I says, "Klapkowski, that's no thing to say." He scared the hell out of Gramari. I was young but Gramari was a kid. I think he was 18 years old. I finally told Klapkowski off. He'd say to Gramari, "We ain't gonna make it. You know what's gonna happen? Someday, the tank's gonna get hit," and he says, "Lombardi's gonna go to get out," he's the first one to get up, he's in the turret there, "he's gonna get shot and he's gonna come down inside on top of me, on top of you, and you ain't gonna make it, and the tank's gonna be on fire," and I, I just blew up, I told him, "Stop talking that way." Because he's making me scared.

Bob Rossi

"We're gonna burn. We're gonna burn." Klapkowski would say this to Gramari, all the time. "You're gonna burn, you're gonna burn." He use to pull the same crap on me. I said to him, "Hey, I burn, you're gonna burn, too." So he had to stop giving me that crap.

CHAPTER 15

Accidents

Forrest Dixon

Following the Ardennes offensive, we requisitioned a total of 69 replacements. When they arrived, they were placed with the companies in different tanks.

About the second day we got word that one of the boys accidentally shot another one of the crew members while cleaning a gun. I went to investigate, and I don't remember the fellow's name, I said, "Now tell me, how did it happen?"

He says, "Well, I picked up the gun and was going to clean it and all of a sudden it fired." He said it went right through this kid.

This gun is what we used to we used to call a grease gun, and there's a cover on it. I said, "Well, soldier, you know where the cover is on the gun, was the cover open or closed?" And he said, "Well, I ain't never seen that gun before." And I said, "Apparently it was closed, because when the cover is open, it's on safety."

Well, he said he didn't know that. He said, "I reached for it," and he didn't know this, but apparently when he reached for it, he shut the door, the latch, whatever you want to call it, and the gun went off.

I said, "Soldier, how long have you been over here?" And he said, "Well, I've been over here about ten days."

I said, "How long have you been in the Army?" He thought a minute and he said, "Sir, I believe just six weeks."

I said, "You mean you've been over here six weeks."

"No sir," he said. "Seven weeks ago I was a civilian."

I said, "It can't be."

And he said, "Sir, it is."

I thought, well, there's no need to make an issue of it, I'd better go find out for sure.

He said, "Major, am I in trouble?"

I said, "If what you tell me is true, you're not in too much trouble, but I'll let you know." So I got my sergeant, and I sent him back to the rear to pick up the records of the 69 replacements. He got back with the records the next morning, and I looked at them, and all 69 were between six weeks and three months from civilian life. I got ahold of Colonel Kedrovsky and I said, "We've got a problem."

He said, "What's that?"

I said, "We've got a bunch of kids that don't know a thing about Army life. They don't know how to do anything."

He said, "Why not?"

I said, "They just came out of civilian life."

He said, "How long ago?"

I said, "From six weeks to three months."

And he said, "Major, that can't be true."

And I said, "I have the soldiers' records. It's true."

He said, "Get ahold of all the companies and get those men up to battalion headquarters." He said, "They are more dangerous than the Germans."

So we put out the order and we got the 69 back to battalion headquarters, and we set up a school, what we called a round-robin school. We had maybe six or eight positions, and we got some of the sergeants that knew what it was all about, and we trained them in the machine gun and the different sidearms, how to drive a tank and how to shoot the 75 and so on, and in 10 days, those boys probably learned as much as when we were learning back in '43, it probably took us six months to get as much as we gave in the 10 days.

Walter Galbraith

Pfc. Walter Galbraith, from Chelsea, Mass., was a gunner in D Company.

The last man on guard at night was supposed to make sure that all the ammunition was out of the guns. We were in Germany, I forget what part of Germany it was, but it was in the winter. Some of the houses only had a wall up, and the GIs put their bedrolls against the walls, to shield them from the cold.

In the morning, I climbed up onto my tank, and my eye caught a glint of brass. I thought, "Who the hell left the ammunition in the gun?"

I had gone into the tank to check on Little Joe. Little Joe is the motor that turns the turret. If you press your thumb on one side you start the machine gun, and if you hit the other side you hit the cannon.

I got in the tank and I saw that brass, so I removed the shell and I cleaned out the chamber, and then I threw the round back in.

Then I reached over to check on Little Joe, and when I did my hand came up, and I hit the button for the cannon.

The periscope was in front of me, and I saw the whole road blow up in front of the tank. I blew the whole goddamn road up. And I thought, "Oh, my God, did I kill somebody?" That's the first thing I thought about. So I reached up, I raised my seat, and I looked out. I didn't see anybody walking around with no head on, and I felt good, I didn't care what they did to me, I hadn't killed anybody. And all of a sudden the company commander, the first sergeant, all the guys are walking up to that big hole that I made in the road, and I figured I'd better go face the music. So I walked up there, and I was just gonna say, "Well, that's the way the cookie crumbles," when the first sergeant says, "Jesus. I drove over this road three times this morning and that goddamn mine didn't blow up."

CHAPTER 16

The Angel of Mercy

Jim Flowers

There was this angel of mercy, this Army nurse, she was about forty years old. After they got me settled in a bed, she came and said, "Lieutenant, how long has it been since you've been bathed?"

"You mean, a real bath?" I said. "Well, they wiped me off down at the field hospital at Southampton."

She says, "Soap and water." Hmmm. I think the last real bath I had was on board the LST going from Weymouth over to Utah Beach, and that's been six weeks ago now. And she says, "M-hmm. How long has it been since you've been off of your back?"

"Since the 12th day of July."

"How long have you been wearing that catheter?"

"Since the 12th of July."

"We'll be back in a bit. We're gonna get you off of your back, we're gonna scrub you good, and we're gonna remove that catheter and all that adhesive tape."

I said, "I'll be grateful if you will."

She was a gal of her word. In a bit she and a younger nurse came back and they partially pulled the curtain around my bed, and she says, "Now, we're gonna turn you on your side. It's gonna hurt." She says, "We'll be as gentle as we can. We just want to warn you, though, that you're gonna have some discomfort."

They put out a draw sheet, and they gently rolled me up on my left side, and everything was exposed on my right side; they scrubbed me good, like they was scraping hair off of a hog.

First, they took the catheter out. I thought she'd pulled my guts out, but boy, it was a blessing to have it all done quickly.

After they finished bathing me, they made me as comfortable as I'd been in quite some time.

As I think back I'm looking at some of the fellows that are in that ward with me. I especially remember one boy who was right across the aisle from me and down several beds, he was moaning about the low blow that fate had dealt him. Before the war, he was a pianist. He had aspirations of being a concert pianist. His left arm was completely paralyzed. I suppose that he eventually lost that arm. Imagine a pianist with only one arm. It's hard to accept that.

I stayed in that hospital several days, and then they moved me to Salisbury, to a hospital group. Two medical-surgical units and one convalescent or rehabilitation unit.

There I saw Paul Hamilton. He was across the aisle and down two or three beds. He was ambulatory by then. He walked over and he said, "You're the tanker."

I said, "I sure am."

He told me who he was. We were glad to see each other.

On the same side of the ward that I was on, down about four beds, was one J.Q. Lynd from Stillwater, Oklahoma. He was a University of Arkansas ROTC product, and had been a 90th Division officer also. He got hit in the first three or four days after the landing.

In the bed next to me on my right-hand side was a young captain who had a terrible wound. He had been shot through his left foot. The top of his foot. Ruined his shoe.

I was sympathizing with him, and some of the other patients looked at me. I asked him how he got that wound, and he started telling how he got shot through the left foot, and somebody says, "That's an S.I.W," a self-inflicted wound. And I looked at him and I said, "Did you do that?"

He said, "Well, it was an accident."

"You yellow cowardly son of a bitch!" Everything that I could get my hands on off of the bedside table, I threw at him.

One of the nurses heard the commotion and she came down to see what the problem was. Then they took that old boy's bed, wheeled him out of there, and she came back and said, "You'll not be bothered with him anymore."

J.Q. Lynd, he's a professor of agronomy at Oklahoma State University, he remembered that incident a hell of a lot better than I did, and he enjoys telling about it.

Over on the bed next to me on the left side was a young fellow who had a through-and-through wound in his chest. Through his chest, lung, everything, and out the back. It was almost a foregone conclusion that this man was a terminal case. He'd lay there and he'd cough and spit up blood. They had a four-by-four gauze bandage over him. He'd smoke cigarettes, and smoke would come out under this bandage. Isn't that a hell of a thing? He wanted to live, though, he really wanted to. It wasn't a matter of just three or four days, he was gone.

Another one that I recall on that ward was a big, handsome fellow who had a spinal cord injury. He was finding it not just difficult but almost impossible to accept the fact that he was going to be a paraplegic. The moment he got hit, that altered the rest of his life. There's no repair for spinal cords. He sure took it hard. But a lot of people took it hard.

Jim Gifford

They took me to a big farmhouse, and in back of it there was a barn with a lot of manure, some cows, and a couple of wounded guys were laying there, they laid them out because it was sheltered there. I went over and I sat down, then I laid down. I was feeling lousy.

While I was laying there, Tony D'Arpino and one of the other boys came up to see how I was, and about that time an ambulance started backing in. So I got up and I got in the ambulance, and there were some German guys in there that had been badly wounded. There were about six or seven of us in that ambulance. The war was over for both of us. One German guy was carrying on kind of bad, and we'd try to comfort him. You know, even though he was the enemy, you become a human being when you get into the hospital.

We went back to Luxembourg, and we went to the main hospital, and they unloaded us there. Some of the guys were on stretchers. I was a walking patient, and then, when I got into the hospital, I fell down, and they put me on a stretcher.

There was a big, wide staircase going up to the second floor, it was probably ten feet wide. It circled up. There was a veranda up there, and every single step had a stretcher case on it.

They put me on one of those steps, and the German soldiers were on other steps, and the doctors and nurses were all running around, they were trying to evaluate who was wounded, who to wait on first and second, because they were pouring into that hospital from the whole front, and they were overwhelmed with wounded. Guys were laying there, some of them died, some of them had half their leg off and a tourniquet, it was a mess, and they were working like crazy those doctors and nurses, all of them deserved medals, they were really doing their best.

Because of my bullet in the head, they took me right up to an operating room. There was a doctor from Long Island, I don't know what his name was -- at one time I remembered, I've forgotten it now -- I was on the operating table, and two or three doctors were looking at my eye, and they were saying, "Take the eye out, get the bullet and take the eye out," and I was just laying there, whatever they do, that's it, they know more than I do about it, and the one from Long Island says, "No. We can save this eye. No, no, we're not going to take the eye. We can save it."

The next thing, I was in a room. Whatever clothes we had on when we were operated on was the clothes that we wore. There was no such thing as going into a hospital and getting out of your clothes and getting into something else. I've got a blank from the time they operated on me until I ended up in a room somewhere, so they must have knocked me out, because I don't even remember them operating on my head. But then I had patches, the side of my head was all patched.

They put me in an ambulance and took me down to a field hospital. Then they transferred me, the next hospital I was in was in Paris. How I got there -- I think I went by train, I don't remember. I was in bad shape. But I ended up in a hospital in Paris. Oh, no wonder I don't remember: By the time I got to Paris I was blind. I went blind somewhere after the operation.

I was laying in the head injuries ward in the hospital in Paris, and they had ropes going from behind your bed to different locations. If you want to go to the bathroom, you follow the rope that was the thickest. Whatever the size of the rope was told you where you were gonna end up. If they allowed you out of bed, you could do that. They allowed me to follow those ropes to the bathroom so I didn't have to use bedpans.

Then one day I was laying in bed, and everything was grey, and all of a sudden I saw something up above me, a square. And the next thing I saw a grill. And I just hollered. I didn't move my head or move my body, I just hollered to the guy in the bed next to me, I said, "Tell the doctors I can see! I can see a square." They came running in and they propped up my head. They said, "Don't move." The coagulation of the blood behind the optic nerve was breaking up, and so they immobilized my head for the rest of the day and into the night, and the vision came back in my left eye.

Until then, I was prepared to study braille. I thought I was going to be blind for the rest of my life.

So it cleared up. And then I stayed there for a few days.

There was a guy in the bed next to me that came in with me, he had been hit in the face with a hand grenade and he was all bandaged up.

The doctor came in one night, and he's got the flashlight, you know, the war's on, at night there's no lights in the hospital, so the doctor came in and he's got the flashlight in his armpit, and he's trying to redo the bandages on this guy's head. So I got up, I said, "Give me the flashlight, Doc, I'll help you."

He said, "Good, okay, hold it right there." So he starts unraveling this guy's -- the guy was 19 years old, I'll never forget it -- he started taking the bandages off, and I have never gotten sick at the sight of anything in my life, never, but standing there, when he took those bandages off and I saw this kid's face, there was no nose, no left eye, no cheek, no upper teeth, a couple of broken bottom teeth, and I looked right down into his lungs practically, he was a mess, he was a mess. And his tongue was there, and he was saying, "I'm scared."

I said to the doctor, "Doc, do you want to hold this light a minute?" And he took one look at me, I guess he knew I was, I said, "Just hold it a minute." He said, "Oh yeah, it's okay." He understood. I walked over, there was a door there and I stepped out into the snow and took some deep breaths, and then I came back and I was all right. I held the light, and he bandaged him up.

Jim Rothschadl

In the hospital, they put me on intravenous feeding. That was in July. I didn't eat solid food until ten days after Thanksgiving, I got one egg. When I went to France, I was a pretty strapping fellow, I weighed 191 pounds stripped. Then I went down to 122. I never got back to 140.

After quite a few months in England, they took me into a dental unit. They had operated on my leg and fixed that up, and they had to operate on that again on Thanksgiving morning, because it grew a great big piece of flesh, half the size of a tomato, and green. So they operated again. Then they put me in a dental unit and I had bridgework done. You won't believe this, but the thing that ran the drill was a foot pedal. There was a GI sitting on a bicycle. That was the GI's duty. But the dentist did a beautiful job.

When I was in the hospital in England, I was looking around for people that I knew. It was a huge place, and on the end of every bed was a tag, with name, rank, serial number, and religion. And they gave the units also. So I was looking for guys from the 712th, or the 90th Infantry Division, or the 82nd Airborne. I was going back and forth there, and one day, by God, I ran into a guy from my company. A fellow by the name of Coleman [Guy T. Coleman]. He was the second cook in the kitchen all the while we were in Benning.

I said, "What the hell happened to you?" He had a big cast all the way down his leg.

"Well," he said, "them sonofabitches. One day they got short a loader and they stuck me in a tank." He never was in a tank. He said, "They showed me what the hell to do," and god damn it, he got his knee in the way of the recoil from the breach, and it smashed his leg. It smashed his whole knee up.

Another guy I got to know in the hospital, his name is Fred Czarny. He was in the bed next to me in the hospital. I was already married at the time. I had gone home on a furlough in 1943 and got married. And my fingers were stiff, like pieces of board. I couldn't write. I couldn't bend them for a long time. This Fred Czarny, I would dictate to him and he would write for me.

He was kind of heavyset, and he got hit by an artillery shell that made a rut, like an indentation, on his right side, and he lost control on that side, so he wrote with his left hand.

He stayed over there in the hospital, and he said, "When you get back to the States, send me a fifth of whiskey," he even named the kind he wanted. So when I got to Halloran General Hospital in Staten Island, I was going to keep my promise. I said to the nurses and doctors, "By God, I want to send this guy a fifth of whiskey." But there was a rule, you can't send whiskey overseas. You can't do it, the doctor said. I begged him. But I couldn't do it.

We still have a lot of the letters. They were mostly love letters. I did write one serious letter home, though. Not to my wife but to my younger brother. I had an older brother, Fred, who was in the service, but he didn't get overseas. And I had a younger brother, Richard, he wrote me one letter when I was in the hospital in England. He said, "All my friends are going in the Army," and all this sort of stuff. He said "I'm going to go in the Army." And of course I knew what hell it was over there. Well, I wrote him a letter. And he saved it. He showed it to me after the war. The censors really blocked it out. Oh, God, they massacred it. Because I was going to discuss it and disillusion him. I had been laying in the hospital for months, and at the time, instead of grafting skin, they used a live tissue culture. My mouth was burned real bad, and they wanted it to grow back, they had a hell of a time with that. Twice a day they'd put this live culture on. One of my buddies was laying there, he was burned worse than I was. They did his whole face, over the months. And then one morning, before they shipped me home, I noticed something different about him. His body rejected it. He was purple and green and red and white. They scraped the whole damn thing off. About 40 percent of the guys they used that process on it worked, but on about 60 percent it didn't, so eventually they went back to skin grafts.

I wrote this letter to my brother, and it's funny they didn't toss me in the hoosegow. I told him to stay the hell out of it. I said there's two of us brothers in here now, that's enough.

I told him, "Don't do it." And I told him some of the things that happened and how bad it is, and how cruel humans can be to one another. It's terrible. The censors butchered the letter, but he got the understanding of it. He didn't sign up. Of course, by the time he would have got trained the war would have been over.

CHAPTER 17

Habscheid

Feb. 8, 1945

Bob Rossi

We subsequently got a new tank, and Sergeant Holmes [Eldon K. Holmes] became our acting platoon leader. He had been the platoon sergeant. On Feb. 8, 1945, we were knocked out again, at Habscheid, Germany. We were in a wooded area; they called us during the night.

Tony D'Arpino

We argued about it. If you move the tanks at night, Jesus, they make too much noise, they draw artillery fire. But the infantry officer said, "I'm giving you an order."

Bob Rossi

When light came, it seemed like everything opened up at once. They knew we were there in the woods, and they had mortars, artillery, machine gun fire.

I could hear the shrapnel hitting the outside of the tank. All of a sudden, Sergeant Holmes fell down into the turret, and I was yelling, "Holmes, Holmes, are you hit?" And Spahr says to me, "Sure he's hit."

We picked him up and put him in a sitting position behind the gun. Shrapnel had gone through his steel helmet. He had several long cuts the length of his head, and the o.d. towel he used as a scarf was soaked with blood.

I said to D'Arpino, "Give me the first aid kit." And with that, he can't open it. The darn thing was rusted shut. So with a chisel he opened up the first aid kit, and I bandaged Sergeant Holmes as best as I could, and as he's laying on the floor he called up Sergeant Gibson [Maxton C. Gibson] on the radio. He says, "Gib, I'm hit, I'm getting out of here."

And Gibson called back, he says, "We're all getting out of here." With that, Gibson started up the hill, and this is when we found out that the Germans had the hill zeroed in.

Gibson then led us up the hill. He stopped to see if we were coming behind him, and just as he stopped, the Germans fired two rounds just in front of his tank. We could hear him say on the radio to his driver, "Kick this tank in the ass and let's go."

We came up the hill next, and an armor-piercing round hit us and went from the rear to the front of the tank, and landed between the assistant driver's legs. Jim Sessions was the assistant driver. He was a recruit, I think it was a day before or a day after his 18th or 19th birthday. He later told us his left leg was on top of an ammunition box because it was all wet down there. If his leg had been down, it would have been blown off.

I could see the shell lying there. It was red, fiery hot. In the meantime, we were on fire, because the 88 round had gone through our gas tanks. I turned to pull the inside fire extinguisher, and I got hit in the face with flames.

I yelled, "Let's get out of here!"

Tony D'Arpino

I knew there was another tank behind me to get out, so I tried pulling over to the right to give him room to get around me, and of course nothing was working.

Sessions, the assistant driver, was new, and he grabbed a fire extinguisher. I says, "Jump, you crazy bastard, jump!" Matter of fact, I didn't even unplug the radio or nothing, I just got out.

Ed Spahr

He [Sessions] never did attempt to get out 'til I got ahold of him. I jumped back up on the tank and I grabbed him.

Bob Rossi

One tank was already knocked out in the woods, and we had taken two guys from that crew into our tank, so there were five of us in the turret. The other three guys from their crew were laying on the back deck of Gibson's tank. Now they've got the better tank with two hatches, but Gibson wouldn't let them in. This is the way we should have done it, because we only had one hatch in the turret. This was the old cast-hull model. The tank I was in with Gifford, I had my own hatch, but this tank had only one hatch.

The two men were Bob Gladsen and Cecil McFarland. And this is the funny part of it: McFarland's carrying a carton of cigarettes with him. He told us their bogey wheels were shot off, they can't move, and he takes the carton of cigarettes with him!

When we got hit, I was the last guy to get out. I was on my hands and knees, waiting for the others to get out. I no sooner got out of the turret than the ammo started to explode and started to make smoke rings from the turret.

It had been raining the night before when we got the order to move. Sergeant Holmes said to me, "Rossi, get out and lead the tank," and he handed me his tank commander's watch, which had luminous dials. Now I'm running in front of the tank in the rain, holding it up as I'm running so D'Arpino can see the watch in the dark. After we got knocked out the next morning, I said to myself, "Thank God my clothes were soaking wet." I think that's what saved me from getting burned to death in the tank.

Tony D'Arpino

It's taking a while to tell this story, but it all happened within seconds. When that projectile hit and I saw it land beside Sessions' foot, it came right alongside the transmission. The transmission was between the driver and the assistant driver. The projectile was red hot, and it was laying right down by his left foot. I put my hand outside and tried to pry myself up, and that tank was just as hot as a stove.

Ed Spahr

When they hit us, it felt like it drove the tank ten feet forward.

Bob Rossi

Just before I got out of the tank, the other tank, just about on our left rear, they got hit. But they weren't as fortunate as us. La Mar, who was the driver, was burned pretty bad. I can remember when they took that stocking mask off it took some of the skin right off his face. And Whiteheart [Gary L. Whiteheart], the type of tank they had, they had ammo stacked in back of the assistant driver, it shifted, and hit him right in the back.

Van Landingham [Carl Van Landingham] was the tank commander, part of his heel was torn off from the shrapnel.

Grayson La Mar

Grayson C. La Mar, from Trinity, N.C., was a driver in C Company.

We were on top of this hill, and we were taking orders from a 90th Infantry Division lieutenant. Since we hadn't run into anything the night before, he wanted to go on down to the bottom of the hill, in the valley. But at daybreak, when we started out, all hell broke loose. We had four tanks and a tank destroyer. They threw a shell in the tank destroyer, killed all of the crew. One boy, they broke his leg or something, he was trying to climb out when they threw another round in and finished him off.

Then they got the second tank, I believe it was. When they got that, that left three tanks. Sergeant Gibson, he didn't know what the rest were gonna do but he's gonna get the hell out of there, and he's the only one that got out.

When he left, Sergeant Holmes' tank followed him. I automatically backed up and followed Holmes. When I got to the top of the hill, Holmes' tank was sitting in the middle of the road burning. So I couldn't get around. I had to go off into a field, and when I did my back end blew up. The shell came in there and set me on fire.

It took three tries to get the hatch open. The hatch would hit the gun barrel. The gunner was killed, so nobody could operate the gun to get the barrel out of the way. Finally, on the third try, I got it open enough to squeeze out. If the gun was a quarter-inch further I'd have never got out.

The force of the shell had blown my steel helmet off. I still had my tank helmet on. When I got out, there were blazes all around and I had to keep my eyes shut.

I heard the tank commander, he was hanging over the side, he said "Help me." He had gotten his heel blown off. I dragged him off into the snow, and I just fell in it, too. There were about ten inches of snow. I drove my head into it.

Tony D'Arpino

We crawled all the way down that hill, got down to the bottom, and Van Landingham was missing. He's still back up there. So I don't know who the other guy was and myself, we grabbed a stretcher, we went back up, we crawled back up. They were shooting right over our heads. I thought that was my last day, I had three tanks knocked out from under me, and out of all of them, I thought that was it. I had it.

We crawled up there with a stretcher to get Van Landingham. We finally get to him and he's moaning and groaning. I'm looking for blood, I don't see nothing. He's got them combat boots on. I looked, and he goes, "Ohhh, ohhh," real sharp, now he must have been hit someplace, I don't know where. I couldn't see any blood. We're trying to get him on that stretcher, and we're trying to crawl on our hands and knees with the stretcher, get him down over the crest where they couldn't see us. They had that place zeroed in. We'd go a few feet, and "shooom," we'd drop the stretcher. The third time the stretcher hit the solid ground, Van Landingham, "Oooooh," he would groan. Anyway, God willing, we got him down to the bottom, and I don't know who that man is today, I've thought about this a million times, but an officer saw me and whoever else had that stretcher, and he took our names, he thought we should get the Silver Star for what we had done. I was told later on that this man was called back to England, he had to be a witness in a court martial. I don't know who the officer was. He wasn't in our outfit.

Bob Rossi

Later on we were kidding, it was bad, but we kidded, "That German gun crew must have all got the Iron Cross and a three-day pass." Two tank destroyers had also been knocked out, and we lost practically the whole company of infantry that we were attached to. The Germans kept pouring on the artillery, mortars and small arms fire.

After we abandoned tank, we ran from pillbox to pillbox. Gladsen threw his .45 down, because he was afraid of being captured. I still had Gifford's .45, and it fell down on the inside of my combat pants. I'm running with that thing down around my ankle, and I'm thinking if I got captured they'd think that I was trying to hide the gun, they'd probably kill me.

I gave the gun back to Gifford when the war ended and we were stationed at Amberg.

Ed Spahr

I remember there was a sniper, and this captain pointed to an infantry boy and said, "Get up there and get that son of a bitch." And that infantry boy handed him his M-1, he said, "Here, you get him."

Bob Rossi

We were running from pillbox to pillbox to get out of the line of fire, and the infantry was dug in foxholes. They said, "Don't run on the road, it's mined. Don't run in the gully, it's mined." We finally got to this one pillbox, and I think it was a major or a lieutenant colonel, he wanted American wounded put outside because he complained that they were in the way of him conducting business. And we were PO'd at him. I was so mad at the time, I was only a kid, but I was so mad I felt like shooting the German prisoners who were there because they did this to us.

About that time, somebody said to me that I had blood all over me. It was then that I noticed that I had Holmes' blood all over my left sleeve from when I had bandaged him in the tank.

He was evacuated, and finally our company jeep driver came up to make several trips to get us back to the rear.

We left the pillbox where the first aid station was and waited for the jeep driver to come back for us by a bombed-out house. There were several German dead in there. Then a self-propelled artillery crew set up their position next to the house and started drawing fire from the Germans, so we got the hell out of there.

Finally, the jeep drove us back to the rear.

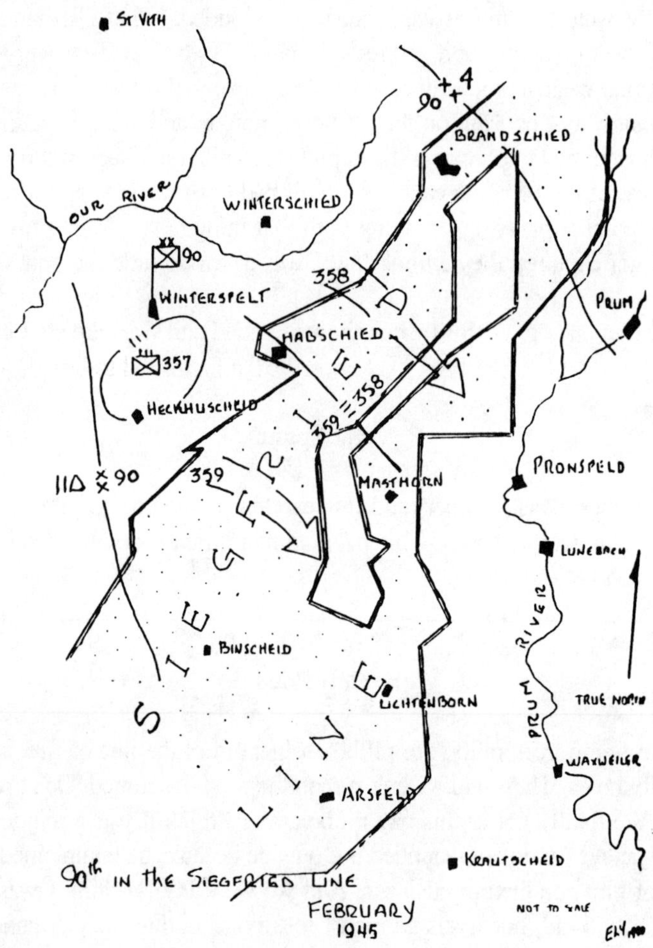

REPRINTED WITH PERMISSION FROM "WAR FROM THE GROUND UP" BY JOHN COLBY

CHAPTER 18

The Telegram

Jim Gifford

I was from Gloversville, N.Y. There was a fellow from Albany in my outfit, Fred Putnam, he was killed at Mairy. He was a bow gunner, or a driver in George Peck's tank. An armor-piercing shell came in and went through him, killed him instantly.

Then the tank burned, so they didn't bury Putnam. There was nothing to bury.

After the war, I went to see his mother. She asked me how he died. I told her some of the details, but I didn't have the heart to tell her he was cremated. I said there was a church nearby, and there was a cemetery in the churchyard, a walled yard with a cemetery in it, and that he and some other soldiers that were unknown were buried there, and the people in that church tended to the graves.

She said to me, "Oh, I'm so glad, I wondered what happened to him." I didn't have the heart to tell her. It gave her something to live with, you know. I don't know if I was right or I was wrong, but I think I was right.

Lester Suter

I had to send the personal effects of all the KIAs back to their wives and mothers and friends. A lot of them had wives, and they'd have pictures of girlfriends that they had met in England or even in Germany or France. I knew this because they'd have a picture of their wife and then maybe two of girlfriends. So I would go through their wallet and pull out these girls, so it would never be known to their wife. I thought that was only a fair thing to do, since he was dead and gone, it didn't matter any, why should they know what he did when he's gone? I thought it was a benefit to them, although they were dead.

Joe Fetsch

Pfc. Joseph R. Fetsch, of Baltimore, Md., drove a truck that brought gasoline to the tanks.

There was an old guy who delivered the government telegrams in my neighborhood. We lived in a row house, what they call town houses now, in Philadelphia. My mother and my sister had gone out of the house, they were going up to the store, it's getting late in the evening, and they see him with a flashlight. He hits our house and hesitates. And he hits the next house and he hesitates. And he comes back and looks at ours. The kid next door to me, he went in the service maybe a year after me, and ended up in the infantry.

My sister's telling me this, now, she says, "I couldn't hold onto Mom."

Finally, the old man went next door, and he had a telegram that said, "Your son is missing in action."

So Christ, a week later here comes another telegram, "Your son was killed in action." Well, my mother went over and nursed this lady for a week to get her back on her feet.

That was in January, around in the Bulge time is when he got killed. Here comes April, the first part of April, and here comes the same little guy again, he's got his light out. And my mother sees him coming up the road. It made her sick, she damn near died. She damn near died. Then she was scared to open the envelope, that telegram. My sister opened it, and it just said that I was wounded.

CHAPTER 19

Battle Fatigue

Jim Gifford

One of our lieutenants, I don't know if the boys told you this story, I got the 90th Division newsletter just recently, and isn't his name there in the obituaries. We were on the Saar River, and the Germans were across the river, in the high ground. There were woods over there. We were in an orchard on this side. We had our tanks dispersed.

We were getting shelled real bad, and the ground all around us was blowing up all over the place. It was dusty, just like going across a desert. When they start shelling, the shells explode on the ground, and all that dirt turns to dust. If they do enough of it, you get a hell of a dust cloud going.

The periscope was up, and I'm looking around, because we're all buttoned up. When you're moving, you open the turrets because a mine will kill you if you're inside. So we'd close the hatches when we were in a standing position and let 'em shoot, we don't give a damn, those shells used to hit the side of the tank and rock the tank but never bothered us inside, because it was high explosive, and not armor piercing.

So I'm looking out the periscope, and Geez, I see this turret hatch suddenly come up in the middle of all this dust, and the lieutenant comes flying up out of it, lands on the back, jumps down into the dust, and he runs off, out of sight, towards the road.

I don't know, I figured he had some good reason, maybe somebody's hurt in the tank, I mean, I never questioned it. But it turned out that he -- I don't like to use that word -- he just blew his cool, and they found him about three miles up the road in a farmhouse in the cellar. We went down in the cellar, and he was in there in a corner, crouched in a corner.

The guy was a brave man. Prior to all that we had no problems with him at all. But I guess there's a breaking point.

I felt bad, because one time, he showed me a letter from his father, he says, "Look at this," and I read it, and his father was calling him "My warrior." Little old father, you know. That always bothered me, because I remembered that letter.

Claude Pittman

Claude Pittman, from Gainesville, Ga., was a gunner in A Company.

You had to keep your sense of humor, or you'd go crazy. Everybody always teased me about my southern brogue, me being from Georgia, they all kidded me about it. But after we got out of Fort Benning I told them I didn't want to hear 'em kid me about Georgia anymore, that was the best place in the world.

We had one boy in service, I won't say he went crazy -- after he got out of it he was all right, but I've seen him go to pieces at the time, he didn't hardly know what he's doing. After it was over with, he raised a family and all.

What's funny about him, at Fort Benning he used to tell me about running white lightning, and the police is shooting at him and shooting at him, and he'd outrun 'em and get away from them. Then, when we got over there, the Germans got to shootin' at him, and it's different than the police shootin', he went all to pieces. I mean, that's kind of comical to me.

CHAPTER 20

Tigers

Jack Sheppard

We weren't looking for tank battles. One time we were coming over a hill down towards this shallow valley with a creek in the bottom of it. Up the other bank, almost to the top of the hill, was a German tiger tank shooting its 88 at anything that moved on our side of the hill, and our powers that be decided that we had to knock it out.

So we fired everything we had at it. The artillery fired everything they had. The corps artillery, which included 155-millimeter and eight-inch guns, fired them at it. It never moved, and it continued to shoot.

Eventually it quit shooting, and when we finally took the area, I personally climbed into the tank. It was out of gasoline. It was still usable, and the forest was cleared for a hundred yards all the way around it. There wasn't a tree left standing.

There were dents in the tank where rounds had hit the metal and ricocheted off. Didn't even break the track. They just let it sit there as a pillbox, used up their ammunition and left.

Bob Hagerty

We were in Oberwampach, which was just a crossroads with some farm buildings and a few little homes. We needed an outpost, and I went up on a side road and pulled off to the right. There was a little culvert where the farmer had cut a path through to move the wagons and horses.

We could see up ahead. There were some buildings on fire. Sometimes things like that are set on fire by the infantry, maybe they create a kind of a super searchlight, and then the Germans aren't going to come through and expose themselves while they're highlighted liked that.

The fires were up the road, the road was kind of a gentle rise, and an infantry guy came running toward us. He said there's a halftrack coming. So we thought, "Halftrack, boy oh boy, where is she?" Big Andy was my driver. He eased the tank back off of the road.

A fellow named Ted Duskin was my gunner. He swings the gun out, and lays it up the road. And through this smoky haze that the fire is making, here comes this German, but it ain't no halftrack. It's one of the big tanks. And I just remember thinking, "God, this is gonna hurt." Because he saw us I'm sure as soon as we saw him. Ted shot right away, as soon as that bulk came through the haze, and he must have hit the turret, there was a big shower of sparks. They were heavily armored in the front, and they were only really vulnerable in the rear.

About a second after we fired, he fired, and a big lick of flame came out of the muzzle of the gun, and it hit our tank. It seemed to hit it down low in the carriage, it made a hell of a sound, and suddenly, the German began to move backward into the smoke. How lucky can you be? We quickly took a look at our tank, and one of the bogey wheels appeared to be almost severed. He hit us down low. It glanced off, fortunately for us, and with the track still being intact, Andy could ease her back, and we eased her back down that slope, and this German didn't come after us. But talk about being scared, before he made that first shot. ... They had the firepower. They could penetrate us; we couldn't penetrate them until we got a larger gun.

After we backed down, around a little curve in the road there was a little rock wall, and there was enough room for us to get in there. Ahead of us, against the same rock wall, was a tank destroyer. They had light armor, but they had a bigger gun than we had, so they could knock out a German tank, which we couldn't. So as soon as we got behind the destroyer, I ran out and told the destroyer's tank commander what was probably going to be coming down the road, so he could get a good shot at it. The German doesn't know the tank destroyer is here.

First thing you know, we could hear little click-clicks. That's about all the noise their tracks made, click-click, they were real quiet. We would make lots of noise, and we'd give ourselves away. He's coming down here, and he has a dismounted soldier leading him. Imagine having that as your job, because this guy's dead the first time he's seen. But he's gonna take the fire and spare the tank. So this foot soldier comes down here with a rifle, and as the tank creeps up behind him, the guy in the tank destroyer fired too soon. It went right across the front of him, missed him, and with that, the Germans threw it in reverse, and went back up the hill. And of course the tank destroyer didn't go after him because he couldn't afford to take a hit, he would lose. But I think Andy and I were genuinely scared, when we saw that halftrack turn into a big German tank.

Claude Pittman

We landed in Normandy on June 28th. We were under some fire, but the beach was pretty secure. I was back over there a few years ago, and now I tell people I was on

Normandy beach on June the 6th, but I don't tell 'em what year. I'm just kidding about that. But we did go back over and were on the beach on June the 6th.

I'd rather be in a tank than in the infantry. I was sorry for the infantry boys. I was so thankful that I was in a tank, for I felt safer in a tank than in the infantry. But after getting a tank shot out from under me, I was a lot scareder from then on than I was before.

It was early one morning. We'd knocked out a German tank within twenty feet of our tank the night before. We'd set it on fire, and it set there and burned. Then the next morning they started pulling tanks in on us, and it was just shoot them and they shot us. I don't know how many we got of them or they got of us.

A shell ricocheted off my tank. It never did penetrate, it just ricocheted off, enough to set the tank on fire. That's how I got burned. Just the exposed skin on my face and hands got burned. Where I had clothing on didn't get burned, but I got first and second and third degree burns on my hands and face. That was in August.

When I got wounded I didn't have sense enough to be scared, I hadn't been at it long enough. I guess after I got back, I was scared. I've seen the time I was shaking all over, when we'd get artillery firing.

CHAPTER 21

Pfaffenheck

March 16, 1945

"I haven't much to tell, except that I have joined an outfit," Private Billy P. Wolfe wrote in a letter to his family dated March 5, 1945. "As a lieutenant told us, 'The best goddamned outfit in the world.'

"I don't know much about its history as yet, but it played a major part in smashing the Siegfried Line and has fought since D-Day and drove the Nazis from France. It is the 712th Tank Battalion. I am in Company C and in Germany now. ..."

Billy Paige Wolfe was a fresh-faced kid of 18 who grew up in Edinburg, Va., on the banks of the Shenandoah River. He had a small collection of Indian flints and Civil War bullets that he picked up working in the cornfields, and he loved to fish and hunt, although the first time he had an opportunity to shoot a deer, he couldn't bring himself to pull the trigger.

"If I were to be blind after today," Billy wrote in a high school essay, "I would want to go off by myself in the mountain, climb to the highest cliff, and look out across the valley at the towns, farms and farmhouses.

"I would want to picture each native tree in my mind, the rough bark and the shapely green leaves.

"I would want to see the squirrels running and leaping from one walnut tree to another, and the birds flying.

"I would like to see the deer run and jump swiftly and gracefully and leap across the fences, and lie in a tree that leans across the water and watch bass laying under the rocks and dart out after a fly.

"I would go through the house from one room to the other picturing each piece of furniture, every corner and everything, in my mind.

"I would like to see all my sisters, brother and parents together as we were, and picture each as they look for future reference."

Although there were seven Wolfe children -- five girls and two boys -- there was a special bond between Billy and his two younger sisters, twins Maxine and Madeline. Billy was two years their senior, but because he broke his hip one year and came down with pneumonia another, he was in the same class with them at Edinburg High School.

When his brother Hubert was drafted, Billy tried to enlist in the Army Air Corps, but was turned down. Maxine and Madeline do not know the precise reason why, but Madeline says "he wanted to get in so bad he didn't know what to do."

Billy was drafted on Aug. 23, 1944, and went to Fort Mead, Md. From there he was sent to Fort Knox and trained as a tanker.

He wrote home faithfully, describing the chow that was to put 15 pounds on him before he was sent overseas, asking about his friends, requesting his swimming trunks and more stationery, chiding the twins about their weight, and sprinkling his letters with words like "damn" and "hell," knowing full well that they would cause his mother, Anna May Wolfe, who taught Sunday School, to have a conniption.

Billy sent one of the twins a small pin in the shape of a tank. "Dear Madeline," he wrote, "Here is your pin. Take care of it, and no boys are to wear it. Also I want a big letter of thanks, understand? That costed me a big pile of money, you old soak. You never write. Maxine does. Well, don't be too bad, now. I am in a hurry. So long, Love Bill."

Billy came home on leave before going overseas. On Jan. 30, 1945, the twins walked him up the mile-long country road to Route 11, where he caught the Greyhound bus.

"He walked between us and there was snow on the ground," Maxine Wolfe Zirkle says. "I'll never forget. That snow lay for it seemed like weeks, and every day, when we went to school, we would walk in his tracks. That's how sentimental we were."

"When he left," Madeline Wolfe Litten says, "he said 'So long, kids, and if I never see you again, goodbye.' And he waved all the way down the road."

"Twins, I think you are having a birthday soon. Sweet 17, isn't that right?" Billy wrote in the March 5 letter. "You can be glad you are not boys, or there would be a possibility of you getting in this mess, although I don't think, and hope, it won't last that long. Happy birthday, Twins, and many, many returns of the day..."

The letter arrived on the morning of March 16, 1945. With the time difference, it was afternoon in Pfaffenheck, Germany, a small town east of the Moselle River and west of the Rhine. Billy Wolfe's tank, which was hit by an armor-piercing shell, had been burning for several hours.

Bob Rossi

After my tank was knocked out at Habscheid, I was assigned temporarily to the second platoon. This is March of '45.

One day I'm on guard duty, the early hours of the morning, and I'm looking all around -- we're parked alongside the houses in this town -- and these German soldiers are coming out of the woods with some girls, and I whisper, "Everybody up, Krauts! Krauts!"

With that, Martin [Otha Martin], who was the gunner, he pushes me down, and he gets up and starts firing his tommy gun at them.

Otha Martin

Sergeant Otha Martin, from Leguire, Okla., was a tank commander in C Company, Second Platoon.

We had just made our second crossing of the Moselle River. We crossed it under artificial moonlight -- which they made by bouncing huge lights off the clouds -- on a treadway bridge, and went on to a village that I can't tell you the name of. We pulled in before daybreak, and were lined up.

Just as it began to break day, there was a bunch of haystacks stuck out there, and the Germans were in 'em. They began to come out of there, and there's one running toward Number 3 tank, that Lloyd Heyward was the tank commander on. That's the tank that Billy Wolfe was in.

I'm in Number 5 as the gunner that day. I was normally a tank commander, but Jack Sheppard had said, "We've got a man here who can do that but I don't know if he knows a damn thing about a gun or not, would you be the gunner in 5?" I said "Yeah."

So we pulled in there, and Bob Rossi was on guard; he was the loader that day. I was sitting on the gunner's seat, kind of dozing, and he just had his head up out of there.

Several years ago, when we had a reunion in Orlando, Rossi said to me, "I'm lucky to be here."

I said, "How come?"

He said, "I thought you were gonna kill me."

I said, "We never had no problem."

"Oh, no," he said. "But that one time you jerked me out of that hatch up there and slammed me against the wall of the tank, I thought you were gonna kill me." Well, that tank wall is solid steel. Here's what he was doing: He hadn't been with us so long, but he was saying, "Heinies, Heinies." He saw 'em. But he wasn't doing anything. So I grabbed him and I jerked him out of that hatch so I could get up there, and I had a Thompson sub laying on the radio. I slammed him down into the tank, and I got up in there, and that German was running, he had a long overcoat on and it was flopping. I started to work on him with that Thompson sub. Well, they'd always said if you could shoot a man anywhere, even in the hand, with a .45 it'd knock him down. That's not true. I like to cut that one in two with .45 slugs and he finally did fall behind the tank, and Hayward hollered at me, "You got the sonofabitch." He was going to our tank, I don't know if he intended to throw a grenade in there or what.

So we stayed there. We moved up and had a little firefight, it wasn't real bad, and got that under control and stayed there that day and that night.

Sometime before daylight the next morning, on the 16th of March, somebody come after us. The infantry had tried to take Pfaffenheck and got treated bad. There was a crossroads there, and an SS outfit was holding the crossroads. It was troops from the SS Mountain Division.

Snuffy Fuller [Lieutenant Francis A. Fuller] wouldn't move. He said, "When it's daylight, we'll move. But we're not moving in the dark."

Byrl Rudd

Byrl E. Rudd, from Elmer, Okla., was the platoon sergeant in C Company, Second Platoon. I did not interview Rudd, who passed away in 1993. The following is from a letter he wrote in 1986 to Ray Griffin, who had asked him for details of the action at Pfaffenheck.

Having crossed the Moselle River, we spent most or all of the day clearing the high ground on the east bank. There were two companies of infantry with the second platoon of 712th, Company C (me) as support for either infantry company that might happen upon a machine gun nest. The Germans were backing up, supposedly, for a last stand at the Rhine River. We were giving them plenty of time because our left flank was lagging behind. From the sound of rifle fire, they were meeting more resistance than we were.

We moved slowly eastward all day. About sundown, we hit a spot of open terrain. This area was three to four miles square.

On our right flank, the trees extended to a small village approximately two miles ahead, so there was no problem to get there with cover all the way. This village was Edenhausen. A little farther east and one to one and a half miles north was another village, Pfaffenheck.

After a powwow, Snuffy Fuller informed the infantry companies that the tanks would not be split. One infantry company would occupy each town for the night, with all tanks in the higher town of Edenhausen. A blacktop road ran north and south on the east of these two towns, and there was not one building on the east side of the road. There were tall pine trees 25 yards or less east of the road, and on our left flank buddies were still progressing too slow for me.

So here we are, mission accomplished. Two towns exposed to a blacktop road and miles of tall pines. I checked to see if all the tanks had a good field of fire and where the infantry outposts were. Nothing to worry about. The Germans have crossed the Rhine. WRONG!

Guards are out. The infantry is bedding down. Lieutenant Fuller looks out. I am looking out. He looks at me and I at him. Nothing is said. I feel like ducks on a pond, and so does he. Good houses to sleep in, but I am up making a noise. Guys are griping. Then, about 2 a.m., I hear people running near the rear of the town. I jump on my tank and listen. An infantry guard stops them. All are excited. They wake the officers and convince them of a horrible massacre in Pfaffenheck. Those boys, five or six of them, are the only survivors of the company. The infantry officers are furious and want to attack right away. Lieutenant Fuller and I have a powwow. We present our plan to avoid the road and attack five tanks abreast with the infantry on the back of the tanks across the open ground at full speed to the apple orchard. The time would be just at sunup. We are hoping that the big guns would be looking at the blacktop road. Plan accepted and carried out.

The apple orchard was full of SS troops. All had American guns. The second section soon cleared the orchard and three houses on the left side of the street for the infantry. I then had to go forward to get a field of fire down the street. It curved or made a couple of angles. The infantry was taking a beating, which I thought was coming from the right side of the street.

There was no big stuff up to now. At the first intersection, I saw Lieutenant Fuller moving and firing at the second intersection. I saw him stop. We were both firing across the blacktop road into the tall pines that were thick with Germans. We had them running, I thought.

Lieutenant Fuller's tank was hit by an antitank gun. He got out and made it to the buildings. About the time he got there and looked back, Lloyd Hayward came out of the top hatch. One of his legs was limp. Lieutenant Fuller started after him. Machine gun fire stopped him.

The fifth tank was not able to fire in that direction. I jumped out to go get Lieutenant Fuller while my gunner kept them pinned down across the road. I got Lieutenant Fuller to go back down the street to find a medic. I found Russell Harris, the tank commander, was slowly dying from a bullet that had just grazed the top of his head while he was in the orchard. The medic told me his life might be saved if we could get him to a hospital within four hours. The boys had got him out of the tank. He seemed to be in no pain. They tried to get to him with a jeep, but the SS drove them back. They tried later with a halftrack, and the SS drove them back again. While I was there, I learned that the driver of the No. 2 tank had been killed about 50 yards after leaving the orchard. This man was Jack Mantell. Those SS troops were tough.

Being under strength going into this action, the infantry company was very slim in men able for combat. I had seen their officer killed. Upon getting back to my tank, I found the roof of the house that was protecting me to be on fire. Lots of the SS were moving around in the pines. I decided to try the antitank gun again. He was still there, and he knew where I was. Time to try something else.

The field artillery had been firing all day, but their shells were going too far to help me. I went to find an infantry non-commissioned officer who knew where the phones were. He would not call the field artillery, so I called someone and got to talk to the field artillery fairly soon. He finally agreed to bracket one gun. The first shell hit between me and the No. 5 tank. I told him to raise it 200 feet. Since the two tanks were the only men near the road, he agreed, with a promise to pull it down if the SS tried to come back into town.

The field artillery went on until an hour or more after dark. The SS had quit shooting at us. They were still milling around in the trees across the road.

After doing my job on the ground, I got back in the tank. The roof had fallen in on the house protecting me from at least one antitank gun. While trying to get my nerve up to try him one more time, I noticed that the one rifleman to my right was not an infantry man but was a tanker. This man was Aaron C. Brown, who had gotten out of No. 5 tank and had picked up a rifle and came up where my tank was. Standing at the corner of the house, he picked off several SS men when they moved from one tree to another.

After more than an hour of field artillery fire, I got nervy and decided to try to get one more shot at that antitank gun. He knew what I would do and was waiting. If I had pulled out one more inch, he would have gotten my gun shield. Then I tried backing up again, but the space between the two houses was too wide. He would have gotten two shots at me. There were probably two of them, anyway.

After dark, I got my tank backed up to the disabled crews. I organized three tank crews ready to go full-strength. Then with the few infantry boys left, we set up our defense for the night.

I called the field artillery again. I told them our position and said that I would tell them, if the SS tried to reenter the town, to shell the east half of the town.

We had accomplished our mission. However, at dark there were a lot more men on the other side of the road than there were on our side, so every man pulled guard all night long. We got no information or instructions from anyone all day or that night. The medics finished what they could do by about 2 a.m. (too late for Harris).

The next morning, the first thing we saw move was 12 or 15 American tanks coming down the blacktop road from Edenhausen toward us like they were on a pleasure cruise going to Koblenz. When they stopped, we found that everything movable in the woods was gone. There had been two antitank guns where Lieutenant Fuller was firing when he was hit. One was knocked out, I'm sure by Lieutenant Fuller. The other had been towed away.

That morning we were informed that 3,200 SS troops were in the woods when we attacked. It scares me to think what might have been had we attacked down the blacktop road that morning.

I'm almost sure about the fourth boy killed in Pfaffenheck, but I will check with Wes Harrell. He was the driver of Snuffy's tank. Three boys were wounded, but I don't remember who they were, either.

Otha Martin

It wasn't far to Pfaffenheck from this little village, maybe three kilometers. We moved across country abreast, not in a column, and Number 3 tank was the first one hit. I don't know if Number 1 or Number 2 was hit next, but Number 3 was hit first. It was in an orchard. We went through the little town, but the Germans had dug in on the road and had their guns camouflaged, and they knocked out Number 3. And they cut Heyward's leg off below the knee, I remember him holding it and dragging it with him. He got out on the ground, and they cut him down, they machine-gunned him on the ground.

Billy Wolfe, the shell hit him somewhere in the midsection, and he burned in the tank. He was dead. Heyward is on the ground dead.

Wes Harrell, who was from Stonewall, Oklahoma, and lives in Hobbs, New Mexico now, he was the driver. He got out. And the bow gunner was a little Chinese boy named Moy. Koon L. Moy. We called him Chop Chop. He got out. And the gunner was John Clingerman. He got out without a scratch. But then he got on Snuffy's tank. The reason I know that was the first tank hit is because Snuffy's tank wasn't hit yet. Clingerman got on it, and when it was hit he lost an eye. And it killed Jack Mantell. He was the loader in Snuffy's tank.

In that crew, Carl Grey was the driver, a Mexican boy named Guadalupe Valdivia from Topeka, Kansas, was the bow gunner, and he wasn't hurt. The gunner was Russell Loop, he lives at Indianola, Illinois, he's a farmer. Jack Mantell was the loader, and he was killed. The shell came through the gun shield.

Snuffy was the tank commander and lieutenant, the platoon leader. So that's 1 and 3. Now Number 2 tank -- which was my tank, but I was the gunner in Number 5 tank that day -- they put a man in there that had come in fresh from Fort Knox named Russell Harris, and he was one of these gung-ho type fellows, he told me the first time I saw him, "I'm not afraid of the damn Germans. They'll not make me pull my head in."

I told him, "Harris. You're a fool. These people here, they're not necessarily afraid of the Germans, but they respect them. They're good soldiers. They'll kill you. If they shoot your head off, you're done. But as long as you can stick your head back out and fight again, you're worth something."

Well, that's just what he did. He never pulled his head in and they shot him in the head with a 40-millimeter gun.

There had been only four men to begin with in that tank. John Zimmer was supposed to be the loader, but he had gone to the medics back across the river, and he wasn't there. The driver was Leroy Campbell from Meridien, Mississippi. The bow gunner was Lloyd Seal, but he had got up to be the loader in the turret in John's place. And the gunner was Clarence Rosen, he was from Ogilvie, Minnesota, and one of the top-notch gunners, too.

Now that's three tanks gone. That just left 4 and 5. I was in 5. Byrl Rudd was platoon sergeant, and he was in the No. 4 tank. Well, the Germans had him hemmed in behind a house with a big dug-in gun up there, camouflaged.

So he's hemmed in up there. That just left the Number 5 tank. And we were the only one that could move. The Germans tried for the whole day to come back across the highway, but they never did get back. But I burned the barrel out of a .30-caliber air-cooled machine gun, we changed barrels. I never counted them, but we stacked up a whole bunch of SS troops.

Although we just had two tanks left, the next morning we moved out with three, and I never knew where the third tank came from until the reunion at Niagara Falls [in 1987], and Snuffy Fuller was there. I said, "I've thought about this for a lot of years, I want to know where we got the third tank to move out."

Snuffy said Sheppard got it from A Company. And that answered that. But he came to me that day and said, "Say, do you want to be my gunner today?"

I said, "I ain't put in no application for it but I will." So we put Loop over in Number 5, and Rudd's tank was still intact. And we moved out with three tanks, and moved down through the woods. The Germans had pulled out in the night, took their guns with them. And we pulled through the woods, out on a point of a ridge and could look across the Rhine.

That's the 16th day of March that the fight was in Pfaffenheck. Billy Wolfe was killed. Russell Harris was killed. Lloyd Hayward was killed, and Jack Mantell was killed. And we lost three tanks.

Russell Loop

We went across an open pasture and got into this town. We were staying behind buildings. We pulled around the buildings and got on the road, where this 75-millimeter gun was just across the road and down, and I could never get that thing in my sight. It was too low down. I couldn't get my gun down. I never could get it down that far. I could have knocked that silly thing out, saved a lot of trouble, if I could have got my gun down. But I couldn't do it.

Then they started firing a lot of footballs [panzerfausts], we called them. So we had to back out of there. We backed out, and thought we could pull around behind these buildings and then come in facing them. Well, that was a mistake. They'd already knocked two tanks out there and we pulled out and we were the third. But ours would still move. So we backed around behind a building, and Snuffy and I went out to pick up one of the boys that had both of his feet shot off, one of the other tank commanders. He had managed to crawl down over the back of the tank, and we got out there, and got him up between us, but they hit him about a half a dozen times right between us. So we let him back down and took off pretty quick.

That gun crew that knocked our tanks out, I went into a building with the infantry, after we couldn't get that sergeant back, I went up with the infantry and I went to an upstairs room. I had an old M-1 rifle, and got me a chair, and I sat down in it, and I picked them suckers off one by one. Every one of 'em.

I think Jack Mantell was just about the closest buddy I had over there. Just a night or two before he got hit, we were setting in a house, and Jack said, "I'll make a deal with you." He had a wife and a little boy. And he said, "If I get killed, will you go tell my wife and little boy what happened? Exactly."

And I said, "Well, I'll make you a deal the same way. Will you go tell my folks?"

And I reckon that was about, he was about the closest, really. I did go and tell her. She lived in Milwaukee, Wisconsin. Took me a while to get the nerve up, but I did go tell her, finally.

Before we moved up to Pfaffenheck, Jack was standing guard outside a house. He was a replacement, and I thought I had him on the stick. A shell came in, and the house had a tile roof. It hit a corner of the house, and some of the flak went through his helmet, cut a pretty good gash in his head. I said, "Jack, this is your chance. Say your head's killing you. Get the heck out of here." Another quarter of a mile and he was gone.

Francis Fuller

I did not interview Lieutenant Fuller for this book. The following is a letter that he wrote to Hubert Wolfe.

"To PFC Hubert L. Wolfe Jr.[1], Company M, 310 Infantry, APO 78, 14 July, 1945,

I hardly know how to start this letter, as you don't even know who I am. Anyway, Lieutenant Seeley, the adjutant of our battalion, received a letter from you asking the facts about your brother, Billy Wolfe. As I was his platoon leader and was there when he was killed, he has asked me to try to give you the information you requested.

Captain Sheppard has already written your mother, but perhaps he has not told her exactly how he died. But I am trusting that since you are a soldier, I can tell you the true facts, and then perhaps you can tell your folks what you think they ought to know.

To start off, our battalion has been attached to the 90th Infantry Division since July 3rd, 1944, which as you probably know is in the Third Army. My platoon, the second platoon of C Company, 712th Tank Battalion, was attached to the second battalion of the 357th Infantry Regiment.

[1]When Billy Wolfe was killed, his company commander sent the family a letter saying that he was buried in Germany. Further inquiry by the family brought a letter from the War Department saying Billy had not been seen to leave the tank. Hubert Wolfe never showed this letter to anybody in his family. As he lay daying of cancer in 1980, Hubert told his sisters where the letter was and that they should read it. He passed away the next day.

Your brother joined my platoon on the 4th of March while we were driving to the Rhine River, following up the 11th Armored Division. We drove to a town called Mayen, and then changed direction and started driving to the Moselle for the second time.

On the evening of March 14, we crossed the Moselle and found that the infantry that had preceded us had gotten into a jam and lost over half of their men and gotten cut off, so we were called upon to rescue them.

We succeeded in reaching the town where they were, and cleared it okay, and stayed there the rest of the day, and stayed there the night of the 15th. Then, on the morning of the 16th, we were told to attack the town of Pfaffenheck, which was about 2,000 yards north of where we were. The TDs started into the town first, but as they rolled over the crest of a hill, the lead tank destroyer was knocked out by an antitank gun. They withdrew, and succeeded in knocking out the gun and another.

We were then ordered to try to enter the town, and by going down a draw, I managed to get into the east side of the town.

Your brother was in No. 2 tank[1], which was commanded by Sergeant Hayward, with Johnny Clingerman as gunner, William Harrell as driver, Koon Moy as bow gunner, and your brother as loader.

As I said, all of the tanks got into the town okay except No. 3, which encountered a 40-millimeter AA gun, which killed the tank commander.

We took all but three houses, when the infantry got stopped by firing from the woods east of the town. In order to knock out the gun that was holding up the infantry, the tanks started to move out to get a firing position. I sent the second section along the backs of the houses, while I took the first section into an orchard. My tank was in the lead, and the tank your brother was in was on my left flank, slightly behind.

Just after we had passed an opening between two houses, my loader told me No. 2 tank had been hit. I looked over, and the men were piling out, and the tank was blazing. The shot had went through the right sponson, puncturing the gas tank.

I didn't know then how many men had gotten out, so I tried to get my tank into position to rescue the men, but as I moved into position, my tank received a direct hit through the gun shield, killing my loader. Fortunately for the rest of us, my driver was able to move the tank before the Heinies could fire again.

After giving Clingerman first aid and getting the rest of the boys calmed down, I took my gunner with me and we crawled out to where Sergeant Hayward lay wounded. I found that he would have to have a stretcher to be moved. I went back to get the medics, and then I learned from the rest of the crew that your brother never got out of the tank. As the tank was burning all this time, we could not get near it. I don't know if you have ever

[1]Otha Martin calls this the No. 3 tank. Although some details, such as the manner in which Lloyd Hayward and Russell Harris were killed, vary in the differing accounts, I have left them they way they were remembered.

seen one of our tanks burn, but when 180 gallons of gas start burning, and ammunition starts to explode, the best thing to do is keep away.

When I got the medics back out to Sergeant Hayward, I found he had been killed by a sniper. The other section of tanks finally took care of the Heinies, and we secured the town.

Your brother's tank continued to burn all that night, but in the morning we were able to go out to investigate. We determined that your brother had been killed instantly, as the shell had hit right above his seat. There was nothing visible but a few remnants of bones that were so badly burned that if they had been touched, they would have turned to ashes.

As for personal effects, you could not recognize anything because the intense heat and the exploding ammunition had fused most of the metal parts together.

The accident was reported to the GRO of the 357th, and as we moved on to the Rhine the next day, I didn't think anything more about it until two weeks ago when I received a letter from the Third Army asking for information. I sincerely trust that by this time they have everything straightened out. If you ever get into the neighborhood of that town, the

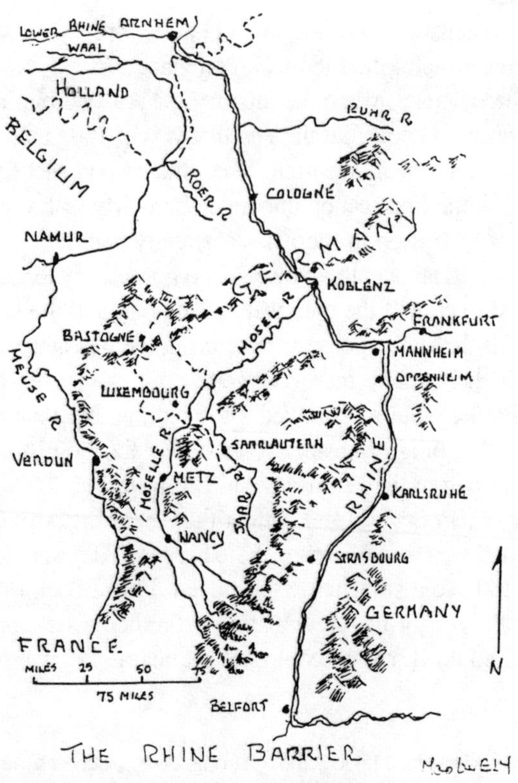

REPRINTED WITH PERMISSION FROM "WAR FROM THE GROUND UP" BY JOHN COLBY

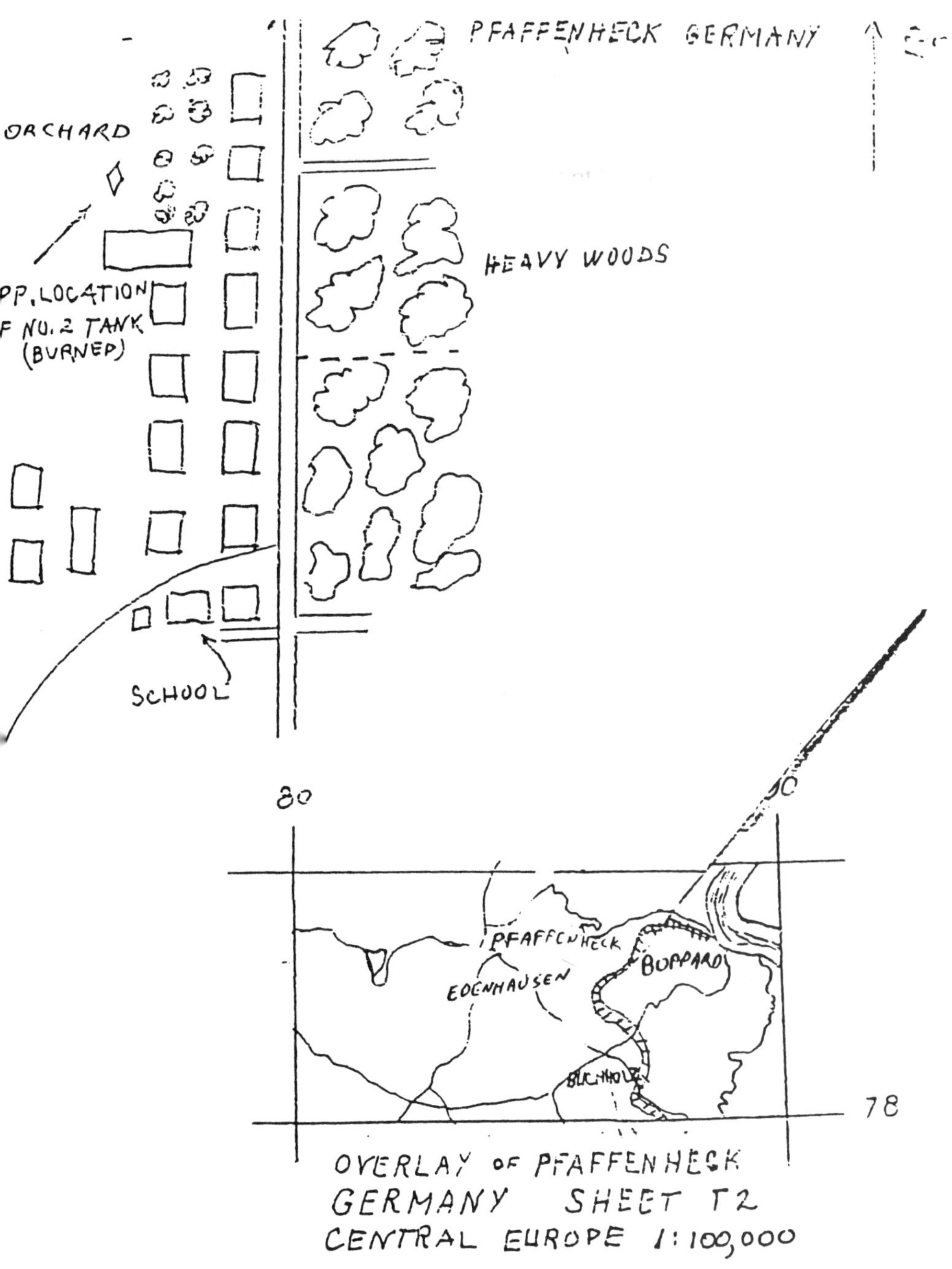

SKETCH BY FRANCIS FULLER

tank may still be there. The town of Pfaffenheck is about 13 miles south of Koblenz on the main autobahn that runs straight down that peninsula formed by the Rhine and the upper Moselle.

Maybe I have told you more than I ought to, but I really would like to help you in any way that I can. Your brother was very well liked by all the rest of the crew, but he was so doggone quiet that we hardly ever knew he was around. Of the other members of his crew, William Harrell is still with me, as is Koon Moy. Clingerman lost his eye and had his legs filled with shrapnel and is now back in the States. That was the worst day I had in combat. I lost three tanks, had four men killed and three wounded. But that is the way things went. It might be interesting to you that in the town there were seven anti-tank guns, one 40-millimeter antiaircraft gun, plus plenty of determined SS troops. We counted 92 dead Germans and had 23 prisoners.

I am enclosing a snap one of the boys took which has your brother on it. I will also try to draw a sketch of the town, so if you ever get there you can find the place.

Incidentally, you will have to use your judgment as to how much of this story you want to pass on to your mother.

Don't forget, if I can be of any further help to you, I will be more than glad to hear from you at any time. There is no use in trying to tell you how sorry I feel, because you have been through the same things yourself, so I'll just say so long and good luck.

-- Francis A. Fuller, First Lieutenant

Otha Martin

Billy Wolfe and Jack Mantell came to us the same time, they were just youngsters. The first or second day they got there, they were talking to me. They were concerned about how they'd do in combat. I said, "Boys, I don't know how you'll do. But the fact that you're concerned about it, I believe you'll be all right." Well, they both got killed in just ten or twelve days, but they didn't get killed because they were bad soldiers. If a man had been there twenty years he'd have got killed if he was in their spot. When one of those big shells hits you, you're dead, it's not your fault either, you just don't weather that.

CHAPTER 22

Buddies

Wayne Hissong

Wayne Hissong, from Argos, Ind., was a sergeant in Service Company.

When I went into the service, there were four of us went in together. One of the fellows, John Charles Mitchell, he and I graduated from high school together. He was in B Company, I was in Service Company. We went through everything, we got overseas, and he was one of the first ones in the battalion to get killed.

His mother wrote me, I don't know, two or three letters overseas and wanted me to detail to her what happened. But your letters were censored, you couldn't tell much. And I really couldn't tell her too much anyway.

Then when I got home, my dad met me at the railroad station, about 2 in the afternoon, and we went to our house, in the little town of Argos, Indiana. Then we went to my brother's house.

After awhile, I said, "Well, I'm gonna go uptown, Dad," and he said, "I'll go with you."

On my way uptown, he says, "Now, I want to tell you, Mitchell's mother is waiting for you."

She worked in a dry goods store on the corner. There was no way I could get around her, absolutely no way, hell, I could have went forty different ways and she could still see me, and I'm walking down the street, and boy, here she comes across the street.

She wanted to know how it happened. And man, I could just tell her so much.

He was a tank driver. At one time, he was considered one of the best tank drivers there was in our battalion. As I understand it, they came around a bend in a road that was blind on his side...and he was engaged to a girl in England, and had written to his mother that he had gotten engaged, and his mother got the ring, and his sister sent the girl a wedding gown.

Seeing his mother was about the hardest thing I had to do.

Smoky Stuever

Shorty was my buddy in the cavalry down on the Mexican border. We'd go to town together with some other fellows. A lot of times we hitchhiked a ride. We were 50 miles east of San Diego on the Mexican border, in a very remote area, there was no bus transportation available. If the trucks weren't going into San Diego you had to find a ride there and back, and you had to make sure you got back on time, because we were under scrutiny of some old time sergeants that served in the Philippine campaign and the Cuban campaign. They were very rigid.

Shorty [Marion Kubeczko] and I stayed together through the cavalry. Also Kenny Wallace from Southern Illinois. There were some other fellows that we buddied with, but the three of us from Illinois, we always managed to stay together, and we were in the same tank crew together, Wallace, Kubeczko and me. We were joined by Eugene Sand of Nebraska, and Patsy Barchetta and Ed Chieleski. That was my recovery crew.

Shorty was an eager driver. When we were leaving England, we brought up the tail end of the column, and we had to repair a flat tire on a truck. It only took us five minutes but it made us drop way back and we had to try and catch up. Well, the truck could catch up, but we didn't. We kind of dropped back, but we were going at top speed, and when the MPs realized who we were, they made a sudden right turn in the middle of this town, and Shorty made this turn at high speed but he couldn't stay on the street, he went through a cemetery. We went right over the graves.

Shorty was killed on Hill 122. We were sent to retrieve a tank that was knocked out, and as we were going up the hill we encountered a heavy mortar barrage. I heard this one coming right at me, and I ducked, because my chest was about ten inches from where it exploded. It hit the front end of my turret, and Shorty didn't have his cover down. He had it wide open, and he was down under, using the periscope. And the base of the shell went through his right shoulder and came out his abdomen, and shrapnel flew all around in the front end of the tank.

Shorty was laying on the accelerator, going up the hill in low gear. And the tank retriever was headed right for a big pile of gas cans. I steered it out of the way, trying to shut that darn thing off. I shut the master switch off and that damn thing kept running. By that time, a paratrooper grabbed me by the feet and pulled me off of that tank and said, "He's gone. Let him go." He shoved me down in a foxhole and I said, "Get off of me, I need some air." As soon as he let me go, I ran up there and got on that darn tank, and all around the turret was burning. I pulled the fire extinguisher and put the fire out inside, and then it dawned on me: Ground the damn magnetos. And so I ground the magnetos, and it killed the engine. The engine was going at top speed in low gear, and we were going to the top of the hill.

Then I helped them take Shorty out of there, and gave them his belongings. And then this colonel that was in charge of that operation, he was from the airborne group [the 82nd

Airborne], he said, "Let's get this damn tank off of this road, who can drive a tank around here?" Well, they had me down on the side of the road, trying to give me a morphine shot, and I wouldn't take it. So I said, "That's my tank, and I'll get that damn thing out of here." And I made a U-turn with sparks flying in every direction.

That night, the Germans were laying some mortar fire on us, and Tony Skolarus gets up out of his foxhole and he goes out in the middle of the field, and he says, "Come on, you Germans, kill me. You got Shorty," so I grabbed him and shoved him down in a hole, and he says, "What can we do? What can we do?" And I said, "Start praying, that's what your mother's doing."

We had a guy in the other tank retriever, that was on the other side of this open field, his name was Whitehead. He was an atheist. He was always in arguments with Kenny Wallace about religion. Back in California they would argue and I would get in trouble because they're arguing after hours, and at Fort Benning, all over, those two were always arguing about religion. Kenny Wallace would always get into these religious discussions with many people, wherever he went. I admired him. He was quite an evangelist. I could never shut him up.

So when Whitehead woke up that next morning, he says, "I want everybody to hear me. I prayed last night."

Tony D'Arpino

One of the drivers in Lieutenant Flowers' platoon was a guy named Paul Farrell. He came from Haverhill, Mass. A handsome guy, had red hair, he was married. We were very friendly because we both came from the Boston area. When we were at Fort Benning, we used to go to the bars together.

Farrell was in the first platoon, and I was in the third platoon, so we didn't get to see each other that often.

We came together one day, and I asked for Paul Farrell, and one of the guys says to me, "He's sitting in the tank, he won't get out." So I go over, I drop myself down into the assistant driver's seat, and he says, "Hi."

I said, "What's the matter?"

He says, "We ain't gonna get out of this alive."

I said, "You really believe that?"

He said, "Yeah."

I said, "If I thought that," I says, "I'd get up, take off. Go back. Over the hill." I said, "You're gonna get out of it alive, don't worry about it."

"Nooo," he says. "Never."

That was the last time I ever saw him. And that guy there, even in the States, when we had guard mount, they always used to give a 24-hour pass to the best-dressed. The best informed. Best-dressed, Farrell got it every time. He was just made for uniform, he had the build, the shirt fit just perfectly, like a model.

I can remember, we had a young kid -- young kid, we were all young kids -- the loader on our tank was Luigi Gramari, he came from Utica, New York, and he was probably a year and a half younger than I was. And we had the honor to go back up Hill 122 after Flowers got knocked out, we were gonna go up there and take it.

We were in Lieutenant Lombardi's tank, and Gramari threw a tirade. "You stupid sonofabitch," he's saying, now Gramari, he weighed about 110 pounds, he says to Lieutenant Lombardi, "You're gonna go up, all the goddamn first platoon just got killed and you're gonna go up there?"

I grabbed him, I said, "Get in the tank, will you, and be quiet." He'd heard about all these guys that, you know, and now we're going to go do the same thing, how crazy can you be? He was telling Lombardi, but Lombardi was taking his orders from the infantry.

It was getting dark, and Gramari thought we were going to go right then and there, but we waited until the next morning. By the next morning everything turned out pretty good, we made out all right.

Louis Gerrard

Harold Gentle and I were both from Philadelphia, but I didn't know him before the war.

The day I was drafted, we were down at the Reading Terminal, and we got on the train. He said, "Is this seat taken?" and he sat beside me. And from then on, we were buddy-buddy.

From there, we went to New Cumberland, Pennsylvania, where we got all our shots, and the next day we were put on trains, and everybody said we were going to Florida. The guys looked out the window, they said they saw palm trees.

They asked me when I went in the service, at New Cumberland, what would you like to go into? I told them I'd like to get in the Air Corps. They said, "Okay." The next day I was in tanks.

Fort Benning, Georgia, that's where the palm trees were. We were all in tanks.

We were in Benning for over a year. Gentle and I, we really hit it off. I was an usher at his wedding, in Manionk. He married somebody from Philadelphia. We both got furloughs, and he married her on the furlough. Her cousin was an ensign, and he had to be the best man. Gentle wanted me to be the best man, but she wanted the ensign. He said to me, "Would you mind?" He fought like hell with his wife, he wanted me to be the best man. I said, "Harold, don't do that, I'll just be an usher, I don't care." So I was an usher.

After they were married, we were in Fort Jackson, and she came down and stayed with him.

Her mother was a pain in the neck. One time Gentle's wife was on the phone with him, she says, "My mother wants to come down," to Fort Jackson, oh, he got on his hands and knees and prayed, and said, "No, please don't have her come down." I was there watching him on the phone. So she never came down.

Gentle's wife remarried, I found out. When I got back from overseas I went over to see her in Roxboro. I went over there, and the father-in-law, he understood, I told him what happened. He said, "They were all killed in a tank?" He was classified as being missing in action. But they were all killed in that tank. They were all ablaze, and they can't get out of them tanks.

Bob Anderson

Generally when you were up on the line all you got to eat was what we called C rations, but then when you got back for a 10-day rest you'd do most anything. There was one time a bunch of us guys was having fun, we'd throw hand grenades in the creek, they'd go off underwater and we'd get fish, clean the fish and eat them.

Then we got crazy enough we were taking and unscrewing the cap of the grenades and knocking all the powder out, and then we'd pull the pin and toss them over to somebody. Well, I did that to one kid whose name was Bynum, I said, "Here, Quentin Bynum," well, I didn't have all the powder out so the thing exploded. It didn't have strength enough to hurt him but that made us quit doing that stuff. He could have got hit in the face.

One thing I'll say about the outfit I was in, we grew up as a group of men that stayed together. I can list several of us that stayed together and went through the 10th Armored, and went to the 712th Tank Battalion, we fought together and we came home together. Earl Apgar lives up here in Rockford, Illinois. Jule Braatz lives in Beaver Dam, Wisconsin. And there were several boys out of Chicago, we all stayed together after we got out. We became like brothers.

Quentin Bynum, shucks, him and I we fought and had one heck of a good time. Percy Bowers from Chetack, Wisconsin, we were the best of buddies.

Percy Bowers was killed at Avranches. He was killed in a cemetery. His tank was knocked out. Pretty near all of us were out of ammunition. His tank was knocked out, he got out of his tank and was carrying a white flag, crawling back, and some German shot him, with a white flag, crawling back.

Quentin Bynum, who was better known as Pine Valley, was killed in the Argonne Forest. He'd still be here today but they had a new lieutenant.

I heard it all over the intercom -- they were in this forest, and the Germans were laying artillery, and the shrapnel was coming down and hitting the tank. And this Lieutenant Lippincott said, "Abandon tank."

And Bynum said, "No, Lieutenant, that's just shrapnel. Just sit still."

"I said abandon tank."

And they all abandoned tank but one man, his name was Shagonabe [Frank Shagonabe]. He stayed in the tank, and he's the only live boy out of that crew. The rest of them, Bynum -- I don't know why Bynum obeyed -- but this Lippincott, if he would have listened to an older man, they all might have been alive today.[1]

About two or three days later, they asked me if I'd go back and identify Bynum. I would just say you could recognize him, he was full of shrapnel, and laying in the snow [this may have been in the Ardennes, rather than the Argonne].

A few years ago I went down and saw some of his folks, and his mother -- I don't know why I didn't go down there when we first came out -- his mother didn't believe in burying him underground, he's buried on top of the ground [in a mausoleum].

I went up to Chetack, Wisconsin, to see Bowers' folks. They didn't have him brought back. When I was back in Germany, it must have been about 17 years ago, I did go to Bowers' grave.

I went all the way through the service, I got three Bronze Stars, knocked out tanks. With my luck I never got a Purple Heart. That kind of, it just gets you, now.

[1] Shagonabe was later killed in action.

CHAPTER 23

Blood and Guts

My father heard General George S. Patton speak once. The line he remembered was that Patton said not to worry about saving ammunition, they could always make more.

George Bussell's encounter with Patton came after the battalion's first of two Moselle River crossings. The river was at flood stage, and Patton would call it "one of the epic river crossings of all time."

"We went across on pontoons," Bussell recalls, "and they had the pontoons sunk in the water about a foot deep to keep the shells from busting them up.

"After we crossed the river, Patton was there waiting for us. Sure as hell was. I was as close to Patton as I am to you. He said, 'Give 'em hell, boys. Give 'em hell.' Yessir. I'd have followed him to Japan if I'd had to. To me, he was a general. The one and only."

Doc Caffery

The first time I saw George Patton was on a hillside in England where he assembled all the non-commissioned officers, right before we went into Normandy.

He gave one of the typical George Patton talks. By the time you got through listening to his speech, you wanted to go out with your bare hands and kill Germans.

But I'll never forget. He had a high-pitched voice. He said, "Let me tell you one thing. After this war is over, when you get home and are bouncing your grandchildren on your knee, you can tell them that you fought with George S. Patton, and you didn't shovel shit in Fort Polk."

He kept on and on in that vein. When you left, you just thought the guy was a born leader.

Wayne Hissong

I was taking three trucks with gas on them to A Company during the breakout from St. Lo when I came to a crossroad that wasn't marked as to whether it was cleared of mines or not. So I was sitting there debating what to do, when all of a sudden I look up and I see all these stars shining. It was General Patton, and he wanted to know who was in charge of the trucks.

I told him I was, and he said, "Well, what the hell are you sitting here for?"

I said, "I'm taking gas up to A Company. I know where they are, but I don't know whether that road is cleared of mines."

And he said, "Well, you take this goddamn truck and drive it down that road, and we'll find out whether it's cleared of mines or not, won't we?"

So I went down the road, at about five miles an hour, every moment wondering if it was going to happen. Needless to say, it must have been cleared of mines or there were none there to begin with, because we made it. We found the tanks and got them gassed up.

That was my encounter with Patton.

Russell Loop

One time we had just pulled up on a four-way crossroad and were waiting for further orders, and here comes Patton and his jeep.

He got out, and he walked right by the officers and went around and shook hands and talked with nearly every one of the enlisted men.

While he was there, a German plane strafed that crossroads both ways, twice. And he just looked up and said, "They must know I'm here." But what he wanted to know was, "Are you getting plenty to eat? Are you getting enough ammunition and gasoline? And is there anything that I can do to make it better?"

And of course we all said, "Yes, send us home." But I got to shake hands with him on the front line.

Doc Caffery

When we broke through in Normandy, the battalion was acting as a point and protecting the right flank of the 90th Infantry Division as we went down through Avranches. The Headquarters Company had an assault-gun platoon.

We came to this bridge, and I was in charge of the assault platoon. I deployed the assault platoon vehicles in what I thought was the proper method to protect the bridge site, and just about five minutes later, George Patton approached. He came up in his jeep, and I very quickly ran to him and saluted and told him what the situation was, and his words to me were: "Get the god damn tanks across that bridge on the east side and do it now!" I saluted very hurriedly and did that right quickly.

Red Rose

Walter Hahn, he was Colonel Randolph's jeep driver, said Randolph came down with pneumonia somewhere on the road, and he wouldn't turn himself in. Some of the officers reported him real sick, and the doctor checked him and ordered him to bed. And Hahn said when Patton found out Randolph was in bed -- "Now I was standing right there with the jeep, right next to the old building where they had Randolph in because he had pneumonia," Hahn said, "and Patton went in, and he came out in a few minutes," and said Patton stood and looked at him and said, "You know, I'd give anything in the world if the Third Army had as much confidence in me as the 712th Tank Battalion boys do in Colonel Randolph." And he said tears came into Patton's eyes.

Smoky Stuever

General Walker from the First Army called Patton and asked him to send up a recovery crew to remove a gun that missed a curve in the road and went down a cliff. It was a 155 Long Tom, towed by a big truck full of shells that stood five feet high and were eight inches in diameter. This crew of five was on top of that truck when it rolled over, and there were five bodies under that mess. That was our first job, to turn that truck over, get the weight off, and bring those bodies up that hill.

I met General Walker in a little cabin up in the woods across the road, and we agreed that I could have the road for three hours. I wanted four. Then he said, "You have the road from midnight on." So it was getting daylight. Removing the bodies and getting them up the cliff took longer than we expected. Everytime the men would pick up a body they'd start vomiting, they had dry heaves. So I said, "Throw the canvas over them and roll them in it. Out of sight, out of mind." And we dragged the bodies up to the road that way.

Just as I had the gun up near the edge of the road, a sergeant from the medics came to me and he said, "I understand you're in charge of this operation. I've got 20 ambulances back there, and if they don't get to a doctor in an hour there's gonna be a lot of dead people."

"Bring 'em through."

And this colonel that was in charge of the gun said, "No you don't. You get that gun up first."

I said, "Those men back there are more important to me than that dang gun there. Lower them cables, fellows." So we lowered the cables and they laid flat on the road, and I moved the ambulances through. I moved them all through. And this colonel said, "I'm going to court martial you for refusing a direct order." I didn't hear him.

So we got all the ambulances through and then we got the gun up on the road, and I said, "Okay, you want to see General Walker about that court-martial?"

He said, "Aw, go to hell."

And I said, "The same to you," and I saluted him. Then I went in and talked to General Walker. He had a bottle of Canadian Club on the table and I said, "God, can I have a shot of that?" I was shaking like a leaf. And he said, "What's the matter?" And I said, "Ah, there's a redheaded colonel out there, he wants to court-martial me for refusing a direct order," and I told him what had happened.

"You did the right thing," he said, "Those men had to get through." So I had a shot of Canadian Club and he said, "How about another one?" Then he said, "You see old George, give him my regards."

Bob Vutech

Lieutenant Bob Vutech, from Corpus Christi, Texas, was a platoon leader, and later company commander, of B Company.

I was invited to a conference in Austria. It was a critique, and we sat with a whole bunch of colonels and generals. I don't know how I was chosen. I got to go, and maybe one more person from the battalion. It was after the war in Europe was over, but we were still fighting in Japan, and we didn't know for sure whether we were going to go over there or not.

We discussed the war day by day, and the generals would ask us questions. Why did you fire this type of ammunition? Should we change our tanks?

General Patton asked us how many times we sighted a gun when we fired. The more we were in combat, you didn't take the time eventually to fire like you think a sharpshooter would fire, you fired. You got the first round in if you could. You had a sense, you knew where it was gonna go, you didn't have to be told. When I grabbed a machine gun I never had to fire four or five rounds until I saw where the tracer was going. All the sights that were put on these guns cost money. In his eyes, the question was, do we need them? If you were a sharpshooter, yes, you would need one. But when the average boy fired, our answer was no. We critiqued the entire war that way.

At the end of the critique, Patton asked if there were any questions. And I asked him why the armored divisions got the first crack at the new equipment, why didn't we get some?

He asked me what I thought.

I said we should have gotten some of the new tanks like the armored divisions were getting.

He paused and said, "Politics, son. Politics." It was a good answer.

Afterward we had a social. Patton's niece had come over, she was a Red Cross girl. She attended the cocktail party, and a young major took a fancy to her. Then it came time that the general wanted to leave. Well, when the aide tells you that the general is leaving and he's got his niece with him, you let the niece leave. But this major kept talking, and

Patton had to wait. The major was doing all the talking, nobody else. The next day he was transferred to the Pacific.

CHAPTER 24

Mainz

Late March, 1945

Budd Squires

Budd Squires, from Winona, Minn., was a replacement in A Company.

At Mainz, there was a building that was walled in, with a courtyard, and our tank was parked right in front. I don't remember who I was with, but the two of us were on guard, and Ted Duskin and somebody else came up to relieve us.

Ted said, "I couldn't find my gun, can I have yours?" So I gave him my tommy gun and started to go toward the building, and just as I went through the gate all hell broke loose. An American ambulance had pulled into the area and a bunch of German soldiers piled out of it and started firing. One of them was chasing me with a machine gun, and I didn't have a gun.

I ran into the building and went up the stairway, and there were some infantry guys up there.

They started running down to the entry, and I said, "Don't go down there, Christ, a guy just chased me through there with a machine gun."

I went upstairs and was looking around, trying to find a gun, and everything is going like hell outside.

I found a gun and went back down into the courtyard. When I got around to the courtyard, the Germans must have thrown some concussion grenades, and all the shingles came down off the roof. They were slate shingles, and they knocked me out.

When I woke up, there was still firing going on outside. I got up and was wandering around, and somebody hollered "Halt!"

I said "Don't shoot! I'm a tanker, a tanker."

It was this tank destroyer outfit, this TD lieutenant was in the building there. So I went in the building and they had a Kraut in there and they were beating the hell out of him, trying to find out how many people were out there or what the hell was going on.

Clarence Steuck, he was on his first day with the outfit, it was right outside of Mainz. He took his German pistols and he threw them away, he must have got them from a German prisoner.

So I went in that building, and I said, "I've got to get to my tank. It's right outside the gate there." Ted was in the tank. And the lieutenant said to me, "Hey, there's nothing out there, they're all dead." But Ted was all right, what he was doing was throwing hand grenades out of the tank.

Then it came morning, and my tank was all right. Ted and the guys were still in the tank, they were fine. But the TD across the street had got it, and the 4.2 mortar outfit behind us and a bunch of other ones got it, and Sergeant Martin [Lloyd Martin], he had his tank parked behind the building and he had the breach open, and a Kraut threw a grenade in, blew his arm off.

In the courtyard, there were Germans dead all around. And right by the main gate was the body of the sonofabitch that was machinegunning me going through that gate.

I went over to him, and he had a square flashlight, it had a little slide you could pull down for a night light. I pulled it off, and it said "A.O. Nuskie," and that's my mother's name! She's from Germany. I never followed up on it, but I probably should have. My mother and her mother are from Germany. Hell, it might have been a cousin.

CHAPTER 25

Lieutenant Forrest

Heimboldhausen, Germany, April 3, 1945

Joseph Fetsch

Delivering gas to the front was a little hairy, but I never had a problem. When it would get too hot, they'd run me off. They'd say "Get that damn gas truck out of here." All you'd need was a piece of shrapnel to hit one can, and I'm sitting there with a two and a half-ton truck, no canopy or no top on it. Three hundred cans, five gallons apiece, about 1,500 gallons of gasoline, and just one little piece of shrapnel and I'm sitting on dynamite, I was gone.

We lost a few. In fact, my own truck, when A Company's headquarters got blown up, my truck got demolished. Actually, it didn't burn or blow, but a building fell on it. That's when Lieutenant Forrest got killed.

Although I was in Service Company, I was attached to A Company most of the time. I felt like an A Company man.

Their headquarters section got blown up on Easter Monday, April 3, 1945. A plane had been following us all day. There were two empty tank cars in a little railroad depot near the headquarters, and two boxcars filled with black ammunition powder that we didn't know about.

Somebody hollered "Here comes a plane!" and this airplane that had been following us all day came at us and started strafing.

I jumped on the truck, which had a .50-caliber ring-mounted machine gun. I knew it wouldn't hit him. But before I could get the gun around, the plane hit the cars with the black powder and he blew everything, the whole town. I think there were 32 of us in that area, and out of 32, there were only four guys able to move.

Only Lieutenant Forrest got killed. He had been wounded twice before.

I was injured all over the face and head. I didn't have a steel helmet on. I had a knit cap, backwards, one of these damn ol' Army knit caps, and everything came down on my head, and a steel girder came in behind my legs and held me up, or I'd have been under that rubble also.

Forrest Dixon

I was leaning on a halftrack talking to Dr. Reiff, and all of a sudden the channel opened up, "O.O.O., Dixon-Reiff, quick, Able Company." And just then we saw a big pall of smoke, and I said, "A Company's in trouble." So Reiff got his group and I got my group and we beat it there.

This is what happened: A German airplane came with a little bomb, and here everybody's shooting at it. And the airplane jettisoned the bomb, hit two carloads of black powder right in front of the house that Forrest had used for a command post, and it buried him. I think he was the only one from A Company that was killed.

"O.O.O." means everybody else get the hell off. When you heard a message in the Army back in World War II and it started off O.O.O., everybody that hasn't got business gets off and listens. And it said 'Reiff, Dixon, Able Company.' So Reiff and I took off, Reiff with his medical section and me with my maintenance section.

It was along towards night and we found out that everybody was accounted for except Forrest, so I got ahold of the burgomeister and told him that I wanted fifty men with shovels up there in the morning. So I was there at daybreak, and the burgomeister had fifty men with shovels, and we found him.

Hell of a nice fellow. He was a little bit like Colonel Randolph. Very quiet, unassuming. From Stockbridge, Massachusetts.

CHAPTER 26

Hof

Forrest Dixon

We captured a German ordnance truck. It was a GMC. It had a lot of cabinets in it, and I used that as my headquarters. We moved the cabinets to the rear and cut a hole in the side of the truck and put in a mattress and we used it to sleep in.

When we got into Hof, Germany, near the Czechoslovakian border it was permissible for us to move the Germans, so my warrant officer, Baker, found a house in which there were some feather mattresses, and he said, "We're gonna sleep on a soft bed tonight." So we moved in, and we were shelled -- we didn't know with what at that time -- and we moved our mattress under a big oak kitchen table so the plaster wouldn't hit us, and we thought we'd be comparatively safe. In the morning before we got up, a fellow comes in all excited, and he said, "Did you see where we were almost eliminated last night?"

And I said, "No, where?"

He said, "A big shell hit right in front of the front door, and there's a hole thirty feet across and fifteen feet deep, and it didn't even wake us."

And I said to him, "Wait a minute." I thought he had exaggerated a little bit. So we went over there, and so help me, this hole was at least thirty feet across and fifteen feet deep. One of the boys opened up the front door and was going out and almost fell in the hole, it was that close. And it never woke the remainder of the maintenance section. I had my whole maintenance section, which is about 30 men, in that building.

We found out later that it was a railroad shell. A railroad gun, with a 240-millimeter shell. They thought that Lucky Forward, which was code name for Third Army headquarters, had moved into Hof and they were shelling it. We got the royal treatment, but nobody got hurt.

The only damage they did was they got my German truck, and they put a hole in front of the housing where my mechanics were sleeping, and the other four or five shells went into the cemetery and there were bones in every direction.

CHAPTER 27

Greener Pastures

April 1945

Otha Martin

I'll tell you how Lieutenant Fuller got the name Snuffy. His name was Francis A. Fuller. We had a boy from Layton, Ohio, in the No. 4 tank, Byrl Rudd's tank, he was the cannoneer [loader], name of Wesley Haines.

Haines would bend his elbow if it was cognac, schnapps, champagne, any alcoholic beverage, Haines would take some of it. So, when he'd get drunk, well, you know how drunks are, they insult anybody. Haines told Fuller, "You look like Snuffy Smith in the comics." And it stuck, from then on it was Snuffy Fuller.

One Sunday morning we were in a town, this is along toward the end of the war. It's beginning to get in spring, the weather had warmed up, it was nice. We'd taken this town, and Snuffy, he had the flour and all the ingredients, and he was in this house, a real nice home there, he was baking a cake.

We all were out there soaking up that sunshine and not in a fight, that was one of the few times we weren't in a fight, and they had some big Belgian horses, they were huge, in a stable back there. Well, Haines had done imbibed some, and he was getting the horses out and riding them. He tried to make them run -- well them ol' horses' feet were so big, they were big ranch horses, and they were liable to fall down and hurt you if you made them run.

Snuffy saw him and he came and said, "Haines, put them horses up. Let 'em alone."

Well, he put 'em up. So I'm settin' out there soaking up the sunshine, and resting kind of easy. But I had had nothing to drink, in fact I wasn't a drinker.

Haines put the horses away for a little while, and then he got one of the horses out again, and he was trying to make him gallop. Snuffy comes out there and tells him, "Haines, I told you to put that horse up and I mean put him up and leave him up."

Then he said, "Martin, I'm giving you a direct order. If he gets that horse out again, shoot him."

You know, I'm not gonna, I don't want to shoot one of my own men over a horse. Well, Haines put the horse up. Then he comes around and I'm settin' there, and he got up close, he says, "Say ol' buddy, you wouldn't shoot me, would you?"

Russell Loop

Snuffy Fuller wouldn't wear his bars out where you could see them, and he always kept the bar on his helmet covered with mud. He didn't want anybody to know he was an officer, especially the Germans. He was of German descent, and he could speak real good German.

One night they sent us out on patrol. I was the gunner in his tank. Well, we got lost. And we rode and rode and rode. Didn't know where we were. It ended up that we were behind the German lines. And just when it got daylight, we looked back, and two German tanks had fallen in on our column.

So Snuffy, he didn't know what in the world we were gonna do. And he bailed out of the tank, went back, and talked to them in their language. He told them that they were in our territory. Well, they weren't. We weren't, either. But he convinced them to follow us on in. And by George, we captured two tanks without firing a shot!

Tony D'Arpino

Toward the end of the war, they made Sergeant Gibson a lieutenant, and they made me a tank commander. I had the fifth tank.

At that time, we could see the end was in sight. And they told us, if you go into a town, any house that had a white flag out the window, don't shoot, because they didn't want to ruin the people's homes.

So we're taking this town, I don't remember the name. Gibson's going down this little road, and he tells me to get on his left flank. We're going in a line formation, five tanks into this town. And it's all field leading up to the town.

Now I look way ahead of me and I can see that one place there the grass is a lo greener than anyplace else.

I'm not paying any attention to this. I was trying to do everything right the first time I'm a tank commander. I'm telling the driver, "Stay on course," and I'm telling the gunner "Keep looking to your left," there's no sense in him looking to his right because the other tanks are over there, all he had to worry about was looking to the left and behind us.

Then all of a sudden we hit this green thing, and the tank sank right down to the hull. The whole track was sunk.

It was a manure hole. And the grass had all grown green over it. So there we sat, and we had to wait for the tank retriever to come and get us out.

CHAPTER 28

Anne Marie

Ellwood Willard

Edwin E. Willard, from Lebanon, Mo., was a lieutenant in Headquarters Company.

We had a young fellow who had three women claim him as their husband. So the battalion commander told me, "I'd like you to sit down with him and let's work this thing out," because the office of dependency benefits is not going to pay three women.

So I called him in, I looked at his service records, and I said, "Tell me when you married Jane."

"Well, I started living with her," he said. "Then I ceased to live with her, and I started living with Mary," and he had one child with Mary.

"I ceased to live with her, and I started living with..." He was from Mississippi or Alabama, they were common-law marriages, none of these things were actually in the eyes of the law, but I guess the law down there does, too, recognize common-law marriages.

When I got all these names down, I looked at his service records, and there's another woman's name there. So I said, "How about her?"

He said, "Don't worry about her."

I said, "What do you mean, don't worry about her?"

He said, "She's not gonna bother us."

I said, "How do you know she's not going to bother you?"

And he said, "Well, she's dead."

I said, "My gosh, when did she die?"

And he said, "Oh, she was dead when I came in the service."

So I said, "How come you told everybody that was your wife?"

And he said, "Well, I knew she couldn't cause any trouble."

So we had a problem deciding which one of these wives was entitled to his benefits, but he was pretty unconcerned about the whole matter.

And you know, a lot of fellows really stewed about those sort of things, and there were a lot of them who figured they weren't gonna make it home anyway, so why bother thinking about it?

Bob Hagerty

My grandmother had a number of children, many of whom she lost in childbirth or later, through smallpox or diphtheria. She actually raised two boys, including my father, and two girls.

Of the two girls who survived, one's name was Anne, and the other was Marie.

At one point, there was a fellow named Medich, Joe Medich, who was a huge man. Those huge guys always seemed to wind up as drivers. Joe was taking some pictures one day, and I think I was standing alongside his tank just balancing on my elbow. His tank was named by him, for whatever reason, they had printed on there "Anne Marie."

He took my picture alongside his tank, and later gave me a copy, and I must have sent it on home. My father ultimately showed it to my grandmother, and she said, "Praise be to God! The boy's named the tank after the girls!" She just assumed that immediately, and no one said otherwise, and she was delighted.

She never got to tell me about it, because she died before I got home. But that little mistake gave her a lot of pleasure.

Ellwood Willard

There was a fellow in Service Company named Raffi who was kind of an interesting character.

Raffi had a young lady he met over there that he paid a lot of attention to. He told her he was going to bring her back to America with him.

She found out he was married, and he told her it was no problem, because his wife was broad-minded, and back in the States, she'd understand. He told her everybody in America has more than one wife.

So it turned out this gal writes a letter to his wife, only his wife couldn't read it because she wrote it in German. But Raffi's father-in-law got ahold of the letter and he could read it. Raffi said the old man wrote to him and said, "You know, you might as well get killed over there because if you don't, I'm gonna kill you when you get home."

CHAPTER 29

Prisoners of War

Wayne Hissong

I was wounded and captured on Easter Sunday.

We were taking the trucks to get some gas, and we came up a little knoll in the road, and there was a pocket of Germans. We just never dreamed they would be there. And they hit us.

Arnold Marshall and I were in the lead truck, and a bazooka came right through the side of the truck. Fragments from it hit me on my arms, and I was knocked out of the truck. Mutt -- Mel Paul -- was right behind, and when I fell out of the truck, his truck stopped on my ankle. I hollered, "Mutt! Move the truck!" And luckily, he moved it enough that I could get out from underneath it.

Marshall and I, we laid in a ditch there. I was hit, and Marshall, luckily he didn't get hit. The Germans put me up on this horsedrawn artillery. I had to help myself up, I could hardly get up, I crawled up behind these horses to get up on this seat, and they took Marshall down the road.

They had searched all my pockets and everything, took everything, and I had a P-38 shoulder holster. Luckily, I threw the P-38 away, but I still had the holster. And I had a German pocket knife that they didn't find. When we were going up the road, I showed it to the driver, and he said, "Ach, keep it."

When we got to this little burg, they dropped me off and they took Marshall on. They put me out in a barn, and there were two other fellows from another outfit, I don't know what outfit they were out of. The guy that owned the building, he could talk a little English, and the only thing he asked was that we didn't smoke, we could set the barn on fire.

The next morning, they carried us into the house. In the meantime, one fellow had died during the night. So they carried this other fellow, he had been shot through the knee, and they made stretchers and carried us in the house and laid us down on the floor, and there was a German soldier in the corner to guard us.

About 9:30 in the morning, this woman German doctor came in. She was dressed in a full Nazi uniform, I mean Nazi everything. She talked to this other guy, and she could speak fluent English, better than you and I can. She asked all kinds of questions, and we didn't tell her anything. So she gave me a morphine pill to stick up my butt, and she said, "I'll be back."

She left, and pretty soon she came back, and when she came back this time, she had taken off her Nazi uniform. She was dressed -- skirt, blouse, nylon hose, high heels, I mean, she was a beautiful woman. Then she went out and she got some hot water and she came in and dressed my arm.

When she came in with the pan of hot water and set it down, imagine now, you're laying flat on your back, you can move a little bit, but here she is with long blonde hair, and she comes in with this damn skirt on and she kneels down and she pulls the skirt up when she kneels down. I'm flat on my back and because of my injuries I can't move. And she says. "Would you like to have a cigarette?" I said, "Yeah, I'd like to have a cigarette." She gives me a Lucky Strike cigarette out of a green package. She lights it with a Zippo lighter which I had tried four goddamn years to get one. And then she starts asking me all these questions about what outfit are you out of, and blah blah blah blah blah. All I would tell her was my name, rank and serial number, and she said, "If you just tell me what your folks' home address is, I'll write them and tell them where you are and how you are" and the whole works, and I just give her name, rank and serial number, that's all I would give her."

She went over and talked to this other guy, but she didn't spend too much time with him.

She said, "I know that you Americans like your fried potatoes." And she went out in the kitchen and she fixed us a breakfast, fried potatoes and eggs and bacon. Then, after we ate that, she came back in, and she went through this whole rigamarole again with the questions, how she would get in contact with the Red Cross and get the word to our parents that we were all right and all this, and I wouldn't tell her anything else.

So finally she says, "I'm gonna leave, but I will be back."

She never got back. And I have often wondered whatever happened to her. Man, I'm telling you, she was a beautiful woman.

The next night, I could hear these tanks coming. I didn't know whether it was our tanks or their tanks or who it was. And all of a sudden, this tank stopped out front, and the next thing I remember is this great big black lieutenant busted through the door, and as he busted through the door, right over in this corner sat a German soldier with a rifle guarding us, I said to the lieutenant, "Don't shoot him. He hasn't hurt us."

I remember writing home to my uncle, and I told him it was a hell of an Easter parade I was in. But the hell of it was, they sent a telegram to my folks, and the first telegram that they got said that I was missing in action. Then they got a telegram that I was a prisoner of war. Then they got another telegram that I was wounded in action.

When I got hit, my mother was in the hospital. So when Dad got the first notice, he went to the doctor and he said, "Doc, how are we going to explain this" to my mother? "She looks for a letter from him about twice a week."

"Weeellll," the doctor says, "you just leave that to me. I'll find some way to explain it to her."

So he got these telegrams. Three telegrams. Dad got two one day and then one the next day, all of them conflicting with one another.

So Doc, he went in one morning to my mother, and he sat down beside the bed and talked to her, and examined her, and he said, "Boy," he said, "you know, that son of yours, he is one tough sonofabitch."

And my mother said, "What?"

"Well," he says, "you know, they kicked the hell out of him, but he's all right. He's gonna make it. Don't you worry now. He got beat up a little bit, but he's gonna make it all right."

Bob Rossi

In April 1945, we were in a column and we had reached our objective for the night. It was near a bridge, and these two German civilians came up on bicycles and told us there were American prisoners in the next town. So we called up and said we wanted to proceed into the next town. They said American wounded, American sick.

We proceeded into the town, and naturally, where do you think you'd go to see wounded, we went to the hospital. There was only German wounded in there, no American prisoners were in the hospital. They were across the street. They had these guys laying on the floor of the schoolhouse. There was straw on the floor. These were the guys from the 106th Division, they were captured during the Bulge.

Every one of them was a stretcher case. Every man. A guy told us that all they had for three months was potatoes, that they would put a wire through and hold it over an open flame, and weak tea, that's what they had for three months. They used to torture one another, like make up a menu, every time they made up a menu for one another, it always had sugar, something sweet.

One guy pulled up his pants to show me his long johns, I thought they were o.d., they were brown from the dysentery.

This one guy came from Connecticut, his family owned a roller skating rink, and one of the MPs came from that area, this guy kept saying, "God bless you men! God bless you men!" When I walked in, my heart was in my throat, because you can't believe what you're gonna see, these guys were like skeletons.

One guy was buried the night before we got there, and they told us it was the first time any one of them got buried. These guys were being marched away from us, and if a guy died, they just picked him up and put him on the side of the road. The night before we got there was the first time any one of them ever got buried.

So I went out to my tank and I got a box of those Tropical Hershey bars we had. They're called Tropical Hersheys because they wouldn't melt. I was giving the Hershey bars out to these guys, and Dr. Reiff comes in, he starts chewing me out, he says, "What the hell are you trying to do, kill them? They'll get sick." And they promised him they wouldn't eat them fast, they would eat them slow.

The GIs that were with us, they shot two SS guards that were left behind to guard them, but the prisoners told us, "Don't let them shoot the medic," the German medic, "he's a good guy. He was decent to us."

The next day -- we're traveling now, we're still moving, moving, moving -- I'm up in the turret of the tank, when I see these two guys come out of a barn. They were part of a group of 150 that were still being marched away from us. Well, these guys figured this is it, and they hid in the barn, they escaped.

I'll never forget their faces. One guy was a short guy with red hair, and as he's looking at me up in the turret, I could see the tears were just coming down his face. Like he was in a state of shock, like I'm liberated. And the other guy was tall, black hair, had a mustache and wore glasses.

I reached down, I said, "You guys want a butt?" because I used to smoke at the time, and they couldn't reach me, so I jumped out of the turret, and gave them each a cigarette, and as I went to light the cigarette, the little redheaded guy, as he cupped the light, I noticed he had a big, festering cut on his hand. I said, "What happened to your hand?"

"The Krauts cut me with a bayonet and they refused to dress the wound."

I called "Medic! Medic!" Again, Dr. Reiff comes -- they mentioned him in the newsletter, he just got remarried -- Captain Reiff comes down, he said, "What's the matter?" and I told him. With that, Captain Reiff asks the redheaded kid, he says, "What happened to your hand?" He told him, and Reiff says, "The sonofabitches," and he starts putting sulfanilamide on his hand and bandaging it, and Dr. Reiff says, "Okay, son, we're taking you back now." And with that, he can't move, like he's stunned. So Streeter, Dale Streeter, who was Gibson's driver, he was a pretty big guy, he threw a blanket around him and picked him up and put him in the jeep.

CHAPTER 30

Flossenburg

Jim Gifford

When we got back to England we were in a hospital, I can't remember the name of it, north of London. Then they gave me what they call a Zone of Interior, if you want to you could go back to the United States, or you could go back to your outfit, and I said Jesus, the war was still on, I want to go back to my outfit. So they said okay. I signed a whole bunch of papers releasing the hospital. I wanted to get the hell out of there and go, because I was feeling good enough. They gave me a patch for my eye, and told me to keep the patch on as much as possible.

They gave me two or three days before I would go back, so I went into London. This was in February. While I was there, I was walking down this street near Piccadilly, and all of a sudden sirens went off and everybody started running. Well, I had just come off the front and bombs didn't bother me. I just wanted to see where they're gonna land, so I didn't run anyplace, I just stood there in the middle of the street by myself, looking around and looking up in the sky.

I counted 14 of those little airplanes, I forget what bomb they were called, it was either the V-1 or V-2, one of them was up and you couldn't see it, not that one, these were little airplanes, and they had 500-pound bombs in them, and they would fly over and the motor would shut off, then they would come down, and whatever they hit they hit[1].

I counted fourteen of those things, I would follow them with my finger in the air. Then suddenly, a little putt-putt engine would shut off, I can hear it now, and down she'd come, and you'd see these big explosions, all over the place.

That night I stayed in a rooming house, and I was in the front bedroom, the people rented the room out for peanuts, and Jesus, during the night, suddenly the windows, and

[1] John Colby, author of "War From the Ground Up," points out that the bombs Gifford remembers were V-1s. "The V-2s were huge rockets," Colby says. "I recall both clearly. We tried to shoot down some V-1s aimed at 3rd Army HQ in Nancy, and we saw, during the winter of '44-'45, rockets rising at night in the distance. They were the V-2s. Also, when we were fighting through the Eifel Forest in Germany, we found a crumpled V-2 that had obviously tumbled in flight and crashed down on its side without exploding. In fact, some of the men in my company discovered it contained a tank of alcohol. They drilled a hole in it and drank 'V-2 cocktails.' I had one myself. Pretty potent stuff."

the side of the building all shook and the glass broke. There was a fish market up the street, and the people were queued up there, and the god damn bomb dropped into that intersection there, and it killed a whole bunch of people.

Then the next day I had my orders cut to go back to the front, and they sent me down to a train station. When I went into the headquarters in the railroad yard, they had a whole bunch of American soldiers, forty or fifty of them, lined up.

They said to me, "Lieutenant, you're going to be in charge of these 50 Americans, you're taking them back to Bonn, Germany, on your way back to your outfit."

Well, it turns out these forty or fifty guys were all prisoners, Americans that had gone over the hill, and they had a choice, either go to jail for ten years or go back to the front, and they decided they would go back to their outfits.

We got to the boatyard in Southampton and they were put on a small British cruiser. They also gave me nine guys as guards. These men had been wounded like myself and were on their way back to the front. they weren't trying to get out of anything. They were legitimate fighting soldiers, and they didn't have much sympathy for these guys.

It's amazing, I forgot all about this until just now, it's been laying in the back of my brain all these years. There was a big coal pile in the boatyard, and as we're marching by it, all of a sudden one of them bolted, and the other prisoners were all going, "Hey, hey, hey," for him.

As he ran through the yard, two of the guards ran after him, and he couldn't go one way, he couldn't go the other, so he started to run up the coal pile. He got almost to the top to go over the fence when the coal gave way and he comes tumbling back down. And all the other prisoners laughed and clapped, and they booed the shit out of him when they brought him back and got him in line again.

We landed in Le Havre, and they put us in a freight car on a train. And then we started going towards Bonn.

I'll never forget, we were going along and suddenly one of the guys fell off the train. He really jumped off. So one of the guards hollered, and I swung out the door of the caboose. I had my tommy gun. That old tommy gun was always with me. So I swung the tommy gun, the guy now is trotting behind the train, and the train isn't moving too fast. So when I swung out the door I put the gun on him and I said, "Catch the train." And he looked at me and he didn't know whether I was going to shoot him or not, he wasn't sure. I wouldn't have shot him. He started running, and he's running, and the train's picking up speed, and he's running his ass off, and he's scared to death now, I could see he's really frightened. He started falling on the track. He tripped, fell a couple of times, he'd get up and run and try to catch the train. Then I reached up and I pulled the brake, and the train stopped. And the guy came up and got back up on the train, and all the other prisoners are laughing and booing him.

We stopped at a place where we were being fed, and there was a guardhouse there with a man and his wife. So we get back on the train, we're ready to leave, and there was a soup kitchen there, and this old lady came running out, crying. She said somebody stole her wallet. I said it's one of those bastards. So I told all the guys, "Listen." I stopped the train, and I said, "Somebody stole that old lady's wallet and in it is the only picture she's got of her son who was killed in 1940," this is what she told me. So I said, "We want that wallet. I'm not going to do anything. I want to see that wallet." The next thing we got the wallet. Either they threw it out or somebody said "Here's the wallet," and we gave it to the woman. She was crying and hugging me, she was so happy. She was an old French lady with a black outfit on. That bothered me.

Then, as we got closer to Bonn, during the night, we were all laying down in the car to sleep, and all of a sudden we hear all this machine gun fire. The train kept going, and of course, I didn't know what was going on. When we got out, we saw that they had machine-gunned the train, and luckily they didn't hit anybody. They were wooden cars, the bullets went right through the goddamn car but nobody was standing up.

When we got to Bonn, I turned the prisoners over to the constabulary. I went in to meet the guy who was in charge of the military police in Bonn, because Bonn was already occupied by the Americans, and isn't he a colonel from Texas and his name is Gifford, and I said I'll be damned, he was probably a relative of mine, and we both had a big chuckle out of it.

Then I said, "Listen. The reason I'm here is that if you need MPs, these nine guards are excellent, top-rated guys. I said they're really, really good guys, if you need anybody. They did an excellent job."

I had to wait to get a jeep to go back to my outfit, and the next day, Geez, I see an MP coming down the street, it was one of my guards. He said, "They're going to make us MPs. They took us all."

I said, "No kidding."

"Oh, thanks," he said. "We were only going to get killed at the front. This is great. We'll be MPs back here." I was happy about that.

Then I got a jeep and I went back to the 712th. I met up with them in a place called Chamm. I stayed with the outfit and we continued right straight through into Czechoslovakia. I remember the German 11th Armored Panzer Division gave up to us. The whole 11th, all their tanks and everything came down the road and surrendered to us. This was getting towards the end of the war.

While we were in Chamm, a German fighter plane circled and dived on us. He was coming straight down at us and we all ran and threw ourselves into a ditch. There was a little river there, and he crashed right into the river. There was a big splash, and he's there today I guess, there was nothing left, that water splashed back down in that river.

Then we hit Flossenburg. That was in the woods in Bavaria.

At that time I think I was in an armored car or a jeep. We came up to the gate, and the gates were locked, and we broke the gates open. There were some guys in there, some prisoners, with black and white stripes on them. We went in, and other personnel came in, and the next thing they flooded the place with help, and we were told to move on to a further location.

There were a few very skinny prisoners that were still in some of the buildings, but the majority of them were gone. I don't know what happened to them, but I think that as we approached, the German personnel just took off and left those in there, and they just were so happy to see us. I was surprised they didn't want to run out the door, but they didn't. I took some pictures.

There was a big, high fence that went around the camp, and on one side of the fence there was this long brick building. It was maybe 50 feet, 75 feet long, and one story high. As you go into it, the whole wall is just furnaces, you open the furnace doors and there's an iron tray in there, and that's where the bodies were put.

In front of the building was a little railroad track, and it went underneath the fence, and down into a location where there was a pit. The pit was at least 10 or 12 feet deep, and one end of the pit was one solid mass of human bones, and none of them were more than an inch long, so how many people were in that pit God only knows because their bodies had been reduced to these little chips of bone, and it was pretty depressing.

Then our backup companies came in. Because we were a fighting company, we didn't stay at that location. We continued on.

Paul Wannemacher

Paul Wannemacher, from Johnstown, Pa., joined Headquarters Company as a replacement in Normandy.

I remember when we went into the concentration camp. We came up to this little block building, and we stopped the jeep and walked into the building, and there was Lieutenant Gifford from C Company standing in front of an open oven door. I've got a picture of him standing there.

We heard water running, and we didn't know what it was, so we followed the sound. There was a room right next to the entrance, and there was a guy standing there with a hose. It looked like he was spraying the room, so we got over and we looked closer, and what he was spraying, there were a bunch of dead bodies in there. They were just stacked up in the room, there must have been 25 or 30 of them. I guess they were getting ready to cremate them, and they were trying to keep some semblance of sanitation at the time. They were all naked and he was just spraying them with the hose.

Then we got the hell out. We saw the two big buildings where they gassed them, and at the foot of one they had a huge pile of shoes, and there was a big pile of eyeglasses, just laying there, a huge pile. We got pictures of all that.

Forrest Dixon

The furnaces were still burning when we went in, but they had evacuated most of Flossenburg three days before our arrival. Then we took out after them, and we caught up with them after dark. The fighting units took all the Germans prisoners, and then, I think there were about 1,600 inmates that went amok. We took the Germans at a poultry farm, and I'll never forget, all night you could see these little fires, and they kept sending people around, "You're going to kill yourself eating." We lost several that night from overeating.

Then the next morning they found a dairy farm, and they killed all the cattle and ate them.

CHAPTER 31

The Monument

Ellsworth Howard

Captain Ellsworth Howard took over from Clifford Merrill as A Company's commander. Howard was wounded at the Falaise Gap, but later rejoined the battalion.

One day I got this letter that came down through channels, from Eisenhower on down, I think. Lieutenant Lund's [Arnold Lund] mother and sister had written and were asking how he was killed.

I guess I hadn't answered their letter the first time they wrote. There was some reason they had written again, because this time it came down and it had everybody's signature on it. Colonel Randolph gave it to me and said, "Answer it right now."

I didn't know how Lund had died. It was the situation there at Mayenne. Everything happened so darned fast. We got into a fight we didn't know we were gonna get into. And it had everything under the sun. If we went around this way to outflank the Krauts, they came around that way to outflank us, and we ran into each other. It was a real brawl.

Lund's tank was way out there. You've got the platoon scattered all over the darn place and I couldn't keep track of all of 'em. His tank was way up in the woods there someplace.

Then we got word from Randolph that we're pulling out, get your platoon down here right away. I had Dixon out looking for Lund's tank, and I left him stranded up there.

Forrest Dixon

He left me up there with two medics, trying to get Lund and the crew out of the tank. Good friend of mine.

You know, Lund almost didn't get on the monument at Fort Knox. When Les O'Riley read me Ray Griffin's list of the people killed, he wanted to know if I knew of any corrections. He said he thought there was another but couldn't remember his name.

I said, "You're missing an officer."

He said, "Who?"

I said, "Lieutenant Lund."

He said, "Are you sure?"

I said, "Yes, I'm sure. Ask Howard. He was there."

Then O'Riley asked our secretary, "No, uh uh." He had no record of Lund. And O'Riley came back to me, he said, "Ray says we didn't lose a Lund, but I remember him, too."

I said, "We sure did lose a Lund. Damn near lost Howard and Dixon, too."

So he wired Washington. The name came right back. When he was killed, who he was with, what happened, and who his sisters were. So he got on the monument.

He was assigned to us that morning and he got killed that afternoon. And I wouldn't have known a thing about it, only I was going to help Howard. "Dickie, want to go along with me?"

"Oh, sure, I'll go along with you." So he gets two medics, and we go up. Here's the tank afire. Guay [Roger J. Guay] was one of the crew. Guay, Percy Bowers and Lund, and I don't know who the other two were.

Then Howard got word the company is moving out, and he left without us, so we stayed there a little while. Then the artillery came on target, right on top of us. And I said to the medics, "I guess it's every man for himself. Let's get the hell out of here."

CHAPTER 32

Going Home

Ellsworth Howard

You could only get a replacement tank if you lost one in battle, and the replacement tanks were slow in coming through. We had a void of tanks for a long time.

So I started battle losing 'em on paper. And then the durn war ended before my tanks balanced out. I had four or five too many tanks, and we had to turn 'em in at Nuremburg.

We went to some ordnance place down there and turned those tanks in, and they wouldn't take but just the number listed in the table of operations.

I said, "What am I gonna do with the rest of them?"

"That's not our problem."

So I found a field down there right close by, and parked those tanks, got out and left. A week or so later a guy named Marshall House called, and he said, "Are you by any chance from Louisville?"

I said, "Why, I sure am."

And he said, "Well, this is Marshall House."

I said, "Why, I remember you, Marshall." And we talked about old times.

And then he said, "What about these tanks down here?"

I said, "I can't hear you, it must be a bad connection."

Clifford Merrill

When I returned to the States, I became the provost marshal at Fort Myers, Va.

At Fort Myers, there were 23 generals, and that meant there were 23 generals' wives. That was my biggest problem, keeping everybody happy.

A provost marshal is the military equivalent of a chief of police. You're in charge of discipline, law and order. Anything goes wrong, call the provost marshal. I got calls at all times of the day and night. If they called me at home, I'd tell them to call the office. As long as it wasn't Mrs. Bradley.

Omar Bradley's wife was rather an eccentric type. When I took the job as provost marshal, one of the first tidbits of information I got was that Mrs. Bradley was to be handled with kid gloves.

Well, one day she called the office, and the provost sergeant answered, and he handed me the phone quick and said, "It's Mrs. Bradley."

She said, "Major, there's a great big dog jumping on my little dog."

Well, I thought for a moment.

I said, "Is that little dog a female?"

"Yes, but she's been spayed."

I said to myself, geez, this is a tough one.

"Yes, Mrs. Bradley, no doubt your dog's been spayed, but that big dog doesn't know that."

She cackled, and said, "You're pretty smart."

I said, "I'll come right over and handle it personally." I went over and the dog was gone, of course, but she invited me in to have a Coke. I got along well with her.

Another time she was driving pretty fast. She had a kind of car, it looked like an old Essex, I don't know what make of car it was. Anyway, she made the turn around the post exchange and the car leaned way over, it went on two wheels. The MPs were behind her, because she had really been moving fast.

She called me and said the MPs were harassing her.

I said, "No. They reported it to me, and told me about it. They thought there was something wrong with your car, and they didn't know that they might have to render assistance."

"Ohhhhh...." No more said.

Even among kids, rank was considered. We caught three of those kids one day, one was a chaplain's son, another was General Parks' son, and the other was a full colonel's son. They had somebody's hunting bow, hunting arrows, and they were trying to play William Tell.

The chaplain's son was junior in terms of his father's rank, of course, he had to hold the target, and the others were trying to shoot it with the bow and arrow. I put a stop to that. In the course of doing so, one of those arrows happened to hit them across the backside.

That didn't go over well with Mrs. Parks. I hit 'em all, just went tchchchch, now get the hell out of here, don't ever do this again. General Parks didn't know about it at the time, but Mrs. Parks, she came in, she read me up and down, and said, "This is Mrs. Parks."

I said, "How are you today, Ma'am."

"Don't Ma'am me. That's my son you struck."

"Oh," I said, "that wasn't anything. It was just a reminder to him that he shouldn't be playing with dangerous things like bows and arrows that are steel-tipped."

That toned her down a little, but she told General Parks. General Parks called.

He said, "I understand you had occasion to strike my son with an arrow."

I said, "I certainly did, sir."

He said, "How did it happen?"

I told him.

He said, "Good. I'm gonna whip his ass in good shape."

Bob Hagerty

The guys who drove the tanks had a real spirit, like Percy Bowers, Pine Valley, Des Tibbetts, Big Andy -- Robert Anderson. He survived. In fact, I don't even think he was injured. Which is really pretty neat, when you think of how vulnerable the driver is.

The guys who drove the tanks had this feeling about each other. I think they felt like there were some skills that were honed a little more than the others. A lot of your survival depended on his skill, particularly in avoiding getting bogged.

Bussell was in my platoon, but he was with another tank. I think he was with Goldstein and Charlie Bahrke.

Bussell was so heavy, he had the biggest rear end, and you thought, "That guy is gonna get in my hatch?" He had been a tanker before we came to Fort Benning from Camp Lockett, so he was on the cadre that was going to help train us. We took a look at him, he had this big stomach, and an even wider rear end, and yet, when getting in the tank, he had a shimmy that he did, that he was in there in no time at all. There wasn't any forcing himself, or getting scratched or scraped.

After the war ended, in a short period of time, I'd get a call at random, and somebody would say, "I'm in Cincinnati, tell me how to get out to your house." And it would be some Army person. On one of these occasions, it was George. He was in Cincinnati and wanted to come out.

I don't think I warned my father in advance. My father had this awful habit of asking people, "What do you weigh, son?" He never asked me, he was just interested in huge people. I just knew he was going to ask George, and I was hoping he wouldn't. I thought it might be a sore spot, because George was as big as ever, maybe bigger. And pretty soon, Dad said, "Son, what do you weigh?" And George, he had these real bright blue eyes, he said, "About 191, sir."

Bob Anderson

Every Lent, Bob Hagerty would quit smoking, and then after Lent he'd start smoking again. Then he'd say "God, if I could only quit that. I just wish I could quit smoking."

I would say "Well, Bob, you just did for six or seven weeks."

"Yeah, but that was for Lent," he'd say.

Bob was a good man. I liked him. I got along fine with everybody in the service and I had a good time, and still I wouldn't want to go through it again.

I had a lot more aftereffects after I got home.

We lived a mile down the road from where we live now, and I farmed for thirty years. When I first came home, there'd be nights, say, that I worked in the field late, I'd be scared to go out to the barn to milk the cows because I knew there were Germans out there waiting. So I'd drive up the road, and I knew there was a German tank waiting. My wife will bear this out, there'd be nights I'd lay in bed and just freeze. She'd wake me up, and say "W-w-What's the matter?"

"There's Germans there." I had more aftereffects, and was scareder, than I did when I was over there. But I was scared, and every time after you were back on break, you'd pray that you would never have to go back up to the line. And anybody, I always said this, anybody that was in combat who wasn't scared, they're either a damn liar or they never were in combat."

Tony D'Arpino

I wouldn't say I had nightmares, but once in a while I do have dreams. I think about twice I dreamt I was shot. But other than that, I wouldn't call them nightmares.

I've fallen out of bed. That just happened recently, and I never told Mary what I was dreaming about. But that's what I was dreaming. I don't know where the hell I was, it must have been during the war someplace. I was up against the tank and somebody had a gun pointed at me, and I'm kind of sliding down so he won't hit me, and I hit the goddamn floor. I'm on the floor there, covers and all. About three weeks ago.

George Bussell

When I came home, my dad and mom were both still alive, and we lived over on Pleasant Street in Indianapolis. I had the back bedroom on the second floor, and it had French windows.

One night I was asleep, and if my mom hadn't come in and caught me, I'd have probably jumped out the window, because there was thunder and lightning and I kept saying "Here they come! Here they come! Here they come!" I'd sat up on the edge of the bed, and I was heading for the window. I had the window open. But she grabbed hold of me. After she grabbed hold of me I was all right. That's the only time that ever happened. But I probably would have jumped.

Clifford Merrill

This stuff bothers you, you know, and the reaction was later, not then, you don't have time to think about it, but later I had nightmares. I've killed this Kraut a hundred times, for example, and each time he comes a little closer. I don't know how the nightmares come on, but all of a sudden, I still get them. You'd be surprised how much they shake you up. Then you don't get any sleep. I don't sleep much. If I go to bed at 10 o'clock, I'm awake at 1:30. I might get another hour of sleep, not much more.

It's a good thing Jan and I have a queen-size bed. I'm over on one side and she's over on the other, and if I start slugging, why, I miss her. I haven't hit her yet.

Louis Gerrard

When I finally got back to the States, I was down in Martinsburg, West Virginia, and I had been missing all these paychecks. I was always on the move someplace, from one hospital to another.

One day we were told to go down to the auditorium, because the paymaster was coming in. So he called my name, Gerrard, and he started shelling out hundreds of dollars. I said, "There must be some mistake. I'm not entitled to all this."

He said, "That's what's here." So I took it. I went back to the ward and I told the guys it's not my money. And they were hollering "Keep it."

I went back to the service department in the hospital, and there were a couple of WACs there. I told them about all the money, and one of them said "Wait a minute," and they went and got my service record, and she said, "No wonder you got paid all that money."

It was stamped in my service records, "Killed in action."

I said, "Holy cow," it's a good thing they never sent that to my wife and mother.

Ed Spahr

There was this one incident, near the end of the war. The Germans were getting hard up, and they had horse-drawn artillery, and there were three pieces of artillery coming down the road. They saw us, and stopped.

They turned an antitank gun around on us and they fired. They must have been poor gunners, because they fired three shots at us before I fired, and I could see in my sights that I hit this antitank gun. I hit it with H.E. -- that's high explosive -- and I could see a body flying up in the air. I saw a horse get hit at the same time, when the shell exploded on the front end of this German field piece. The horse was hit in the back end, I guess, because his front feet were trying to drag around. I believe there were four horses attached to this field piece, or maybe it was only two, I forget. But one horse was all right and the other horse was trying to get away, and dragging this other horse, and my next shot ... I took to put those horses out of their misery. I didn't know whether the other horse had been hit, but it probably had some shrapnel in it. I had seen a horse before that was hit, and he was all blown up. He was laying in the field, he looked like he was going to burst, and I thought to myself, those horses, that horse that I had seen, and I had seen cattle that way, too, I thought, I'm not going to let that suffer. So the next shot, I sent a high explosive into those horses. ... That's hard. ... In fact, that's harder than enemy soldiers. But I had to do it.

I don't watch war movies. I've seen a little bit of them, but then if I watch them, I dream about what actually happened. I have nightmares, because you see the people in the movies, you see these shells coming in and hitting right in a group of people, they fly up in the air, then they jump up and run away. That doesn't happen. When that shell hits in a group of people, there might be one or two that get up and run away, but the whole group doesn't do that.

I have one son. He was born nine months before I went into the service. He has two children, a boy and a girl.

They're grown up now. The grandson, this is his second year in college, and my granddaughter, she's out of college. She's 22 years old. My grandson is 19. My granddaughter got married last August.

When they were in school, fifth or sixth grade maybe, my grandchildren would say things occasionally about the war, and ask me things about it, and I would just say, "Somebody else will tell you about it." I'd also say, "You don't want to know anything about this, you'll read it in history. What you read in there will be good enough. That's the way I'd answer them."

I brought back a couple of German pistols. I guess my son was about eight or nine, and I came in the house one day from work, he had come home from school about a half-hour before I did, and he had one of his schoolboy friends with him, and he was showing him these pistols that I had brought home.

The one he had out at that time was a Walther, it was a German officer's, the officer's name was on the holster. It was a shoulder holster. The pistol was a 7.65 caliber, and I had ammunition for it, and he was showing his friend the weapon. I took it away from him and I explained to him how dangerous this thing was, and within a week I had gotten rid of all my German pistols. I gave one to a friend who had never been in the service, and the other to a fellow who had been in the service but he was in the Air Corps, and had never seen ground combat.

Jim Gifford

I had a brother who was in the Navy. He was on a destroyer. And my sister was home, her husband was in the Navy. Matter of fact, he was a radio man on the Intrepid, from the day it was launched until the day it was decommissioned. His name was Carl Armstrong. He was on that ship every day. He was in the radio shack. And he could tell some stories about that ship.

Every year, when he'd come East to visit -- they lived in California -- I was going to take him aboard, and he'd say, "Next year," and doesn't he die this last spring. He got cancer. He had a heart attack, they operated on a bypass, and they found he had cancer also and he passed away.

He was on that Intrepid. And a client of mine who was in charge of the museum on the Intrepid told me, "When he comes in, let me know," because we wanted to roll out a carpet for him, and he never got there.

Tony D'Arpino

When I got discharged, I drove to Brockton, which was probably about five miles from where I lived in Whitman. I still had my uniform on with a ruptured duck. When you were discharged they gave you what they called a ruptured duck, that showed that you were discharged from the service. And I had no civilian clothes that fit me.

I went to a pants store in Brockton, and they had pants, but they were too long. In those days they had cuffs, and they had to be shortened.

So the owner said, "Can you pick them up in a couple of days?"

I said, "No, I want a pair today. I want to get out of the uniform."

So he says, "Well, I'll do you a favor. I'll fix one pair for you today."

I said, "Fine, that's all I want. As a matter of fact, for that I'll buy an extra pair."

He told me to come back about five o'clock, just before he closed, and said, "I'll have them ready for you."

So I had to waste some time, and there was this nightclub named Cappy's. We used to go there during the war when we got furloughs, and he used to have all kind of American flags. It was a good place to pick up women. They had floor shows there. So I said, well, I'll go down there and have a couple of beers while I'm waiting for the pants.

Now this is the first or second of October. It was kind of chilly. I parked the car near the place, and just as I'm going to walk in, this guy, he was strapping, he was bigger than I was, he opens the door, and I walk in.

Right after we get inside, he takes off his topcoat, and he was a state trooper. He says, "This place is raided."

I'm standing there with my mouth open. I said to the guy, "You just let me in!"

He said, "I'm sorry. You've got to stay here. The place is raided."

I said, "What's gonna happen?"

He said, "After we question everybody, the paddywagon will come, and they'll take you to the Brockton police station, and you'll have to go to court, and you'll pay five dollars for being present at the time of a raid."

I said, "For Chrissakes, you held the door open for me!"

He said, "I'm sorry." Then he said to the bartender, "Keep serving."

So I'm in there, and I'm really nervous now, and there's a sailor, I can still see him. He was loaded. There were two or three state troopers behind the bar, they were looking for betting slips, and the sailor was going, "All you goddamn soldiers and sailors that fought the war, this is what you fought it for, these 4-F..." he called the state troopers all kinds of names, and the trooper that held the door open for me kept looking at this guy. After about ten minutes of listening to this sailor spout off, the trooper says, "Listen, punk. I've got more bad time in the Navy than you've got good time."

We were there a good two hours. Then the paddywagon came, and loaded the sailor and four or five civilians. There was one woman in the whole place and she was crying because her husband was on the second shift at the Fall River shipyard and she wanted to get home and make his lunch. I guess she stopped off for a beer before she went home.

Finally, I got out of there, and I went up to get my pants, but the store was closed. Then I couldn't remember where I parked the car. So I took the bus home, and the next day I had to ask a buddy of mine to drive me up to Brockton.

Jim Rothschadl

When we were still in England, this fellow Jim Driskill and I were good friends. I liked the guy, he was a raw-boned Texan, a farmer.

About a month before we went to France, we were each issued a new pair of shoes.

Driskill's platoon, the maintenance platoon, didn't have to stand inspection. The line troops did. So I happened to get a pair of shoes that had a little fuzz on them, they were hard to keep a shine on. I couldn't say, "No, I don't want these," you took what you got. So I was kind of bitching about that to Jim one day, because the day before we had an inspection and the officer bawled me out for not having my shoes polished properly.

And Jim said, "I've got a nice pair of shiny ones," and they were the same size as mine. So we traded shoes.

As soon as we got the shoes, though, you had to stamp your name and serial number in them, with indelible ink. So I had already done that with mine, and he had done it with his.

When I got hit, it blew my shoe off. And when Driskill and his group came up to our tanks some days later to see what they could salvage, he said he was walking around, and he saw a shoe laying there. So he picked it up, and it was Jim Driskill's!

And I hadn't heard from that guy since Day One. So one day several years after the war, here comes the mail and there's a letter from Driskill. Somehow or another he got ahold of my address. And the first sentence, he says, "Where's my other shoe?"

Forrest Dixon

My daughter was six weeks old when I went overseas. She was two and a half years old when I came home.

She didn't like it. She'd been sleeping with her mother, and when we put her in her own bed she got mad. She said, "Go back to Germany."

Jim Flowers

One morning, real early, the nurse came in and said, "Are you ready to go back home?"

I said, "Yeah, I'm ready to go."

I think she had brought me some breakfast. She said, "Eat your breakfast and brush your teeth, and be sure that your toilet articles are all together." I had a little zipper bag that I kept them in. She said, "We'll be right back in a little bit, to start your flight home." She was a man of her word, because it wasn't too long until they came and got me and took me out to Prestwick and loaded me on a C-54.

After the war, those were passenger planes, the biggest passenger airliners we had. I guess they were the first of the four-motored airliners. They were made by Douglass.

I can't remember whether the stretcher cases were stacked three high or four high on each side of the aisle, but they had them stacked kind of like sardines, except on one end they had regular seats for the ambulatory patients.

We flew from Prestwick to Reykjavik, then to Greenland, and then I guess we stopped at Gander. I didn't get off the airplane. We may have gone on over to Goose Bay. Six of one, half a dozen of the other except that they're five hundred miles apart. We went from there to Mitchel Field on Long Island.

There, they put us in a little station hospital. While I was there, I got a real haircut. A barber came up, a real barber. The USO, they just couldn't do enough for you. They were real nice. I was there for three or four days. I didn't know where I was going.

They said there's a big Army hospital, a general hospital, in Temple, Texas, would you like to go? I said, "I sure would, and the sooner the better." The next day they loaded me and some of the other guys on a C-47 and took us down the East Coast, I think we went down to Greensboro, made some stops along the way. And they went over eventually to Love Field in Dallas, and they put me in a station hospital out there.

The nurse on that ward, she called Jeanette and told her I was there, and Jeanette got my mother and father, my little daughter, and my sister, and one of my loudmouth neighbors who I wish they'd have left at home. Imagine, people coming in to a damn hospital and asking you, "Did you see any Germans? How many did you kill?"

I enjoyed it. In retrospect, why, I'd have probably done the same thing.

The next morning, they flew me down to Temple, 130 miles south of Dallas, and took me over to McCloskey General Hospital.

After revisions on both stumps, and almost a year and a half, they transferred me to Percy Jones General Hospital in Battle Creek, Michigan. I was there for almost another year and a half, so all told I was hospitalized for almost three years.

The first temporary prostheses I had were fabricated and fitted about nine months after I was initially wounded. I could figure it out to the day. Roosevelt died on April 12th, 1945. That was the day that I received my first temporary prosthesis. I was wounded in July. That's nine months to the day from the day they scooped me up on a piece of bloody French real estate until I put on my first temporary prosthesis.

I used to kiddingly say Roosevelt had lived a long time, and had a pretty full life. He had done a lot of good things, a lot of things with which I didn't agree, but I'm just one person. Somebody had probably called the president over at Warm Springs and said to him, "Jim Flowers is standing up and he's taking his first steps," and Roosevelt says, "I've heard it all. Nothing further that I care to hear." And he sat down and died.

Acknowledgments

I owe a special debt of thanks to Bob Rossi, who, upon reading an early version of the chapter on Hill 122, suggested that I interview Louis Gerrard and Jack Sheppard, and gave me important leads on several other stories.

Although I'd like to take credit for the title of this book, Frances Griffin came up with it first, for a collection of stories her husband put together for their grandchildren.

I couldn't have written "Tanks for the Memories" without the cooperation and gracious hospitality of the members of the 712th, some of whom put me up in their homes on my travels.

Bonnie Harken of Harken Architects helped greatly with the maps and graphics. I also used some of the drawings by the late Eames Yates that appear in "War From the Ground Up" (Nortex Press), John Colby's compelling history of the 90th Infantry Division.

Several of my colleagues at the Bergen Record deserve some credit: Kathleen Sullivan, who made some excellent editing suggestions; a special tanks for the memory (four megabytes' worth) to Jack McNeely, who upgraded my computer; former tanker Bill "Foxtrot One" Newton for his encouragement; Peter Grad and Laura Paino for formatting and printing out the manuscript; Judy Megaro for her help designing the cover, and Phil Read, who sits opposite me in the business department and had to listen to many of these stories several times over.

Thanks also to Ted Weiss and his staff at Ted Weiss Printers in Bensalem, Pa., for guiding me through the printing process.